POPULAR PROTEST
IN CHINA

China Today series

POPULAR PROTEST IN CHINA

Teresa Wright

polity

First published in 2018 by Polity Press

Polity Press
65 Bridge Street
Cambridge CB2 1UR, UK

Polity Press
101 Station Landing
Suite 300
Medford, MA 02155, USA

ISBN-13: 978-1-5095-0355-1
ISBN-13: 978-1-5095-0356-8(pb)

A catalogue record for this book is available from the British Library.

Library of Congress Cataloging-in-Publication Data

Names: Wright, Teresa, author.
Title: Popular protest in China / Teresa Wright.
Description: Cambridge, UK ; Medford, MA : Polity Press, 2018. | Series: China today | Includes bibliographical references and index.
Identifiers: LCCN 2017056580 (print) | LCCN 2017059364 (ebook) | ISBN 9781509503599 (Epub) | ISBN 9781509503551 (hardback) | ISBN 9781509503568 (pbk.)
Subjects: LCSH: Protest movements–China–History. | Political participation–China–History. | China–Politics and government–1976–2002. | China–Politics and government–2002-
Classification: LCC HN733.5 (ebook) | LCC HN733.5 .W754 2018 (print) | DDC 303.48/40951–dc23
LC record available at https://lccn.loc.gov/2017056580

Typeset in 11.5 on 15 pt Adobe Jenson Pro
by Toppan Best-set Premedia Limited
Printed and bound in Great Britain by Clays Ltd, Elcograf S.p.A.

For further information on Polity, visit our website:
politybooks.com

Contents

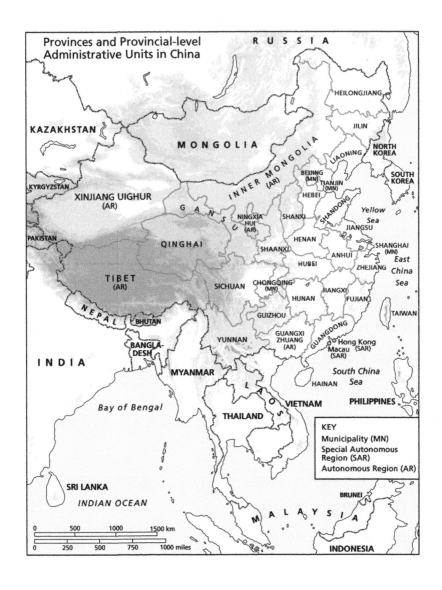

Provinces and Provincial-level Administrative Units in China

RUSSIA

KAZAKHSTAN

MONGOLIA

KYRGYZSTAN

XINJIANG UIGHUR (AR)

PAKISTAN

G A N S U

QINGHAI

TIBET (AR)

NEPAL

BHUTAN

BANGLA-DESH

INDIA

Bay of Bengal

SRI LANKA

INDIAN OCEAN

HEILONGJIANG

JILIN

INNER MONGOLIA (AR)

LIAONING

NORTH KOREA

SOUTH KOREA

BEIJING (MN)

TIANJIN (MN)

HEBEI

NINGXIA HUI (AR)

SHANXI

SHANDONG

Yellow Sea

JIANGSU

HENAN

SHAANXI

ANHUI

SHANGHAI (MN)

HUBEI

ZHEJIANG

East China Sea

CHONGQING (MN)

SICHUAN

JIANGXI

FUJIAN

TAIWAN

HUNAN

GUIZHOU

GUANGXI ZHUANG (AR)

GUANGDONG

Hong Kong (SAR)

Macau (SAR)

YUNNAN

MYANMAR

L A O S

VIETNAM

THAILAND

South China Sea

HAINAN

PHILIPPINES

BRUNEI

M A L A Y S I A

INDONESIA

KEY
Municipality (MN)
Special Autonomous Region (SAR)
Autonomous Region (AR)

| 0 | 500 | 1000 | 1500 km |
| 0 | 250 | 500 | 750 | 1000 miles |

Chronology

October 1949	People's Republic of China (PRC) established under leadership of Mao Zedong
1958–60	Great Leap Forward; tens of millions die of starvation
1959	Tibetan Uprising in Lhasa; Dalai Lama flees to India
1966–76	Great Proletarian Cultural Revolution
1969	Deng Xiaoping purged from Party-state posts
1974	PRC Premier Zhou Enlai convinces Mao to restore Deng and other purged leaders to Party-state posts
January 1976	Death of Zhou
April 1976	Citizens gather in Tiananmen Square to memorialize Zhou, support Deng; Maoist "Gang of Four" orchestrates removal of Deng from Party-state posts, uses official media to deem the protestors "counter-revolutionary"; thousands arrested
September 1976	Death of Mao Zedong
October 1976	"Gang of Four" arrested and sentenced
July 1977	Deng restored to high-level Party-state posts, criticizes Cultural Revolution and calls for a "Beijing Spring" wherein citizens express grievances

March 1978	New PRC Constitution adopted; includes "four big freedoms"
November 1978	Citizens put up big-character posters at "Democracy Wall" in central Beijing and circulate "people's periodicals," criticizing the Maoist period and calling for political reform
December 1978	Deng Xiaoping recognized as paramount leader; CCP Central Committee lays out reform program emphasizing economic reform and promising to strengthen democracy and law. Party-state leaders purged during the Cultural Revolution restored to posts; 10,000 political prisoners freed and cleared of wrongdoing; Official verdict on the April 1976 movement reversed; universities re-opened; crowds gather at "Democracy Wall" in downtown Beijing
1979	Rural collectives dismantled; Ministry of Justice restored; Special Economic Zones (SEZs) established; "one-child" policy established; *Explorations* editor Wei Jingsheng jailed; "Democracy Wall" closed
1980	"Four big freedoms" removed from PRC Constitution
1982	New CCP Constitution adopted; right of workers to strike not included
December 1984	Sino-British Joint Declaration agreeing to return Hong Kong to China in 1997
1986–7	Student demonstrations
1987	Protests in Tibet
1988–9	Tibetan monks arrested; martial law declared in Tibet

April–June 1989	Student-led protests in Beijing and other major cities; worker autonomous federations established; violent crack-down in Beijing June 3–4
1992	Deng Xiaoping's "Southern Tour" of Special Economic Zones
1994	PRC citizens granted the right to sue government officials; Labor Law requires contracts for all workers; owners/residents of urban residential tracts directed to elect "homeowner associations"
1995	Commercial Internet accounts appear in PRC
1997	Hong Kong becomes Special Autonomous Region of PRC; death of Deng Xiaoping
Late 1990s	Privatization of state-owned enterprises (SOEs) and urban housing
1998	China Democracy Party established
1999	Students protest US bombing of Chinese embassy in Belgrade
2000	"Open Up the West" campaign begins
Early 2000s	Rural taxes and fees abolished
2001	China enters WTO
2002	"Three Represents" embraced; private entrepreneurs allowed to join the CCP
2002–3	"Subversion law" provokes protests in Hong Kong
2003	Environmental Impact Assessment law passed
2004	PRC Constitution amendments protect "legally obtained" private property
2005	Anti-Japan protests
2006	"New Socialist Countryside" initiative

2008	Protests and repression in Tibet; summer Olympic Games in Beijing; Labor Contract Law; Liu Xiaobo and others post "Charter 08," calling for fundamental liberal democratic reforms; PRC becomes world's largest emitter of greenhouse gases
2010	PRC becomes nation with highest number of Internet users
2011	PRC citizens granted the right to sue the government for the release of information
2012	Criminal Procedure Law revised; anti-Japan protests; Xi Jinping assumes top Party-state posts
2014	PRC journalists required to pass ideological exams; "Umbrella" Movement in Hong Kong
2015	Environmental Protection Law takes effect

Acknowledgments

When I was asked by Polity to consider writing this book, I was in the final throes of another book (*Party and State in Post-Mao China*, Polity, 2015) and had been looking forward to a break. But, the proposed topic of this book – popular protest in China – reinvigorated me. As a new graduate student in the fall of 1988, I had been captivated by the student protests that had emerged in China 1986–7, and made them the subject of my MA thesis. In early 1989, I excitedly signed up for my first trip to China, for summer Mandarin language study. When student demonstrations again arose in mid-April of 1989, I was glued to the television, following every turn in the developing story. Watching the movement end with a bloody crack-down, I was devastated. I also found that my planned summer study abroad program had been cancelled. In the summer of 1990, I finally made my first visit to China, traveling on my own across many provinces, and doing my best with my still rudimentary Mandarin to speak with the people I met. I wanted to know more about the protests of 1989, and as I began my PhD dissertation research in the early 1990s, I sought out and interviewed exiled Chinese protest leaders (later published in *Protest and Peril: State Repression and Student Activism in China and Taiwan*, University of Hawaii, 2001). I was inspired by these leaders' courage and commitment to ideals in confusing and highly risk-laden circumstances, and overcome by the great sacrifices they had made. Few would ever return to their families back in the mainland PRC.

In the late 1990s, some of the leaders of the protests of 1989 worked alongside leaders of China's earlier "Democracy Wall" movement (1978–80) to establish the first true opposition political party in China – the China Democracy Party (CDP). Intrigued, I interviewed those that I could find, collected a great deal of information about the group, and published some of my findings. Like the protests of 1989, the CDP was allowed to exist for a number of months before its major leaders were imprisoned. But unlike in 1989, when millions joined protests in virtually every major Chinese city, the CDP did not attract a large following.

This lack of apparent public interest in political change – which stood in stark contrast to the late 1970s and 1980s – puzzled me. My attempt to explain it resulted in two subsequent books, *Accepting Authoritarianism: State–Society Relations in China's Reform Era* (Stanford University Press, 2010) and *Party and State in Post-Mao China*.

But in their focus on the reasons why the Chinese public had appeared to become more satisfied with CCP rule since 1989, these books did not sufficiently address the tens of thousands of new and often large-scale non-political protests that had arisen since 1989 – protests that involved a far greater range of socioeconomic groups (most notably, China's vast rural population) than had been the case in the more politically-oriented protests of 1978–89. In addition, these books did not consider the political protests that have been undertaken by Tibetans, Uighurs, and residents of Hong Kong in the post-1989 period.

Consequently, despite my desire to rest after completing *Party and State*, I accepted Polity's invitation to write this book. The research for this book reminded me of the courage in the face of injustice and adversity that I so admired in those who led the protests of the 1980s. It also underscored that the Chinese public is far from passive, obedient, or complacent. To the contrary, Chinese citizens often boldly, defiantly, and doggedly confront authority when they feel that their rights have been violated or that they have been treated unjustly. This is not to stay that they are not careful and strategic in their activism; as you will see in this volume, they are very astute in their protest behavior. But at the same time, they are not cowed by their apparent lack of power relative to political and economic elites, and they do not shy away from confrontation when they feel that it is warranted.

Chinese citizens' commitment to standing up for what is right reminds me of my parents, Pete and Nancy, whose dedication to social justice and community betterment has inspired me throughout my life. I could not be more grateful to them for giving me this gift.

More concretely, I wish to express my sincere thanks to the many scholars that generously took the time to read and provide valuable feedback on portions of this text. They include: Dorothy Solinger, Yongshun Cai, Yanhua Deng, Christopher Heurlin, Anne Christine Lie, Dragan Pavlicevic, Benjamin Read, Christoph Steinhardt, Zhengxu Wang, Ngai Ming Yip, and two anonymous reviewers. Of course, any errors and flaws are mine alone. I also am grateful to the East-West Center for supporting my research with office space and intellectual camaraderie over the course of many summers. In addition, I am thankful for the unfailing support of Amelia Marquez, who has assisted me with administrative matters – and generally has kept me smiling – for nearly two decades. Similarly, the editorial staff at Polity Press – Louise Knight, Nekane Tanaka Galdos, Neil de Cort, and Ian Tuttle – have been an absolute pleasure to work with; professional, reasonable, and supportive. Further, I extend my heartfelt appreciation to Fanyi Yang for our weekly Skype sessions in Mandarin; a more talented and good-humored *jiaoshou* would be impossible to find.

And finally, I am deeply grateful to my daughter Anna, my son Nicholas, and my partner Ty for helping me grow on a daily basis, for appreciating my passion for studying China, for reminding me to prioritize the things that matter most, and for being the best companions a person could ever hope for. I cannot thank them enough for the joy and fulfillment that they have brought to my life.

Introduction

Popular protest has occurred in every kind of political system, and in every country around the world. In contemporary China this is also the case, and often dramatically so. In the 1980s, the most prominent mass protests focused on political reform, including the massive student-led demonstrations of the spring of 1989. From 1990 through the present, there have been no similarly large-scale, nationwide public street protests in China, and very few public acts calling for fundamental changes to China's central Chinese Communist Party (CCP)-dominated governing regime. However, protests of other kinds have been widespread and frequent. Indeed, since the 1990s, tens of thousands of mass protests have arisen in China each year.

Why do people protest in China? What happens when they do? How have protests affected the way that people interact with and view their government? Will popular protests lead to the fall of China's ruling CCP? This book answers these questions. To do so, it comprehensively analyzes the multitudinous protests that have arisen in China's post-Mao period, particularly focusing on the 1990s through the present. To begin, it examines the many causes of protest in contemporary China. In addition, the book describes what people in China do when they protest, how Chinese political authorities at various levels respond to their actions, and how these experiences shape the way that protestors view their government.

These aspects of protest in China have important implications for this book's final question – what do these protests tell us about the stability of China's governmental system? Overall, popular protest in contemporary China has not posed an existential threat to CCP rule. Although collective contention has been a highly inefficient and often violent way to express and resolve social discontent, it has worked adequately to address the public's most serious grievances. Indeed, to the extent that protest demands have been met with sympathy and support on the part of national political leaders, protest actually may have worked to strengthen central government legitimacy.

At the same time, there are three important qualifications to this overall argument. First, these findings apply only to protest within mainland China proper undertaken by the majority Han Chinese population, which constitutes roughly 92 percent of the Chinese citizenry. Protests in China's Special Autonomous Region of Hong Kong have had their own dynamic, as have those undertaken by ethnic minority groups – particularly, Uighurs and Tibetans. These protests have involved fundamental conflict between central Chinese political leaders and protestors, and have the potential to lead to more revolutionary (or separatist) unrest. However, thus far, these kinds of collective contention have found little sympathy among mainland Han Chinese. Indeed, most Han Chinese have seemed to support the central government's repressive actions toward ethnic minority protests. Further, they generally have not viewed Hong Kong protesters' aims as being linked to their own interests.

Second, even when the overall result of protest has been seen by activists as satisfactory, the often highly negative experiences of protestors during the course of their interaction with ruling authorities have made for an unhealthy relationship between aggrieved citizens and governing officials. In part, this is because the intense conflict, trauma, and often violence associated with popular protests have left participants scarred. For, citizens typically have received redress only after grievances have become severe, and only when citizens have undertaken large-scale and sustained actions involving significant emotional and physical commitments and costs. This unhealthy relationship also has been a byproduct of the unpredictable nature of protests. In a context where both regime authorities and citizens have not played by clear "rules," individual political officials and activists have chosen among a number of options within the vague boundaries of what constitutes acceptable behavior. Consequently, each protest episode has been characterized by great uncertainty, with actions on both sides frequently shifting among conciliation, confrontation, negotiation, intransigence, non-violence, and violence. As a result, the development of trust between citizens and ruling elites has been inhibited.

Third, given this situation, efforts by CCP General Secretary and PRC President Xi Jinping to restrict public expression may lead to an explosive situation that may undermine the political stability that the CCP has enjoyed since the early 1990s. To the extent that Xi's repressive measures stifle the ability of mainland Han Chinese to voice their grievances through protest, popular protest may no longer be allowed to act as a crucial social outlet. If aggrieved citizens come to view central political leaders as repressors rather than as allies, the legitimacy of China's CCP-led regime may be expected to decline. Further, because people that have engaged in protest in China have been both empowered and traumatized by their prior protest experiences, and because their relationships with regime authorities have been characterized by unpredictability and flux, they may be more inclined to engage in more revolutionary confrontations.

WHAT IS POPULAR PROTEST?

Before delving into the specifics of the various kinds of popular protests that have arisen in China's post-Mao period, it is important to clarify what this book is talking about when it speaks of "popular protest." Taking a relatively wide approach to the term, it is defined herein as *public collective action directed toward political and/or economic elites.* Within this definition, "elites" refers to persons who hold positions of power relative to the persons that are collectively and publicly engaging in protest, and/or that hold a position of power relative to the issue at hand. An example of an "economic elite" is an employer that controls the working conditions and payment of his or her workers. An example of a "political elite" is a local government official that has control over land use. A "political elite" can also be a higher-level official that has power over lower-level political authorities.

Within this definition, "collective action" refers to coordinated efforts by a group of people on behalf of a shared interest. For the purposes of this book, popular protest is a type of *contentious* collective action that is directed at power-holders who are in positions that give them control over the matter about which the protestors are concerned or aggrieved. Finally, according to the definition of popular protest used in this book, such contentious collective actions must be *public*. At the same time, this book takes a broad view of what is "public," including not only actions in physical spaces (such as street marches and sit-ins) but also public acts undertaken in virtual spaces, such as the Internet.

With this relatively broad definition in hand, this book examines a wide range of popular protests in contemporary China. It includes contentious collective actions on the part of different socioeconomic groups (such as rural residents, urban workers, and homeowners), as well as other kinds of demographic groups – particularly, ethnic minorities. It also looks at protests that focus on issues that are not related to a particular demographic group, such as environmental protests, nationalist protests, and protests calling for political reform.

HOW ARE PEOPLE IN "COMMUNIST" CHINA ABLE TO ENGAGE IN POPULAR PROTEST?

In a country like China, which is governed by an authoritarian regime that self-identifies as "communist," how is it possible for people to engage in public protests that are directed at those who hold power? One might think that in an authoritarian and communist political system, such activities would be harshly repressed, and few would dare to engage in them. However, the situation in China is more complicated than its designation as "authoritarian" and "communist" implies. In fact, there is some legal basis upon which China's citizens may engage in collective protest, and there are some institutionalized channels within China's political system that are designed to accept and respond to popular grievances. Further, when these institutionalized mechanisms fail to satisfactorily address citizen concerns, the aggrieved have been allowed by regime authorities to engage in acts of public contention outside of formal, institutionalized channels.

To more fully understand the context that both provides opportunities for and constraints on protest in China, we must look more closely at what scholars of contentious politics refer to as "opportunity structures." They emphasize that some "opportunity structures" are more open to protest, while others are more closed. At the same time, they stress that opportunity structures are not static, but rather are continually changing. Further, they note that different aspects of changing opportunity structures have different influences on various demographic groups and types of protests. In addition, scholars point out that it is potential protestors' *perception* of opportunity structures that matters the most.[1]

Applying these concepts to China, we can first point to "opportunity structures" related to protest that affect virtually all Chinese citizens, and that have been relatively unchanged over the course of the post-Mao period. Next, we can examine changes in "opportunity structures" during this period. Finally, we can disaggregate the specific ways in which particular aspects of (both changing and unchanged) opportunity structures have differentially influenced particular demographic groups and types of popular protest.

OPPORTUNITIES AND CONSTRAINTS: POLITICAL SYSTEM

The most notable, important, and unchanged feature of China's opportunity structure is that a single party – the CCP – has controlled the Chinese government since 1949. Although China has a formal "state" structure (with a President, etc.) that is "on paper" separate from the CCP, in reality, the CCP created the state to serve the CCP's ends, and the CCP determines who will serve in all important positions within the state, as well as what the state does.[2]

CONSTITUTIONAL PROVISIONS

A feature of China's opportunity structure that has changed somewhat over the course of time, and is much more complicated than the simple facts discussed above, is the legal status of popular protest. Both the CCP and the Chinese state have constitutions that contain statements related to the legality of protest. These constitutions have been amended since Mao's death in 1976, with the result that the constitutional status of popular protest has not been consistent over time. Moreover, both constitutions contain some statements that appear to protect citizens' right to protest, yet other statements that restrict that right.

The current constitution of the CCP was adopted in 1982, but has been amended on several occasions since then. The most recent CCP constitution declares that the CCP "respects and safeguards human rights" and "encourages the free airing of views."[3] But, the CCP constitution does not specify or clarify what it means by "human rights," and it also stipulates that "leadership by the CCP" is one of the "cardinal principles" upon which the People's Republic of China is to be "built." It also states that the CCP must "combat" "bourgeois liberalization."[4] Thus, there is no clear protection for the "airing of views" that might be seen as challenging the "leadership" of the CCP or as promoting "bourgeois liberalization."

The constitution of the Chinese state (technically, the constitution of the PRC) has also been amended on a number of occasions since the death of Mao in 1976. From 1978 through the present, China's state constitution explicitly has claimed to protect civil liberties, even using the same language that is found in liberal democracies such as the US. Specifically, Article 35 asserts that "citizens of the People's Republic of China enjoy freedom of speech, of the press, of assembly, of association, of procession and of demonstration."[5] Further, Article 41 stipulates that China's citizens have "the right to criticize and make suggestions to any state organ or functionary." In 2004, constitutional amendments were added to protect the "legally obtained" private property of citizens, and to protect "human rights."

However, other parts of China's current state constitution place limits on many of the rights listed above. Among them, Article 1 states that "sabotage of the socialist system by any organization or individual is prohibited." Similarly, Article 28 emphasizes that "the state maintains public order and suppresses treasonable and other counter-revolutionary activities." Further, Article 51 asserts that "the exercise by citizens of the People's Republic of China of their freedoms and rights may not infringe upon the interests of the state," and Article 53 warns that citizens "must abide by the constitution and the law, keep state secrets, protect public property and observe labor discipline and public order." Thus, according to China's state constitution, civil liberties are guaranteed, but only as long as they are not perceived by ruling authorities to "sabotage" China's "socialist system" or to "infringe" on the "interest of the state;" to otherwise be "counter-revolutionary" or "treasonous;" or to disturb "public order." Moreover, language that seemed to encourage the public airing of grievances in the 1978 constitution (the so-called "four big freedoms" to speak out freely, air views fully, hold great debates, and write big-character posters) was removed in 1980. In addition, protection of the right of workers to strike was included in the 1978 constitution, but was removed in 1982.

Overall, China's state and CCP constitutions have become somewhat less protective of civil liberties over the course of the post-Mao era. At the same time, throughout the post-Mao period, both constitutions have contained contradictory statements that have given China's political leaders a great deal of constitutional leeway when it comes to dealing with popular protest. Concomitantly, these constitutional contradictions have provided openings for potential protestors.

LAWS, DIRECTIVES, AND GUIDELINES

Laws and other directives and guidelines also can be interpreted to both protect the right to protest and to justify its suppression. Technically, protest organizers are required to apply for and receive legal permission before gathering publicly. Further, a 1998 directive from the central State Council defines as "intolerable:" attempting to overthrow the CCP or overall political system, threatening China's territorial integrity, destroying important infrastructure and facilities, or attacking state agencies. According to China's Criminal Law, the latter can include preventing the operation of a state agency. Further, the Law defines as a crime "assembling the masses to disrupt social order," which can occur when a protest action disrupts work, production, business, or school. "Disrupting social order" can result in sentences of up to seven years, and "attacking state agencies" can be punished with sentences up to ten years. Moreover, in 2004, Beijing municipal officials announced that those who gather or protest in "important" places will be sent by police to official complaint departments, and that persons violating the law will be sent back to the state agency in their place of residence. These rules give the authorities wide leeway in pursuing legal action against protestors.[6]

Yet simultaneously, and particularly since the early years of the new millennium, central authorities have issued regulations seeking to ensure that collective contentious actions are handled professionally, and without violence, and that those who face charges as a result of their involvement in protests have legal protections. In 2002, the central Ministry of Public Security laid out a series of regulations that are to be strictly followed by police in their handling of social unrest, with the goal of avoiding violence or escalation. In 2012, the Criminal Procedure Law was revised to ban extorted confessions and the use of torture to collect evidence, and to require the videotaping of confessions. In 2013, the Supreme People's Court issued guidelines for the elimination of confessions acquired through torture. The fact that these rules have been publicized indicates that the problems that they attempt to address have been widespread. Thus far, there is little evidence that these relatively new regulations have had the desired effect.[7] Nonetheless, they provide protesters with some legal backing, and – especially in cases where police have used unwarranted violence against protestors – these rules have been the basis for higher-level governmental intervention on behalf of protestors.

Adding to the lack of clarity regarding the legality of protest in China, there is no judicial body in China with the power to decide when a citizen or group has exceeded the limits of its constitutional rights, or when a political official has violated a citizen's constitutional rights. Although China does have a judiciary with a "Supreme People's Court," the court system – as with the entire "state" structure – is controlled by the CCP. Thus, if top CCP leaders decide that a particular popular protest action is unacceptable and should be repressed (as was the case in the student-led protests of the spring of 1989), there is no judicial body with the power or authority to rule on the legality of the CCP leaders' decision or action.

Nonetheless, from 1990 through the present, China's central political leaders only infrequently have declared a particular popular protest to be unacceptable and ordered its repression. And in a not insignificant number of cases, central authorities have intervened in support of the protestors. Further, since the late 1990s, officials from the local level through the provincial level have been reviewed annually according to their record of maintaining "social stability," including numerical measures such as how many collective petitions are lodged with higher-level authorities, and how many popular "disturbances" occur within a particular jurisdiction. If officials fail to achieve the goals outlined in these criteria, the evaluation guidelines clearly state that this will result in dismissal. Conversely, promotions are to be given only to officials who meet or exceed these specific goals. Unfortunately, this reality often has led local officials to repress local protests and even use violence against protest leaders. However, these evaluation criteria also give aggrieved citizens leverage, as they know that if word of local unrest gets out, the local officials' reviews will be tarnished. As a result, despite the lack of clear constitutional or other legal protections, many disgruntled citizens have had a feeling of efficacy with regard to engaging in collective protests.[8]

As with many other aspects of China's political and economic system, reliable statistics on the number of popular protests in a given year are elusive. In part, this is because different sources use different definitions of "protest." The Chinese government typically uses the terms "mass incidents" or "public order disturbances," which can include organized crime and other actions that do not fall within the definition used in this book. Further, since 2006, the Chinese government has not published official statistics on such events. However, some Chinese officials have provided verbal estimates, and some Chinese scholars and non-governmental organizations (NGOs) have offered statistics based on their research. Drawing on these sources, the number of annual popular protests in China appears to have risen from roughly 5,000–10,000 in the early 1990s, to 60,000–100,000 by the middle of the first decade of the 2000s.[9] For about the past decade, the number of yearly popular protests is estimated to have remained in the high tens-of-thousands, and according to some mainland Chinese scholars rose to 180,000 in 2010.[10]

These numbers show that the ambiguous legal status of contentious collective action in China has not prevented citizens from protesting. Indeed, the lack of clarity as to when a particular protest action will be tolerated or punished seems to have worked to the benefit of both China's ruling authorities and its citizens. From the perspective of the citizenry, this ambiguity has led to what Kevin O'Brien calls "boundary-spanning" collective contention that is neither entirely "contained" by the CCP/ruling elites nor wholly "transgressive" of rules/laws made by the CCP/state.[11] In other words, China's citizens have used the ambiguous legal status of popular protest, and have capitalized on local officials' career-related vulnerability to protests within their jurisdictions, engaging in contentious collective actions that test – and often push against – the boundaries of what is considered by authorities to be "acceptable" behavior. One specific way in which aggrieved citizens have done so is by pursuing what O'Brien and Lianjiang Li term "rightful resistance" – taking seriously constitutional provisions and laws that purport to protect citizen rights, and challenging regime authorities to make good on these legal claims.[12]

Importantly, central CCP authorities (at least prior to the political ascension of Xi Jinping to the Party-state's top posts) have seemed to accept, and even welcome, "rightful resistance." For, by allowing members of the public to collectively voice their dissatisfaction, regime leaders have been able to find out about public grievances before they develop to such an extent that they pose a threat to the stability of the CCP-led political system. At the same time, however, to the extent that participants in protest actions have experienced violent treatment in the course of their collective contentious actions, they have become both further incensed and more disillusioned with the existing political system. Further, because the "rules" concerning protest have not been clear, the progression and outcome of protest have been unpredictable, as both political authorities and aggrieved citizens have chosen among an array of behaviors within the ambiguous boundaries of "acceptable" actions. To a large extent, their choices have differed according to the idiosyncratic preferences of those involved. As a result, protests always have the potential to spin out of control and destabilize the political status quo.

"LETTERS AND VISITS"

A second element of China's post-Mao "opportunity structure" are the Chinese political system's unique "letters and visits" (*xinfang*) offices. This system was created during the Maoist era, with the intention of allowing for citizen input. Every governmental level from the county to the center has a "letters and visits" office, as does every Chinese court, higher education institution, and state-owned enterprise. Disgruntled citizens have the right to submit letters to or visit these offices to voice their grievances. The system is free, legal, and does not require the complainant to submit formal evidence. *Xinfang* offices are obligated to accept and respond to all petitions to their office. And, higher-level officials track and analyze the number and content of these petitions, taking particular note of grievances that seem to be pervasive, and may be the result of flawed policies rather than simply corrupt or inept behavior on the part of local elites.[13] In some cases, *xinfang* offices send out investigation teams to assess the validity of the grievant's claims.

Very few petitioners have resolved their grievance successfully through the petition process. Typically, *xinfang* officials are very slow in responding. And, not infrequently complainants have been punished as a result of their letter/visit – including being fined, having their homes ransacked or demolished, having their property confiscated, being beaten (along with their family members), and being captured and detained in informal (and illegal) "black jails." When this occurs, aggrieved citizens can

– and often do – move up the political hierarchy, submitting their complaint to higher levels of authority, be it at the provincial level or even traveling to Beijing to contact central *xinfang* offices.

Use of the *xinfang* system rose by an estimated 8 percent per year between 1994 and 2002, and then peaked from 2003 to 2006, shortly after Hu Jintao ascended to the top CCP post. When central leaders became concerned that petitioners coming to Beijing were beginning to disrupt "social stability," Party leaders pressured lower-level authorities to reduce the number of petitioners seeking help from the national government – resulting in the inclusion of the specific evaluation criteria discussed above. Local officials responded mainly by stepping up their use of coercive methods to prevent petitioners from doing so.[14] Nonetheless, every year millions of disgruntled citizens have continued to submit petitions to "letters and visits" offices. In most cases, it is only after citizens have found themselves stymied in their attempt to seek redress through the "letters and visits" system that they have engaged in more overtly conflictual and less clearly legal methods of protest, such as street marches, demonstrations, and sit-ins.

COURTS

A relatively new feature of the opportunity structure in post-Mao China is the court system. During the Mao era, China had no courts (at least not in the Western sense of the word), and law did not exist as a profession. In 1979, under reformist CCP leader Deng Xiaoping, the Ministry of Justice was restored as part of the state structure, and the Party-state began to recruit "state legal workers" to work as lawyers. However, most had no legal training, and all were entirely dependent on the Party-state for their livelihood. In addition, citizens did not have the right to use the courts to seek redress for wrongs perpetrated by political authorities.

Beginning in the mid-1990s, this situation changed: virtually all law firms were privatized, and lawyers became private-sector workers. Since 2001, all new lawyers have been required to pass a "bar" exam. Meanwhile, citizens have been given new legal rights vis-à-vis the government: in 1994, citizens gained the right to sue government officials for abuse of authority or malfeasance, and in 2011 citizens were granted the right to sue the government for the release of information. As will be discussed in more detail in chapter 7, this changing aspect of China's opportunity structure has made it possible for "rights protection" lawyers to emerge.

Nonetheless, for most citizens that have suffered at the hands of political authorities, the court system rarely has been seen as a practical method of seeking redress. In the mid-1990s, use of the court system increased, but since the middle of the first decade of the 2000s, it has plateaued as legal reforms have stalled and even backtracked. In 2008, the new chief justice of the Supreme People's Court (a man with no legal training), reminded China's judges that the interests of the Party supersede adherence to the law.[15] Relatedly, local Party leaders have power over the appointment and promotion of local judges, and these leaders are thus able to dissuade local courts from accepting cases of a politically sensitive nature, to force delays in hearings with the goal of draining the plaintiff's resources, and to prevent the implementation of court rulings. As a result, most citizens have come to the (accurate) conclusion that the odds of successfully filing and winning a case against local elites are low.[16]

OPPORTUNITIES AND CONSTRAINTS: MASS MEDIA

Another facet of the opportunity structure that has changed over time are China's mass media. In one key and fundamental respect, this system has remained as it was during the Mao era: ultimately, the

CCP-led Party-state has the power to dictate what is and is not covered in the media, as well as how stories are covered. Relatedly, those who work in China's mass media outlets know that they may be not only fired, but jailed, if they run afoul of these dictates.

Yet in other respects, China's post-Mao mass media system is significantly different than it was during the Maoist period. First, whereas in the Mao era all mass media outlets were wholly owned and operated by the Party-state and did not have to worry about making a profit, in the post-Mao period, many private media outlets have operated in China, or otherwise have been able to access Chinese consumers on the mainland. Since the late 1990s, even state-owned media outlets have been expected to turn a profit (or at least not operate at a loss). Moreover, in their quest to provide more "marketable" and "popular" content (and thereby attain greater profits), many Chinese media outlets have pursued controversial stories – including those that involve government corruption and abuse. Further, central political authorities generally have allowed media outlets to do so, as this has been a method by which high-level CCP leaders can be apprised of serious wrongdoing among lower-level officials. In this sense, central authorities in the post-Mao era have allowed the mass media to act as a sort of "watchdog" over lower-ranking political officials. Cognizant of this (and not unlike protestors in liberal democratic countries), aggrieved citizens have at times contacted the media in order to publicize their cause and gain the (hopefully sympathetic) attention of higher-level authorities. In the Maoist period, this simply was not an option. Overall, these changes in China's mass media system have made the opportunity structure more "open" in the post-Mao era than it was during the Maoist period.

Nonetheless, Chinese media outlets have remained subject to Party-state control. And, although many stories about relatively low-level political corruption and abuse have been uncovered and publicized, the boundary between what is and is not acceptable typically has not been clear until after a story has appeared. Indeed, numerous media outlets have been punished (such as by being closed down, or having particular employees fired or even jailed) for airing material that later was determined by high-level authorities to be unacceptable.

Beginning around 2008, and further ramping up since Xi Jinping's ascension to the Party-state's top posts in fall 2012, media controls and repression involving both domestic and foreign media outlets have increased. Regime tactics have included: restrictions on permitted reporting locations; visa scrutiny, delays, and rejections for foreign reporters; cyberattacks; direct pre-emptive pressure; and even physical violence. Further, since 2014, journalists have been required to pass an ideological exam in order to be able to legally work. In this environment, many domestic and foreign reporters in China have admitted to engaging in self-censorship.[17] Overall, this aspect of China's opportunity structure has been more closed under Xi Jinping than it was earlier in the post-Mao period.

THE INTERNET

A related aspect of the changing opportunity structure in the post-Mao era is the Internet. Through the end of the 1980s, Internet access in China (as in most of the world) was almost unheard of. In the early 1990s, CCP leaders allowed some of China's top universities to experiment with Internet use, and in 1995 the first commercial Internet accounts appeared in China. Initially, only an infinitesimal number of citizens utilized such accounts. Between 1998 and the present, Internet use has skyrocketed. Since 2010, China has had the highest number of Internet users in the world. At the close of 2016, more than 730 million Chinese citizens were on the Internet – approaching triple the number (just under 287 million) in the US. As a percentage of China's population, this amounts to roughly 53 percent. Further, although at first citizens could access the Internet only via public computer terminals, as of late 2016 an estimated 95 percent of Chinese netizens accessed the Internet through mobile devices. Further, 80 percent of all Internet users frequent WeChat, China's most popular instant-messaging site.[18] In terms of who uses the Internet most, age is a significant factor: as of 2014, 85 percent were under the age of 45, and 62 percent were under the age of 35.[19] Also, as in most countries, Internet use increases with level of education, and is much more common in urban areas than in rural.[20]

Beyond the question of who uses the Internet in China, access to information and the ability to communicate via the Internet have been restricted by the Party-state's "Great Firewall." This consists of a variety of measures designed to prevent the populace from accessing or disseminating information that central leaders perceive as threatening. Some of the most important such mechanisms include: a mandate that all news-providing websites register with the government and relay news only from official news units; the use of firewall and surveillance software to block access to "unsuitable" sites,[21] remove "offensive" content from sites, and filter domestic e-mail messages for "sensitive" content; and the use of human monitors. Since the middle of the first decade of the 2000s, the central government reportedly has hired roughly 20,000–50,000 Internet police to monitor and post criticisms on suspect sites. Provincial and local governments employ thousands to engage in Internet surveillance as well.[22] Further, persons affiliated with the Party-state have made an estimated 448 million fabricated posts on social media designed to distract the public from political criticism and direct the conversation in a direction that favors the Party-state's interests.[23]

However, these efforts have not been as effective, strict, or all-encompassing as many outside of China might imagine. Looking from the bottom up, most savvy and intrepid Internet users have been able to circumvent blockages and access censored sites and content. Further, Internet users and sites track and publicize banned terms, topics, pictures, etc., and create pseudonyms and other alternatives that allow users to evade censors. Looking from the top down, China's top leaders actually have not seemed to want to suppress all political discussion. To the contrary – at least prior to the fall 2012 ascension of Xi Jinping – central authorities appeared to see the Internet as an important means by which they can learn about malfeasance at lower levels, and address it before it spirals into a regime-threatening crisis.

The "openness" of the Internet has declined in recent years. From the late 1990s through the middle of the first decade of the new millennium, access and communication were hindered by the "Great Firewall" measures described above, but – with a few notable exceptions – most determined users did not experience significant punishment, and were able to successfully reach sites and circulate information. From the latter half of the first decade of the 2000s through the present, central Party-state efforts to curtail "threatening" Internet use (as with media coverage more generally), have been greater. This change began in the context of the Beijing summer Olympics in August 2008, which top CCP leaders saw as an opportunity to bolster China's international image. In their minds, this meant that there could be no appearance of public opposition to CCP rule. Also contributing to heightened Internet controls during this time period, in December 2008 a group of scholars and human rights activists posted an online manifesto called "Charter 08," which called for fundamental liberal democratic reforms.

Internet restrictions increased again in the years following Xi Jinping's assumption of the Party-state's top positions. In August 2013, Xi reportedly called on CCP cadres to "wage a war to win over public opinion" and "seize the ground of new media."[24] Shortly thereafter, individuals with large microblog followings were subjected to deletions, locked accounts, arrests, and interrogations. In addition, central authorities closed popular "public accounts" that comment on current events on WeChat.[25] Also in late 2013, China's top judicial officials announced that online speech would be subject to more severe and expansive considerations of what constitutes a "criminal offense," and that criminal defamation charges could result from postings deemed to threaten "public order" or "state interests." If a post is determined to be "false" or "defamatory," and is viewed more than 5,000 times or reposted more than 500 times, the user can be sentenced to up to three years in prison. In this context, hundreds of social media users have been detained and interrogated. Further, in early 2015, Party-state authorities began to successfully interfere with the "virtual private networks" (VPNs) that many users have relied on to circumvent "Great Firewall" blockages.[26] Overall, at the time of this writing, China's "opportunity structure" with regard to the Internet is more "closed" than it was during other periods between the late 1990s and the present.

OPPORTUNITIES AND CONSTRAINTS: ECONOMY

Another aspect of China's opportunity structure is the economy. More specifically, opportunities for and constraints on protest arise from the economic conditions and standing of both potential protestors, and those against whom potential protestors might wish to lodge complaints. In part, these factors derive from political realities. In China, there is an official CCP-affiliated union organization – the All-China Federation of Trade Unions (ACFTU) – that is supposed to have branches in every workplace. It is illegal for workers to form a union outside of the ACFTU structure. In the few instances when workers have attempted to do so (most notably, in the spring of 1989), they have been swiftly punished. However, since the early 1990s, workers have had many other legal rights, including the right to an employment contract, a minimum wage, and a forty-hour work week with fixed overtime rates. Local governments are responsible for overseeing the implementation of these laws. Although workers do not enjoy a constitutional right to strike, there is no law that prohibits them from striking. As will be discussed in more detail in chapter 3, they have done so quite frequently in recent years.

The economic conditions and standing of potential protestors and protest targets have changed as a result of China's economic reforms. In the Maoist era, there was virtually no private-sector in China; nearly all urban residents worked in state-owned or state-affiliated enterprises, and all rural residents were part of agricultural collectives. In the early post-Mao period, agricultural collectives were dismantled in the countryside, and individual families were leased plots of land for extended periods under a new "household responsibility system." In China's cities, through the mid-1990s most citizens with an urban residential permit (*hukou*) (see p. 46) worked in a type of state-owned enterprise (SOE). Through their employment units, they had great economic security, including virtually free housing, food, education, and health care; and generous pensions. Beginning in the late 1970s, CCP authorities allowed private enterprises to form, and established Special Economic Zones (SEZs) wherein joint ventures with foreign firms and domestic private enterprises could enjoy a more-or-less tax- and regulation-free business environment. These developments gave new work options to (mostly young male) rural *hukou*-holders who skirted official prohibitions on moving to the city and looked for urban wage work (which they found mostly in construction). During this period, there were no legal protections for private-sector workers or private business owners. However, most were satisfied with the new economic freedoms that they had been afforded, particularly relative to the much more economically "closed" Maoist era.

From the 1990s through the present, the economic conditions and standing of workers and employers have been quite different. Since the early 1990s, SEZs (and similar zones) have proliferated in China, and private businesses have benefited from increased legal protections. Concomitantly, from the 1990s through the present, the private sector has provided the bulk of China's phenomenal economic growth. Moreover, hundreds of millions of rural *hukou*-holders (a majority of whom have been young women) have flocked to China's cities (particularly those with SEZs) to engage in wage work. In response to this new economic reality, China's Party-state has formulated new labor laws to provide the worker protections noted above. Meanwhile, in the latter half of the 1990s, top CCP authorities announced that most of China's SOEs would be privatized. Consequently, tens of millions of urban *hukou*-holders were laid off. As will be discussed in chapter 3, huge numbers of them took to the streets in protest. Overall, these economic changes have made this aspect of the opportunity structure for popular protest more "open" as the post-Mao period has progressed.

ELITE DISAGREEMENT

Another shifting aspect of the opportunity structure for protest in China is the presence or absence of elite disagreement with regard to activists' behavior and goals. As discussed in chapter 1, in the early post-Mao period such disagreement among top CCP elites facilitated the rise of several large-scale movements directed at central authorities. Conversely, from the early 1990s through the present, the absence of such disagreement at the highest level of the CCP helps to explain why no similar protest movements have arisen in this period. At the same time, in the late post-Mao period China's myriad lower-level leaders have evidenced varied views in instances of protest in areas under their purview. Although generally speaking, lower-level officials make decisions with an eye to their evaluation in terms of economic growth and social stability, individual leaders have different preferences and values that lead to divergences in their response to protest. As will be shown especially with regard to farmer, worker, and environmental protests, in some cases local political officials sympathize with and even lead protests, whereas in others they respond with intransigence or repression. Further, political authorities at different levels and in different governmental bodies have varied perspectives deriving from their placement in the governing structure. In most cases, protests proceed and succeed when activists can capitalize on disagreements among political elites, and they are stymied and/or fail when political elites are united.

EXPANDING OPPORTUNITIES FROM BELOW

As illustrated in the discussion above, opportunities for protest are never fixed or static. Relatedly, opportunities are never just a one-way street determined by political authorities: protestors create opportunities as well, re-shaping existing opportunity structures. With regard to China, this point has been raised most influentially by O'Brien and Li, who found in their study of rural protestors that Chinese citizens regularly "fill spaces that the state and its reforms create," and also "push against boundaries in ways that cannot be read straight off an opportunity structure." By "probing the limits of the permissible," protestors are not simply reactors to opportunity structures created by the state; they are actively involved in the ever-changing process of opportunity structure creation and transformation.[27] This possibility is in part the result of the regime's own proclivity to leave unclear the boundaries of what is and is not permissible. In addition, this possibility derives from the regime's decentralization and fragmentation. China's top leaders in the post-Mao period have allowed provincial and local leaders a great deal of autonomy so that they can experiment with potential "best practices" in terms of economic, social, and political management. As a result, there is a vast amount of local variation in terms of what citizens are allowed to do. Further, because different levels and parts of China's governing structure do not always work in tandem with one another, and because each individual official has his (or occasionally her) own idiosyncratic preferences and values, it is possible for citizens that are disgruntled with one level or part of the government, or with a particular official, to find a sympathetic ear elsewhere within the political elite.

LAYOUT OF THE BOOK

The remainder of the book examines the different kinds of protest actions that have arisen over the course of China's post-Mao period, looking at their causes, progression, and consequences. In so doing, the book uncovers patterns and trends in popular protest, and assesses how popular protest may both support and undermine CCP rule. Chapter 1 compares and contrasts protest in the early and late post-Mao periods (1978–89 and 1990 through the present). Chapters 2 through 9 undertake a much more detailed analysis of popular protest in China's late post-Mao period. These chapters examine the nature of the protestors' grievances, the major demographic groups that have engaged in protest, government responses to different kinds of protests, and the outcomes and impacts of major types and instances of protest – including how the experience of engaging in mass collective contention has shaped protestors' views of their government. Chapters 2–4 focus on protest undertaken by different socioeconomic groups: rural residents (chapter 2), urban workers (chapter 3), and homeowners (chapter 4). Chapters 5–7 look at protests arising around broader issues that cross socioeconomic and other demographic lines: environmental protest (chapter 5), nationalist protest (chapter 6), and political protest (chapter 7). Chapters 8 and 9 analyze popular protests undertaken by residents of China's Autonomous regions: ethnic minority protest (chapter 8), and protest in Hong Kong (chapter 9). The book's conclusion reviews the major types of protest that have appeared in the post-Mao period and assesses their potential to destabilize China's CCP-led political system – particularly under the leadership of Xi Jinping.

1 | Popular Protest in the Post-Mao Era

Popular protest in China has changed over the course of the post-Mao period. From the late 1970s through the late 1980s, a small number of major urban protests arose, focusing mainly on national-level political reform. As noted in the Introduction, these protests climaxed in the massive student-led demonstrations of the spring of 1989. Since 1989, mass street protests aimed at systemic political reform have been non-existent. But, popular protests have been much more frequent, and have encompassed a far wider range of citizens and geographical locations. Indeed, protest has become so common that China has been recognized as a "contentious authoritarian" state.[1] Instead of viewing these protests as a threat, central political leaders seem to have accepted them as a mechanism of ensuring that popular discontent does not become focused on national-level political change.

This chapter examines how protest has changed during China's post-Mao period, particularly in terms of protest quantity, actions, and demands, and their geographic and demographic distribution. The first part of the chapter examines the early post-Mao era, which encompasses roughly 1978–89. The second part discusses how protest in China has changed since 1989. Although the number and frequency of protests have risen dramatically in comparison to the early post-Mao period, the character of protest has been far less threatening to national authorities.

Indeed, inasmuch as China's central political leaders have acted to ameliorate public grievances articulated in mass protests, popular trust in top CCP leaders has been bolstered, and the likelihood of popular support for political protest against the central government has diminished. However, as noted in the Introduction and more fully explored in the Conclusion, if current central leaders make it more difficult for Chinese citizens to effectively express their grievances, the regime may lose its ability to satisfactorily respond to those grievances, and may come to face more serious and widespread public calls for national-level political reform – particularly because sizeable swaths of the Chinese public are now accustomed to participating in collective contentious action.

POPULAR PROTEST IN THE EARLY POST-MAO ERA (1976–89)

In the early post-Mao era, only a few major popular protests occurred. They arose in urban areas, and focused on national-level leaders and policies. To a large degree, they reflected the changing focus of the CCP during this time, as well as factional struggles within the highest ranks of the Party that were related to this change. Each of the major protests during this period emerged when members of the public perceived support for greater reform on the part of some top CCP leaders, and felt that there was an opening to safely prod the Party in this direction. But in each instance, after varying lengths of time, key political elites turned against the protestors, and their actions were suppressed.

The death of Mao Zedong in 1976 ushered in a new era in China. When Mao died, China was in the tenth year of the "Great Proletarian Cultural Revolution." Though Mao ostensibly launched the Cultural Revolution to remove all vestiges of "feudalism" and "capitalism" in China and instill a pure communist culture, the campaign also punished and removed from power all CCP leaders that Mao viewed as a threat. One of them was Deng Xiaoping, who was labeled a "capitalist roader," removed from all of his posts, and forced to do manual labor to "reform" his thoughts. The Cultural Revolution also created chaos within Chinese society, as bands of young "Red Guards" roamed freely, punishing anyone they deemed to be "revisionist" in thought or action. Universities were shut down – targeted as bastions of such activity – and city folk were "sent down" to the countryside to become imbued with communist beliefs through manual labor.

The "April 5th Incident" of 1976

The year of Mao's death was tumultuous. The Party leader that most urban residents expected and hoped would succeed Mao, the administrative and diplomatic genius Zhou Enlai, died in January 1976 – nine months prior to Mao's death in September. In 1974, Zhou had convinced Mao to bring Deng back into the Party leadership, and Deng became the Party-state's Vice-Premier. Meanwhile, Mao's wife, Jiang Qing (and her comrades-in-arms, known collectively as the "Gang of Four") vied to take control of the Party. Evidencing public support for Zhou during the spring 1976 annual commemoration of deceased ancestors, wreaths honoring Zhou appeared in many Chinese cities, including a stack nearly forty feet high at Beijing's central Tiananmen Square. When Deng voiced his support for these actions, little lights and bottles – plays on Deng's name – appeared at the Square. Over the next five days, crowds gathered at the Square, bringing wreaths, singing songs, reciting poetry, and making speeches expressing their weariness and bitterness from their suffering during the Cultural Revolution, and welcoming a new day of stability. But, that day had not yet come. On April 4, police arrived at the Square, clearing away the protestors. The next day, angry crowds returned. They were met by thousands of police and other armed forces. Up to one hundred were killed, and up to several thousand were arrested. On April 7, Deng was stripped of all official posts and branded an "unrepentant capitalist roader." On

April 17, the official newspaper of the CCP, the *People's Daily*, issued a verdict on the "April 5 incident," calling it a "counter-revolutionary" rebellion. In the following months, many thousands reportedly were arrested.[2]

Thus, when Mao died in September, the Party's future direction was uncertain. Temporarily, a relatively unknown and inexperienced Party cadre – Hua Guofeng – assumed the helm. Less than a month after Mao's death, Hua was able to orchestrate the arrest of his main competitors for power, the Gang of Four. In July 1977, Deng was restored to a number of high-level Party-state positions. Deng criticized the Cultural Revolution and called for a "Beijing Spring" wherein citizens could express their grievances. By late 1978, Deng had out-maneuvered Hua, and was recognized as the top leader of the Party.

With this, China's "Reform Era" was ushered in. In December 1978, the CCP's Central Committee laid out a new reform program that emphasized economic modernization, acknowledged the importance of free enterprise, and promised to strengthen democracy and law. The general theme was pragmatism over ideological correctness. Former Party leaders that had been purged during the Cultural Revolution were brought back into positions of power, and an estimated 10,000 political prisoners were freed and cleared of any wrongdoing.[3] The official verdict on the "April 5 incident" was reversed, labeling those who had been jailed as heroes. China's universities were re-opened and tasked with training young people to spur China's economic and technological modernization.[4]

The Democracy Wall Movement (1978–80)

Shortly after Mao's death, and increasingly through 1977 and 1978, people began to publicly post personal appeals related to wrongs they suffered during the Cultural Revolution. In addition to gathering at Tiananmen Square, they affixed "big character" posters on a wall near the Square that became known as "Democracy Wall." When the official verdict on the "April 5" incident was reversed, hundreds of citizens gathered at the wall. In the days that followed, the crowds grew, both there and at Tiananmen Square. People from out of town flowed to Beijing and other major cities to express their grievances.

Most of the participants were relatively young. They included factory workers, students, and junior political officials that had suffered during the Cultural Revolution. Most sought various forms of redress for the many hardships that they had endured. But others moved beyond individual grievances, voicing broader political concerns. These individuals tended to be more educated, and seemed to have connections within the now-pragmatically-focused CCP leadership. Along with putting up "big character" posters promoting ideals such as democracy, science, political reform, and economic modernization, they produced mimeographed "people's periodicals" that they posted on Democracy Wall and even sold. At their peak, there were 55 such periodicals in Beijing, and at least 127 in nearly 30 other cities. Most of the periodicals' editors saw themselves as reformers rather than rebels, voicing support for the pragmatic reforms promoted by Deng. However, a small number took their political criticisms a step further. Most prominently, in late 1978 Wei Jingsheng's periodical, *Explorations*, called for democracy, and criticized Deng by name.

Initially, central authorities – including Deng – responded favorably to these activities. But official reactions changed as the number of petitioners and cities involved grew; the demands of the periodicals became more critical of the Party; and Deng became more firmly entrenched as the Party's top leader. Most importantly, Deng – the most powerful leader in the Party – turned against the movement. In late January 1979, a leader of the petitioners' movement in Beijing was arrested. In February, petitioners and protestors in Shanghai staged a 12-hour sit-in on the tracks of the Shanghai train station, disrupting long distance travel for many days. In March, Deng publicly criticized those calling for "democracy" and announced that all speech, pictures, posters, and publications must abide by the "Four Cardinal Principles" of CCP leadership, proletarian dictatorship, Marxism, and socialism. Shortly thereafter, *Explorations* came out with a special edition entitled, "Do We Want Democracy or a New Dictatorship?," attacking Deng's speech. Three days later, Wei and his staff were arrested. On April 5, 1979, the *People's Daily* asserted that the purposes of the movement of April 1976 had been achieved, and criticized "ultra-democratization." In October 1979, Wei was put on trial and sentenced to 15 years. In December, central authorities announced that Democracy Wall had been closed, and in January 1980, Deng struck from the state constitution the rights to the "four big freedoms" (to speak out freely, air views fully, hold great debates, and write big-character posters). This marked the end of the second major popular protest since 1976.

The Student-Led Protests of 1986–7

For five years, there were no further significant instances of popular protest. During this period, the "ideologues" of the Mao-era CCP's top leadership were no longer in power; all were now pragmatists. At the apex of Party power was Deng Xiaoping and seven other CCP elders. Among them, Deng was the most committed to expanding China's economy through marketization and opening to the global capitalist economy. Yet Deng exhibited only tenuous support for political liberalization. Within the second and third tiers of the CCP, leaders jockeyed for power and disagreed over policy. For most of the 1980s, the more pro-reform faction was led by CCP General Secretary Hu Yaobang and state Premier Zhao Ziyang, both of whom had been placed in their positions by Deng. The other major faction was led by Li Peng, who had been eschewed by Deng as the successor to Party leadership, and who believed that reform must occur slowly.

Throughout the 1980s, conflict between these two groups caused CCP policy to move fitfully and uncertainly between reform and retrenchment in the economic sphere, and opening and constriction in the political sphere. Meanwhile, the suffering and tumult of the Mao years fueled skepticism among university students regarding China's political, economic, and social status quo, and stimulated their admiration of alternative systems – particularly those found in the West.[5] In the latter half of the 1980s, these factors contributed to the emergence of two more major collective contentious actions focused on national-level political reform, led by university students.

The first occurred in the winter of 1986–7. In the first half of 1986, General Secretary Hu Yaobang and other pro-reform CCP elites publicly argued that in order to proceed with China's economic modernization, further educational, political, and administrative reform was needed. Seeing this as an opportunity, students began to collectively voice their support. At the same time, they expressed a number of economic and political grievances. The protests began at the University of Science and Technology (UST) in the city of Hefei in Anhui province. The first public gatherings occurred on December 5, 1986, when UST students met to protest their inability to nominate candidates for the local People's Congress.[6] Four days later, students demonstrated for three hours, and local officials agreed to postpone the election. When the election was held, UST vice-president Fang Lizhi and two students collectively garnered 50 percent of the vote. Students across the country expressed their support – demonstrating, putting up "big character" posters, and boycotting classes. Along with demanding greater participation in local political institutions, they railed against Party cadre corruption – expressing particular indignation at the gap between their "elite" educational status and their low salaries upon graduation, which stood in marked contrast to the relative affluence enjoyed by those with lesser academic credentials but greater political connections. Students also complained about the politicization of their curriculum, and the imposition of small tuition and residence fees at some schools (higher education had been entirely free prior to the post-Mao era). In all, protest activities appeared at 150 higher education institutions in 17 cities and involved up to 100,000 students. At the same time, the students generally did not challenge the legitimacy of the central regime, or call for systemic political transformation.[7]

General Secretary Hu Yaobang quietly indicated his support of the students. However, Deng Xiaoping did not share this view, and instructed Party elites to bring the movement to an end. Fang Lizhi (who at one point during the movement had called for "total Westernization") was expelled from the Party and dismissed from his position. General Secretary Hu was forced to resign from his post, criticized for encouraging "bourgeois liberalization."[8] Yet Hu remained on the Party's Politburo, and Hu's younger protégé, Zhao Ziyang, was appointed as the new General Secretary. Official media outlets propagated a campaign against "bourgeois liberalization," "inveighing against complete westernization."[9] However, the students' demands were not characterized as such. Rather, participants were described as having been led by a "handful of lawbreakers who disguised themselves as students," bent on fomenting nationwide chaos and disrupting stability and unity.[10] On some campuses, selected students were sent over spring and summer break to villages and factories to study the life of the working masses, and in late 1987, military training was re-emphasized on college campuses. Meanwhile, over 2,000 Chinese students that had been allowed by CCP authorities to study in the United States joined a collective petition, expressing concern that political and economic reform were being threatened, and that the chaos of the Cultural Revolution was returning.[11]

Nonetheless, the student participants generally were not punished, and central authorities addressed some of the protestors' grievances. In March 1987, CCP elites announced that People's Congress candidates must be nominated by the electorate (rather than CCP authorities), and that there had to be at least 33 percent more candidates than open seats. In addition, a campaign against official corruption was announced, featuring dozens of prominent arrests.[12] In late 1987, Party-state leaders announced a new law giving all adult rural villagers the right to elect and run for local Village Councils – the lowest level of the state structure.

The Student-Led Protests of 1989

The fourth and final significant popular protest of the early post-Mao period drew massive numbers of participants, and emanated to virtually every major Chinese city, though the most prominent actions were centered in Beijing. As with the prior movements of this era, the protests of 1989 ebbed and flowed along with factional struggles within the top ranks of the CCP, and ultimately were crushed when key political elites turned against the movement – despite the fact that the protestors had called for reform rather than revolution or systemic political change. Indeed, this time, the response of central authorities was so harsh that it broke the cycle of loosening–protest–repression that characterized the rest of the early post-Mao period. After the protests of 1989, CCP leaders changed their approach to social management, becoming more keenly focused on preventing the emergence of political dissent. Concurrently, they embarked on new reforms that led to a change in the types of grievances expressed in popular protests from the early 1990s through the present.

Many of the students that participated in the student-led protests of 1986–7 had been disappointed by the movement's end. Developments between 1988 and early 1989 only made matters worse. During this period, economic and political reform stalled, urban economic inequality widened, and inflation spiraled out of control. The students' top supporter within the CCP, Hu Yaobang, was no longer General Secretary. Although Hu's protégé and successor, Zhao Ziyang, was sympathetic to the students' general demands, by late 1988, economic problems had enabled his detractors within the high ranks of the Party to successfully criticize him and his policies, and Party elders acceded to giving Zhao's economic decision-making powers to his main competitor within the second-tier CCP leadership, the more economically and politically conservative Li Peng.

On April 15, 1989, former General Secretary Hu died unexpectedly, allegedly from a heart attack suffered while giving an impassioned speech to the CCP Politburo. Almost immediately, students (particularly in Beijing) engaged in public acts of mourning, posting "big character" posters and laying memorial wreaths for Hu on college campuses and at Tiananmen Square. Over the coming days, student posters and speeches became more political. Along with castigating CCP cadres (such as Deng Xiaoping's son) who used their political connections to profit from market reforms, students demanded liberal democratic rights such as freedom of association and speech. Yet at base, their political critique was reformist.

Nonetheless, student actions became more contentious as time passed. Many began to boycott their classes. On April 18–19, an estimated 10,000 gathered at Tiananmen Square, during which several thousand attempted (unsuccessfully) to present a petition at the CCP leadership compound adjacent to the Square. In the early morning hours, protestors and security authorities began to push one another, and roughly 1,000 police arrived on the scene to clear the demonstrators.

The students also began to organize, forming new associations free from CCP control. At the time (and through the present), all student organizations were required to have an official Party advisor; by creating their own groups without any Party oversight, students were consciously violating campus rules. By April 22, not only had autonomous student organizations formed on numerous Beijing campuses, but students from a number of Beijing schools had joined together to create an All-Beijing Autonomous Federation of University Students. One of their first major decisions was to hold a massive street march to Tiananmen Square on April 27.

Deng Xiaoping and other more politically conservative CCP elites were not pleased. On campuses with the most activist activities, individual students were called in by campus authorities and pressured to discontinue their plans. On April 26, the front page of the *People's Daily* made the Party's official position crystal clear. Entitled, "It is Necessary to Take a Clear-cut Stand Against Turmoil," the article read,

> During the past few days, a small handful have engaged in creating turmoil...beating, looting, and smashing...In some universities, illegal organizations have formed to seize power from student unions; some have...begun a class boycott...If we tolerate this disturbance, a seriously chaotic state will appear, and we will be unable to have reform, opening, and higher living standards...Under no circumstances should the establishment of any illegal organizations be allowed. We must stop any attempt to infringe on the rights of legal organizations.

Although this ominous editorial caused many students to reconsider holding the planned April 27 march, in the end, they proceeded. The march exceeded their most optimistic expectations: over 100,000 students from virtually every tertiary school in Beijing defied official threats and marched for hours from the university district to Tiananmen Square. Hundreds of thousands of city residents lined the streets to watch and support the marchers. At various points, the students were met by police blockades, but when the students showed no sign of stopping, the blockades dispersed. Buoyed by their success, students held a second mass gathering at Tiananmen Square on May 4. Similar activities arose at virtually every college campus across the country.

On May 13, a group of students marched to Tiananmen Square and initiated a hunger strike. Aware that the CCP planned a gala event at the Square to welcome then Soviet president Mikhail Gorbachev to Beijing on May 15 (in what would be the first meeting of top Soviet and Chinese leaders since the Sino-Soviet split of 1960), the hunger-striking students hoped that their act would press the regime to respond. On May 14, ruling elites conceded to hold a formal dialogue with some student representatives, but the talks quickly collapsed. CCP leaders canceled the welcoming ceremony for Gorbachev as the hunger-striking students remained in the Square. Students from across China traveled to Beijing to join the demonstrations, and protest activities escalated in other major cities as well. Many independent media outlets – most notably, the *World Economic Herald* – supported the students, and even some official media outlets produced sympathetic coverage. On May 17, over one million students and citizens marched in Beijing.

Deng Xiaoping was outraged. Immediately following Gorbachev's May 18 departure from China, he supported a decision to declare Martial Law and to have military units clear the Square. General Secretary Zhao reportedly cast the lone dissenting vote. Subsequently, he visited the students at the Square, apologizing for coming "too late." Yet as the soldiers moved from the outskirts of the city to the center, an unexpected development occurred: hundreds of thousands of Beijing residents spontaneously poured into the streets to block them. With apparently no clear orders regarding how to respond to such a situation, the army retreated.

For the next two weeks, students debated the proper course of action, and pro-repression CCP elites crafted a more fail-safe plan to end the protests. Meanwhile, citizens from all walks of life – including urban state-sector workers from roughly 700 work units (including units within Party and state agencies) – joined the protests, carrying banners identifying their work units.[13] On May 20, a handbill announced the formation of the Beijing Workers Autonomous Federation (BWAF) – a shocking development for CCP leaders, who claimed that the Party was the only legitimate representative of China's working masses. On

May 30, three BWAF leaders were detained. On June 3–4, 1989, Deng ordered the military to clear the Square. Soldiers again pressed from the outer reaches of Beijing toward the city center, and again ordinary citizens flooded the streets to block them. However, this time the soldiers used violent force against anyone who stood in their way. An estimated 2,000 were killed, and many thousands more were injured.[14] In the following days, protest actions occurred in a number of other cities, most prominently in Shanghai, where from June 5–7, students blocked major roads and railways, factory workers went on strike, and students erected biers commemorating the dead in Beijing. Major protests also occurred in Hong Kong, which at the time was still under British rule.

The official verdict in the media was similar to that employed against the student-led protests of 1986–7, but its language was much more vehement: a "small handful" had incited "chaos" and "pandemonium," resulting in a "shocking counter-revolutionary rebellion" – a "struggle involving the life and death of the party and the state."[15] General Secretary Zhao was dismissed from his post and placed under house arrest. He remained there until his death in 2005. Jiang Zemin, the Party Secretary in Shanghai who had managed the demonstrations there without resorting to violence, was appointed the new CCP General Secretary. A list of the "Twenty-One Most Wanted" movement leaders (including mostly students, but also BWAF leader Han Dongfang), was aired on TV and posted in every train and bus station. Some managed to escape, fleeing to Hong Kong, Europe, and the US. Others, such as Han Dongfang and Beijing University student leader Wang Dan, were imprisoned.[16] Many other lower-level student leaders stayed in the country and were not subject to arrest, but had "black marks" entered in their permanent records that made it nearly impossible for them to find work. The *World Economic Herald* was shut down, and several of its staff members were arrested. Two prominent anchors on the official China Central Television (CCTV), some staff members at the *People's Daily*, and a number of other editors were dismissed from their posts due to their sympathetic coverage of the protests. On college campuses, political education was stepped up, including heightened criticism of the West.

In the minds of some key CCP leaders and many foreign observers, university students had become a dissident force bent on fundamental political change. This interpretation buttressed prevalent assumptions in the West that China's authoritarian political system would ultimately fall to popular pressure for liberal democratic change, particularly as China's economy became more marketized, and citizens enjoyed greater material prosperity. Although in reality the students had called for reform rather than wholesale political transformation, these assumptions seemed to be at least somewhat on the mark. For, both college students and other urban residents in the 1980s did indeed hold liberal democratic freedoms and Western cultural values in increasingly high esteem, and they were willing to act publicly and collectively on behalf of these values. In part, this derived from their disillusionment with the chaos and dysfunction of the Maoist period. Moreover, their view of Maoism and their aspirations for stability and modernization dovetailed with the pronouncements and policies of Deng and his chosen CCP leaders, particularly Hu Yaobang and Zhao Ziyang. Thus, students and other urbanites believed that the opportunity for reform was open.

POPULAR PROTEST IN THE LATE POST-MAO ERA (1990–PRESENT)

Realistic as this impression may have been at the time, by the middle of 1989, this opening had closed, and the cycle of opening-political protest-repression that characterized the early post-Mao period came to an end. Since that time, there have been virtually no top CCP leaders who have publicly supported the kinds of political demands that were expressed by students and other citizens between 1976 and 1989. Instead, China's post-1989 CCP leaders have been pragmatically focused on doing whatever it takes to ensure that the CCP will hold on to power. In the early 1990s, this was particularly concerning to them not only because of the protests of 1989, but also because as the 1990s began, communist regimes were falling in Russia and East-Central Europe. Determined to avoid a similar fate, CCP leaders studied what had happened in these formerly communist countries, drawing the conclusion that among the main reasons for their demise were dogmatic ideologies, corrupt elites, stagnant economies, and isolation from the international community.[17] Consequently, Deng and subsequent CCP leaders made a number of bold moves in the other direction. These actions have resulted in the near disappearance of the nationally-focused political protests that appeared between 1976 and 1989.

The most dramatic changes have been in the economic realm. As noted in the Introduction, in the early 1990s Deng encouraged the liberalization and marketization of China's economy. Since then, private enterprises have proliferated and grown. Hundreds of millions of rural residents have moved to cities in search of wage work, and large swaths of previously agricultural land have been converted to industrial use. This process has been facilitated by central authorities' decentralization of economic management, which has allowed local authorities a great deal of flexibility in seeking new sources of local economic growth. Concurrently, local authorities in the post-1989 period have been assessed according to their ability to promote economic growth, giving them a strong incentive to do so. In the late 1990s, central CCP leaders also forced the privatization of most of China's state-owned enterprises (SOEs), many of which had been operating at a loss. In 2001, China entered the World Trade Organization (WTO), further enmeshing China's economy in the global capitalist system. In the decade that followed, China's foreign trade more than quadrupled. Between 1992 and 2014, China's GNP grew by 8–14 percent per year, averaging around 10 percent overall. These developments have vastly improved the incomes and overall material living conditions of virtually all Chinese citizens. As a result, they have been more satisfied with CCP rule, and less interested in engaging in nationally-focused political protest.

At the same time, these economic changes have given rise to other popular grievances that have engendered more localized and economically-focused protests. In the countryside, fiscal decentralization led to the proliferation of taxes, fees and fines by local authorities, propelling widespread unrest. After central CCP authorities outlawed such charges in the early years of the new millennium, rural officials increasingly pursued income by confiscating peasant land and leasing it to private businesses. This has resulted in a new wave of protests that has continued through the present. In urban areas, SOE privatization in the late 1990s led to massive protests on the part of workers who were laid off or forced into retirement. Meanwhile, delayed and underpaid wages, and draconian working conditions in urban private enterprises have spurred numerous protests on the part of private-sector workers, the majority of whom are migrants from rural areas. Further, the rapid pace of economic growth since the early 1990s has been accompanied by severe environmental degradation, and this has engendered environmentally-focused popular protests.

In addition, since 1989, CCP elites have instituted educational reforms that have decreased the likelihood that students will engage in the type of political protests that they led in the 1980s. To begin, since the early 1990s, educational institutions from kindergarten through university have featured a "patriotic" curriculum designed to equate love of China with love of the CCP, and to instill support for China and its governmental policies against attempts by foreign developed nations (particularly those in the West and Japan) to criticize China and prevent it from rising to its rightful international place. This educational campaign has emphasized Chinese tradition and history, as well as the need to protect China's national unity and territorial integrity.

China's historical humiliation and subjugation by foreign powers has been a major focus, as have contemporary "wrongs" committed against China by foreign regimes. Unlike Mao-era "educational" campaigns, this effort has been implemented in a practical and sophisticated way, as CCP elites have recognized that the heavy-handed propaganda efforts of the Maoist period bred resentment and disillusionment rather than persuasion. Indeed, post-1989 regime authorities have studied marketing techniques used in the West to discern the most effective methods of "selling" the Party's "line." Further, both the educational curriculum and the official media have emphasized, with supporting data, how the material lives of Chinese citizens have improved in the post-Mao period, buttressing the CCP's claim to be the best guarantor of China's prosperity and stability.[18] These changes have contributed to the disappearance of nationally-focused political protest, but have fostered new nationalistic protests in the late post-Mao period.

Changes specific to higher education also have pushed in this direction. To begin, the number of colleges and college admission slots has increased dramatically, enabling a far higher percentage of young people to be accepted. Concurrently, however, the central government has cut its funding of higher education institutions, with the result that colleges and universities since the early 1990s have charged often very sizeable tuition and fees. For many students, the cost of a college education has become prohibitively high. The overall consequence of these two changes has been that, since 1989, a much higher percentage of young people from relatively wealthy families has been able to attend college, but only a tiny percentage of regular Chinese youths has been able to do so. Instead, most young people from less well-to-do families have sought work in the private sector. At the same time, in contrast to the 1980s, when the government assigned jobs to most college graduates, from 1990 through the present, college graduates have been on their own. And, because there are so many more college graduates than there were in the 1980s, it has become difficult for those with college degrees to find attractive high-paying and high-status jobs. The ironic result has been that college students increasingly have sought CCP membership as a way to gain an edge in the job market. And because most of them come from families that have prospered as a result of the economic reforms of the 1990s (and often also due to their connections with ruling elites), they have not been pre-disposed to engage in political dissent.

Meanwhile, the CCP has worked to expand its membership to include groups that were excluded from the Party during the Maoist period. In the Mao era, only those with unquestionable class "credentials" and communist commitment were allowed into the Party; generally speaking, this included only people with peasant or blue-collar worker family backgrounds. Persons who came from families that had been privileged in the past (including landlords, wealthy peasants, merchants, factory owners and managers, and intellectuals) typically were not eligible. In the early post-Mao period, between 1976 and 1989, intellectuals and university students were courted by the Party, as its leaders sought a more educated and technocratic membership. However, the fresh and painful memories of the Cultural Revolution caused most to shy away from the Party. As noted above, changes in China's higher education system since the early 1990s have increased student interest in joining the Party, albeit for its perceived material benefits rather than because of students' ideological affinity with the Party. Similarly, in the early post-Mao era, private business owners remained barred from Party membership. In the early 1990s, this prohibition was relaxed, and in 2002 it was formally removed when the Party embraced then General Secretary Jiang Zemin's theory of the "Three Represents," which declared that the CCP represents "advanced productive forces" such as private entrepreneurs. Since then, Party membership among private business owners has skyrocketed; an estimated one-third of them have joined the CCP. The Party's greater inclusiveness since 1990 has diminished the desire of groups such as private entrepreneurs, students, and intellectuals to engage in protests calling for national-level political change. As will be discussed in more detail in chapter 7, only a tiny number of intellectuals have done so in the post-1989 period.

Overall, protest on the part of Han Chinese in mainland China from the 1990s through the present has had a fundamentally different character than the type of protest that characterized the early post-Mao period. Between 1976 and 1989, there were only a few significant popular protest actions. They arose in China's major cities and were spearheaded by urban residents; there were few collective contentious actions of any notable size in the countryside. The significant urban protests that occurred were in some cases quite large – involving well over a million people, and spanning a number of cities simultaneously. This was because their demands were national, not local: they sought central political reform. Further, these protestors engaged in these collective actions because they believed that top leaders within the CCP were sympathetic to their cause. Although their belief was well-founded, in each of the major protests that arose during this era, as time passed key political leaders turned against the movements and the protests were suppressed – in some instances, violently so.

From 1990 through the time of this writing, there have been no significant nationally-focused protests calling for central-level political reform. However, there have been many more popular protests than there were in the early post-Mao period. According to official Chinese government statistics, between 1993 and 2005, the number of yearly "mass incidents" in China rose from 8,700 to 87,000, and it is estimated that there have been at least that many (and perhaps close to twice as many) every year since then. Although these figures may seem to suggest that central CCP authorities have had much more to worry about since 1990 than they did in the years prior, the thousands of protests that have appeared in China in the post-1989 period have not lodged complaints against central leaders, or the CCP-led political system as a whole. Rather, post-1989 protestors have aired local grievances against local elites (both political and economic), and they generally have done so out of a belief that central policies (and leaders) are on the protestors' side. In this respect, protests in the early and late post-Mao periods share one thing in common: a conviction that the opportunity for successful protest exists due to expected sympathy on the part of (particularly high-level) political leaders. The difference is that in the early post-Mao era, protestors believed that particular CCP elites supported their demands, whereas in the late post-Mao period, protestors have been motivated by a more generalized sense that central policies are good. In the former, protestors hoped that by protesting they could get central policies to change, whereas in the latter, protestors have hoped to get corrupt or poorly-behaved local elites to abide by (already good) central policies.

Since the mid-1990s, and especially since the early years of the new millennium, these views have been buttressed by changes in the Party's approach to popular protests. In the early post-Mao period and the first few years after 1989, Party leaders' main goal was to quickly quell protests, and the main tactic for doing so was the use of force. From the early 1990s through at least the fall of 2012, central authorities increasingly accepted that locally-focused protests were not only inevitable, but useful. As a result, the Party has shifted toward a strategy of "containing" and "managing" popular protest. This has involved improved intelligence gathering to foresee popular grievances and preempt potential protests. It also has involved improved training for public security forces, leading to more professionalized crowd control and the greater avoidance of mass arrests and use of violence. In 2003, the CCP's Central Committee called for an increase in the quantity and quality of police substations and local security bodies; the average percentage of local budget spending on public security increased from 2 percent in 1988 to over 6 percent in 2010. In 2011, central leaders announced a new "social management" program, emphasizing the need to alleviate inequalities and hardships among the citizenry, to heighten indoctrination, and to further improve public security.[19] Overall, these changes have improved the ability of political authorities to successfully respond to popular grievances and popular protests. Even so, actions undertaken by Xi Jingping to restrain the ability of regular citizens to publicly and collectively express their complaints may cause this attitude to change.

These differences apply only to protest on the part of the Han Chinese majority in mainland China proper. As will be discussed in chapters 8 and 9, protests by residents of Hong Kong and China's ethnic minorities have evidenced a different trajectory. Both have focused on central CCP leaders, and have overtly called for political reform. However, thus far, few mainland Chinese residents have evidenced any sympathy or support for these protests.

The chapters that follow examine the major types of popular protest that have arisen in the late post-Mao period (1990 through the present). Generally speaking, whereas protests undertaken by Han Chinese mainland residents have buttressed the stability of China's central CCP-led ruling regime, protests undertaken by ethnic minority groups (particularly Uighurs and Tibetans) and Hong Kong residents have undermined CCP rule in these regions. At the same time, recent actions by CCP General Secretary Xi Jinping to rein in collective contentious action on the part of virtually all demographic groups threaten to erode the legitimacy of CCP rule in the minds of mainland Han Chinese as well. Moreover, because people from all walks of life, and across all areas of China, are now accustomed to protest, they may be more likely to act on their potential dissatisfaction with central CCP leadership.

2 | Rural Protest ──────────────

Many demographic groups have protested in the late post-Mao era, but rural residents – who as of 2016 made up over 40 percent of China's citizenry – have been the most contentious.[1] Rural residents' complaints have not been with central authorities or China's overall political system. Instead, rural residents have protested against perceived abuses by local political and economic elites. And, rural protesters generally have not sought to make wider connections with ruralites in other locations, or with other demographic groups. Moreover, their complaints have been of an economic or material nature; they have not been motivated by broader political ideals, and they have shown virtually no interest in pressing for systemic political change. Nonetheless, as long as the fundamental causes of their dissatisfaction are not resolved, rural protests will continue, and the volatility of China's countryside will pose a challenge to central CCP leaders.

THE CHANGING OPPORTUNITY STRUCTURE FOR RURAL PROTEST

Maoist Period (1949–76)

During Mao's rule over China (1949–76), conditions did not favor the emergence of collective rural contention. Prior to and during the CCP-led communist revolution that brought Mao to power, the vast majority of rural residents lived in abject poverty, subject to the vicissitudes of nature and to harsh control by the gentry that owned virtually all of the arable land. Under Mao's leadership, the CCP mobilized China's peasantry, and through their collective efforts gained control of China in 1949. One of the first actions undertaken by the CCP was land reform; land was confiscated from the gentry, and redistributed to the peasants. This policy was incredibly popular; for the first time in their families' histories, many peasants had control over their own land and some measure of economic security.

However, not long thereafter, the CCP collectivized rural land, and individual households had to relinquish their own plots. The size of the collectives varied over the course of Mao's rule, but for most of this period all rural land and capital were owned and controlled by the collective. Further, all agricultural products were bought and sold through cooperatives that were owned and operated by the Party-state. Government authorities set quotas for agricultural produce, with a low price paid for quota items and a slightly higher rate for above-quota items. Typically, very little was left after the basic needs of the collective were met. In some years, even farmers' basic needs were not satisfied. Most egregiously, during Mao's "Great Leap Forward" of 1958–60, tens of millions of farmers starved to death, and many more barely survived.

Part of the reason for these rural hardships was that citizens in the Maoist era were unable to voluntarily change their place of residence or work. Instead, all were issued a residential registration card (known as a *hukou*), which stipulated whether a person was a rural or urban resident, and in which specific location. Citizens could not freely move to other locations – doing so required the official approval of local authorities, and rarely was granted. As a result, citizens with a rural residential card were not allowed to move to the city, or perhaps a more agriculturally productive locality. And if they did so without permission, they would have no legal place to stay, and no access to food and basic necessities.

Certainly, then, rural residents in the Maoist period had many things to complain about. Yet, virtually none engaged in popular protest. Why? Two main reasons stand out. First, although rural residents in the Maoist period experienced many hardships, most still felt that they were better off under CCP rule than they had been prior to the communist revolution. Second, the political system was almost entirely closed to this type of behavior. Through numerous statements, policies, and political campaigns, top CCP leaders made it clear that any and all criticism of the CCP or its policies would be construed as "counter-revolutionary" behavior, and punished as such. Thus, rural residents did not perceive that popular protest would have any likelihood of bringing redress.

Post-Mao Period (1976–Present)

After Mao's death, conditions in the countryside changed dramatically. Although overall, these changes significantly improved the quality of life for virtually all rural residents, the new "opportunity structure" also favored the emergence of rural protests. Perhaps most importantly, the new CCP leadership – particularly Deng Xiaoping, who was recognized as the Party's most powerful leader from 1978 until his death in 1997 – had a different view of its relationship with "the masses." Whereas Mao asserted that the Party represented the will of the masses, and thus that any unrest on the ground must be the work of "counter-revolutionary" or "revisionist" thinking, CCP leaders from Deng on have maintained a more pragmatic view that popular unrest is not necessarily tantamount to treason. Rather, post-Mao CCP elites have seen popular unrest as a potential source of information about what is going on at the grassroots level – particularly when the grievances expressed involve local corruption or injustice and are not targeted at the national political system or its leaders. Of equal importance, even though rural quality of life has improved markedly in the post-Mao period, rural residents have in many instances been subjected to what they believe are abusive and unjust behaviors on the part of local authorities. In this environment, rural residents frequently have engaged in collective protest. Rather than repressing these contentious actions, central authorities have collected information about them, and subsequently have attempted to address rural residents' most serious complaints. In some cases, these attempts have been successful. However, some key issues have yet to be resolved.

CHANGING OPPORTUNITY STRUCTURES AND RURAL GRIEVANCES IN THE EARLY POST-MAO PERIOD

One of the most important changes in the "opportunity structure" experienced by rural residents in post-Mao China has been the dismantling of the agricultural collectives of the Mao era, and the institution of a new land allocation system that leases plots of land to rural households for their individual use. By the early 1980s, virtually all villages had converted to this system. The system created various categories of land, with contracts signed for each. This system was hugely popular with rural residents, and agricultural productivity rose dramatically as farmers felt confident that their hard work on the land would benefit them directly. Although the *hukou* system remained in place, such that rural residents still had virtually no legal geographic mobility, most were happy with the new land allocation system.[2]

In addition, in the early post-Mao period central CCP leaders allowed localities to establish non-agricultural rural enterprises (known as Township and Village Enterprises, or TVEs), which gave many rural residents the opportunity to earn wages on top of the economic gains made through their "household responsibility system" land. This further added to rural residents' satisfaction relative to the Maoist period, and helped to alleviate their frustration with the geographical limitations imposed by the *hukou* system. Overall, most rural residents welcomed the reprieve from the hardships they had faced during Mao's rule, and experienced the early post-Mao period as a time of relative plenty and upward socioeconomic mobility.

However, the rural reforms of the early post-Mao period also had some unforeseen consequences that were very detrimental to some rural residents, and gave rise to serious grievances among them. The fundamental problem was that local governments in some regions no longer had a source of income, as the central government did not provide a funding source to replace the income that rural leaders previously had garnered through the now-dismantled agricultural collectives of the Mao era. In rural areas in coastal provinces near SEZs, TVEs were very successful, and TVE profits provided local authorities with a new source of revenue. However, in China's central and western areas that were far removed from the new SEZs, TVEs were far less successful, and local officials found themselves seriously strapped for cash. In these areas, township and village officials responded to their shortage of funds by adding to legally sanctioned taxes various supplemental fees, assessments, fines, and forced contributions. Peasants were required to pay for government services such as licenses and birth registration, and were penalized for both minor and major infractions – including fines that exceeded the average resident's yearly income for violating the "one-child" policy. In addition, local political elites exacted compulsory assessments for school and road construction, water projects, power station building and maintenance, medical facilities, and public security. In some localities, up to 40 percent of villager incomes were being spent on legal and non-legal fees, taxes, and fines.

Protests and Governmental Responses in the Early Post-Mao Period

In rural areas of central and western China experiencing these "arbitrary" assessments, rural residents became restive. In 1993, central authorities reported over 6,000 cases of "turmoil" in the countryside. In nearly 1,000 of these instances, 500 or more protestors were involved. More than 8,000 deaths occurred, and property worth 200 million yuan was destroyed. Similar waves of unrest swept the countryside in 1995 and 1996. In 1997, nearly 900,000 farmers in nine provinces participated in collective petition efforts and public demonstrations – many of which became violent. In 1999 roughly five million rural residents engaged in public protests, and another two million did in 2003.[3]

Rural villagers' complaints were not with the central policies that had put local leaders in a situation where they felt compelled to levy these fees, but rather with the local authorities that were directly involved in establishing and enforcing these exactions. Further, the protestors' grievances were specific and material: they demanded that these "arbitrary" fees and fines be abolished. Relatedly, these protests were local; participants generally did not make any effort to make connections with aggrieved residents in other localities.

The protests were fueled by farmers' belief that the national government was well-intentioned, but that, when it came to tax/fee disputes, local authorities thwarted the capacity of the center to implement its benevolent policies. As a farmer engaged in tax protests in the late 1990s stated, "Damn those sons of bitches [township and village cadres]! The Center lets us ordinary people have good lives; all central policies are very good. But these policies are all changed when they reach lower levels. It's entirely their fault. They do nothing good, spending their whole day wining and dining. The only thing they don't forget is to collect money."[4] This mentality suggests that farmers during this period believed that the "opportunity structure" for protest was relatively open, as central authorities were perceived to be on the farmers' side. Evidencing this attitude, a survey of rural residents conducted by O'Brien and Li in 2003–4 found that 78 percent of respondents agreed or strongly agreed that "the Center is willing to listen to peasants who tell the truth and welcomes our complaints," and 87 percent agreed or strongly agreed that "the Center supports peasants in defending their lawful rights and interests."[5]

Further contributing to this dynamic was another element of the "opportunity structure:" the governmental system was set up such that fees and taxes on farmers – even those levied by the township and county – were collected by village-level authorities. As related by Bernstein and Lu, because farmers resented these exactions, the local tax collection officials faced a "difficult, time-consuming and frustrating" task that "could only be accomplished by... 'deception, roaring and intimidation'"[6] – and not infrequently spiraled into physical force and violence. This combination of circumstances made for fertile ground for localized protest.

Even so, in most villages the potential for farmer protest lay unrealized. In order for farmers to mobilize, somebody had to take a first step toward action. Frequently, the initial spark occurred when an individual villager or small group of villagers – typically male, relatively educated (with the ability to read the newspaper or government documents and write a petition or informational material), middle-aged or older, and with some sort of leadership experience or standing in the community (such as CCP membership, a Party-state position, or prior military service) – learned about a higher-level government policy or pronouncement against taxes/fees being levied in the individual's locality of residence.[7]

Upon gaining this knowledge, the individual or small group would then relay the information to their neighbors, friends, and relatives. They spread the word in a variety of ways, including making personal visits and having private conversations, holding public meetings, putting up signs and posters in public places, and acquiring loudspeakers and broadcasting information at rural market gatherings.[8] Once a critical mass had been mobilized, protest leaders would write and collect signatures on collective petitions, and submit them to their local "letters and visits" offices. Typically, their petitions were accepted, but did not elicit any serious or helpful governmental response. In some cases, frustrated groups of petitioners attempted to register their complaints at higher-level "letters and visits" offices.

Actions such as these often sparked the anger of local authorities, who did not want to be "outed" to their higher-ups. In many instances, local officials reacted with force and violence. They ransacked petitioners' homes, took their possessions, and in some cases beat petitioners to the point of serious injury and even death. In these situations, conflicts at times escalated into street protests and violent acts of revenge against local leaders; protestors beat local officials, sacked their fields and destroyed their equipment, and raided local government-controlled supplies. Because local state structures had deteriorated in the relatively poor villages in which contentious interactions such as these arose, in many localities diminished public security forces were unable to stop such popular violence or punish the perpetrators.[9] The proximate and ultimate outcomes of escalating protest actions varied. In some areas, higher-level authorities sacked misbehaving local officials, and/or local fee and tax exactions abated. But in many instances, the leaders of the protests were arrested and punished (often with multi-year jail sentences) and the tax and fee situation did not improve.[10]

The prevalence of rural unrest related to taxes and fees did not go unnoticed by central Party-state authorities. For, even though farmers who submitted petitions through China's "letters and visits" system generally did not receive a satisfactory response to their grievances, "letters and visits" offices were fairly meticulous in compiling data on the number and type of petitions received. Moreover, higher-level authorities regularly sought out these data and reports for analysis and review. As documented by Christopher Heurlin, through this process, CCP authorities have been able to identify the most serious "burning issues" within the populace that require governmental attention at a given point in time.[11]

By the late 1980s, the information that had reached top CCP leaders led them to conclude that a "burning issue" had indeed arisen in the countryside – particularly in the less developed villages of central and western China. According to official sources, peasants were exhibiting a "rebellious mentality" and "fierce dissatisfaction," leading to "vicious incidents" and "fierce reactions."[12] Further, central leaders determined that the main source of rural grievances was the "arbitrary" taxes, fines, and fees being levied by local officials.

Beyond occasionally stepping in when a local case of farmer dissatisfaction spiraled out of control, and in some cases firing errant local officials, top CCP elites made concrete moves to resolve the general problems that were causing farmer protests. To begin with, they instituted a new law designed to hold local state authorities accountable to the opinion of the residents within their jurisdiction. In doing so, central leaders hoped that corrupt local leaders would be voted out of office, and more legitimate local leaders would be voted in. This, then, would make the village population more obedient and less likely to rise up in anger.[13] Specifically, in late 1987, central authorities passed a new law granting rural residents the right to nominate and elect the leaders of their Village Council (VC), the lowest-level governmental unit within the Chinese Party-state. Further, the law stipulated that the VC would be answerable to Village Assemblies made up of all adult residents. In 1988, the central Ministry of Civil Affairs worked to implement the new law, establishing province-level guidelines, and organizing publicity campaigns, election work, and training classes. Even so, the law was slow to go into effect, as most existing local leaders did not welcome it, and did their best to delay or block its implementation. Nonetheless, by 1990, "rudimentary" VCs had been established in virtually every Chinese village. And in localities where VC elections were free, fair, and competitive, rural residents became more satisfied with their local governance, and less restive.

However, in many localities, elections did not follow legal stipulations. Further, in cases of conflict between VCs and local Party leaders, the latter typically prevailed. Moreover, the institution of VC elections did not eradicate the fundamental source of the "arbitrary" fines and fees that local authorities were levying: the central government still did not provide localities with sufficient basic funds. Thus, in many villages, "arbitrary" exactions continued, and protests continued throughout the 1990s. In 1997, for example, roughly 100,000 farmers across three prefectures in Jiangxi province engaged in 100 protests that persisted for four weeks and included attacks on government supplies and offices. Meanwhile, in Henan province, approximately 200,000 farmers took to the streets for five days of collective actions that resulted in three deaths and 54 injuries.[14]

CHANGING OPPORTUNITY STRUCTURES
AND RURAL GRIEVANCES IN THE LATE
POST-MAO PERIOD

As central CCP leaders became aware of the persistence of rural unrest and dissatisfaction, they undertook additional measures to address rural grievances. First, they worked to further improve village governance. In 1998, central authorities promulgated a new law that directed VCs to allow Village Assemblies to discuss and decide on matters such as village expenditures and revenues, applications, plot allocations, family planning actions, and collective contracts. The law also instructed VCs to publicize local government allocations and decisions. In addition, the new law gave all adult villagers the right to run for election, to directly nominate candidates, and to recall VC members. According to various reports, the quality of village elections improved in the years following the announcement of this new law.[15]

Second, in the early years of the new millennium, central CCP leaders initiated experimental projects to phase out rural taxes and fees entirely. Based on the results, they announced a new national policy to completely eradicate not only informal charges by local leaders, but also formal rural taxes, by 2006. Importantly, top Party elites made concrete efforts to ensure that this new policy would be realized. To begin with, they gave provincial authorities centrally-prescribed benchmarks, which were then handed down to township and village leaders. With promotion clearly tied to the fulfillment of these benchmarks, local leaders were under pressure to comply. In addition, in some provinces each household was sent a letter explaining the new tax and fee reforms, and told to sign it. With rural residents made aware of the new central policies, it was difficult for local leaders to ignore or circumvent them. As a result, the pace of implementation was surprisingly rapid. By 2004, virtually all rural taxes and fees had been abolished.[16]

These changes eradicated the proximate cause of rural unrest in China's poorer central and western areas. Consequently, protests revolving around excessive taxation almost entirely disappeared. In this respect, the efforts of central CCP leaders paid off. Moreover, farmers' protests resulted in clear and dramatic changes in government policies and practices.

Nonetheless, the abolition of rural taxes and fees did not solve the underlying problem that had spurred local authorities to levy such exactions: the lack of adequate central government funding for local government services. Thus, in China's poorer central and western rural regions, when "arbitrary" exactions were banned, local authorities lost their major source of revenue, and public services further deteriorated. Yet, this development did not fuel new protests in these areas. For, rural residents no longer felt morally and economically wronged by local authorities. In addition, they did not feel propelled to protest against central government leaders, as these leaders had acted sympathetically toward their protests. Moreover, in 2006 the CCP launched a "New Socialist Countryside" initiative designed to improve public services and the general welfare of rural residents, particularly in poorer geographic areas. This initiative included expanded agricultural subsidies, a new "welfare" payment system for the rural poor, improved rural healthcare, and rural consumer subsidies for home appliances. Further, in 2008, central authorities passed a large-scale stimulus package that included roughly US$60 million in rural infrastructure expenditures. Together, these central government-initiated efforts had a notable positive impact on the lives of rural residents in poor areas. As a result, these residents ceased to engage in significant collective protest around basic economic issues.

At the same time, however, new problems emerged in the countryside beginning in the late 1990s – this time in the wealthier coastal areas that had been relatively quiescent through most of the 1990s. The underlying cause of this development has been the fact that local leaders have continued to be evaluated primarily based on the local economy under their jurisdiction. In rural areas close to urban zones, local rural political authorities frequently forced farmers to give up their land, so that it could be leased more profitably to private businesses. Countless "development zones" have been begun in this manner, contributing to the local GDP through fees, licenses, lease agreements, and real estate and construction taxes – and thereby improving local officials' chances of promotion. In the process, many local government leaders also have lined their own pockets.

Rural land requisitions did not begin in the late post-Mao era. However, they were not as common in the 1980s and early 1990s. Moreover, during this earlier period, most displaced farmers were satisfied with their new situation, as they received adequate cash payments and jobs in TVEs, which typically provided them with greater income than they had earned through farming.[17] Thus, during this period, there were almost no collective protests surrounding this issue.

The situation began to change in the late 1990s, due to a variety of factors. First, when many TVEs began to falter as a result of the exponential proliferation of such enterprises, landless farmers typically were the first to be fired. By 1998, Huerlin reports, most resettled farmers had lost their jobs.[18] Second, national leaders put forth a new law in 1998 that dropped the requirement that displaced farmers be given job resettlement. These uprooted farmers – particularly those in their forties and older – found it difficult to find new sources of income, as they had spent most of their lives working the land. Many became unemployed, or found undesirable work as migrant laborers, earning in some cases only one-eighth of what they had made through farming.[19] Third, the pace and extent of land-takings picked up dramatically around the turn of the millennium; according to official statistics, the amount of land transferred every year quadrupled between 2000 and 2003.[20] Since then, numbers have only continued to rise.

Although national leaders have stipulated that farmers who are removed from their land must be provided with alternative housing, in many cases, rural residents have been dissatisfied with what they have been offered. Whereas such families once enjoyed relatively large living spaces in houses built alongside their fields, their new local government-provided housing typically has been in hastily-constructed apartment buildings that are shoddy and cramped, and inconveniently located.

These developments have angered many farmers in rural areas that are relatively close to coastal urban zones. In addition, as with the "artibrary" fee exactions of the 1990s, land requisitions have provided affected rural residents with a clear target of their ire: local political authorities. Further, as was the case in the early post-Mao period, farmers have had good reason to believe that central government leaders would be sympathetic to their plight, as national authorities repeatedly have ordered local political leaders to cease such activities.[21] For example, in 2006, central officials directed provincial governors and local leaders to reduce government requisitions of land that had been allocated to rural residents; in 2008 farmers were given the right to lease and transfer their land; and in 2014 the State Council issued a document emphasizing that farmers have the right to seek a mortgage on their land, on the understanding that the land is not to be transferred or land use changed. This combination has created fertile ground for collective contentious action.

Protests and Governmental Responses in the Late Post-Mao Period

Indeed, by the early years of the new millennium, farmer protests centering on issues related to land requisitions had become widespread. Between 2003 and 2005, official and scholarly reports estimate that farmers submitted to "letters and visits" offices 6–10 million collective petitions related to land disputes. In 2004 alone, 87 percent of known cases of rural disturbances reportedly arose from land disputes, and government sources reported nearly 47,000 cases of "illegal land activities" nationwide within only six months. Since 2005, the government has not released statistics on the frequency of popular unrest, but both official media reports and independent observations have suggested that farmer uprisings focused on land requisitions have remained frequent and widespread. One study published in 2012 found that land disputes constituted 65 percent of all social unrest in China.[22]

As with earlier farmer protests focusing on tax and fee exactions, even when the "opportunity structure" might seem open to the emergence of protest, unless one or more individuals decides to take action around their grievances, collective contentious action will not emerge. In the case of land requisitions, the mobilization process has been shaped by an additional feature of the "opportunity structure" for farmers. The lowest level of village organization is the "small group." Typically, planned land takings are first announced at a special meeting attended only by small group leaders and Party members. In some localities, the small group as a unit must agree to land taking, and land acquisition compensation is distributed to the small group rather than to individual residents. Thus, if there is opposition to a proposed land acquisition, or to the compensation and relocation offered to the affected farmers, collective action generally begins within the small group.[23]

As with the farmer protests of earlier decades, the individuals who step up to initiate or lead a protest action are almost always relatively educated older males with some sort of prior standing in the community. Often, this is the small group leader.[24] In some localities (particularly in Fujian province), the leaders of village old-persons associations (typically local retired cadres, teachers, and other individuals who had a respected position prior to their retirement) act as mediators between disgruntled villagers and local authorities.[25]

The process by which collective actions have developed around land takings also mirrors the progression of farmer protests in the 1980s and 1990s. First, one or more leaders publicizes the situation. Along with using methods common in earlier decades (public posters and broadcasts, flyers, etc.), since the start of the new millennium farmers increasingly also have used cell phones (and to a lesser degree the Internet) to communicate their grievances and planned collective actions. Although most farmers still lack easy access to and facility with the Internet, virtually all have cell phones that they can use to send information via text.[26]

Second, the aggrieved farmers submit a collective petition to the local "letters and visits" office. Similar to earlier collective petition efforts by farmers, these rarely have resulted in redress. For example, a 2005 survey of 17 provinces found that in 68 percent of petition cases (virtually all of which concerned land takings), the government either refused to increase the peasants' compensation (36 percent) or took no action at all (32 percent).[27] Further, as with contentious collective actions on the part of farmers in the 1980s–1990s, the local authorities targeted in such petition efforts often have responded with violence. In a survey of villagers in two provinces conducted in 2003–5, over 60 percent of petitioners had been subjected to one or more forms of local repression, including being subjected to fines (roughly 28 percent); having their homes demolished or destroyed (nearly 22 percent); having their homes ransacked, properties confiscated, and valuables taken away (over 31 percent); being beaten, or having their family members beaten (nearly 47 percent); and being detained, arrested, and sent to labor camps (roughly 41 percent).[28] In another study conducted between 2005 and 2008, farmers in many villages in Hebei, Jiangsu, Jilin, Shaanxi, and Sichuan provinces reported that "local officials offered political shelter and financial assistance to criminal groups," which were used to help keep villagers "in line."[29]

In response to local intransigence and repression, farmers in some localities have taken more confrontational action. Among other things, they have set up blockades on roadways and railways and at development sites, refused to vacate land slated for requisition, and occupied and destroyed government buildings. And, they have used the cell phones and the Internet to relay information, photos and videos of their protests. In so doing, protestors have made purposeful, and often successful, efforts to attract wider attention to their cause – from other citizens, mass media outlets, and higher-level authorities.

In cases where rural protests have become sufficiently long-lasting, geographically expansive, and/or violent that higher-level political officials have taken notice, they sometimes have intervened. When they have done so, they typically have acted in support of the protestors. Not infrequently, the local authorities who were the target of the farmers' ire have been removed from office, moved to another locality, and/or imprisoned. In some cases, development projects have been halted, and/or farmers have been offered compensation. Concurrently, however, the leaders of the protests often have been harassed, arrested, and jailed.

A case that exemplifies many of these features occurred in the village of Wukan, in the city of Lufeng, in Shanwei prefecture in Guangdong province. In Wukan, the decades-long Party secretary and Village Council leader, Xue Chang, had blocked implementation of national laws regarding democratic Village Council elections. In 1993, Xue received approval from the Lufeng city government to turn a large swath of village land into an industrial park. Over 250 plots of land were taken from villagers, who were offered only roughly US$80 dollars in compensation.[30]

In 2011, villager Zhuang Liehong distributed a flyer around the village, containing information about the "illegal" land sale, and providing a QQ (instant message) number to contact.[31] Zhuang reportedly had been working in a village outside of Wukan, where he had learned about village elections and shared profits from land sales.[32] Discussions proliferated, and Zhuang and other villagers brought over ten collective petitions to "letters and visits" offices in Lufeng, Shanwei, and Guangdong.

On September 21, 2011, roughly 4,000 villagers gathered at the Village Council building; rebuffed, they marched to the industrial park compound, and then to the Lufeng government offices, where authorities promised to respond within ten days. When the protesters went to Wukan and could not find village Party secretary Xue, they ransacked the village government office. Some also threw bricks, blocked roads, and destroyed buildings at the industrial park compound. The next day, the Shanwei government sent roughly 200 police to Wukan. Villagers wielding bricks and steel pipes surrounded the police station, overturned nine police vehicles, and clashed with the police. Dozens of protestors and police officers were injured.[33]

Villagers then filed documents declaring that the Village Council had been unlawfully elected, and demanding new village elections. They also elected a Villagers' Provisional Representative Council,[34] which submitted a report to the Lufeng Party Congress Standing Committee. Lufeng authorities promised to investigate the matter, but also sent officials to collect signatures from the villagers attesting that the

September 21 "incident" had been resolved. Angered, the Provisional Council announced (both online and through posters and in-person broadcasts) a second march. On November 21, approximately 4,000 protesters traveled to the Lufeng government offices, where an officer accepted their petition and promised to respond. Concurrently, however, Shanwei authorities declared that the Provisional Council was an illegal entity. In early December, four protest leaders (including Zhuang) were arrested without warrant. One of them was violently beaten and died while in custody. Outraged, villagers erected barricades around the village. As police surrounded the village, reports and images were circulated in foreign and domestic media outlets, and through social media.[35]

In December, Guangdong provincial authorities negotiated a settlement with the village board. The police were withdrawn, several protest leaders were released, village Party secretary Xue and other village authorities were detained, the Provisional Village Council was recognized as legitimate, and a new Village Council was elected. Many of the protests' leaders were elected, and one of them became the Village Council head and village Party secretary.

Subsequently, some of the newly-elected leaders resigned when higher-level authorities refused to support efforts to return the disputed land. In early 2014, some new village leaders were arrested on corruption charges. Zhuang fled China and sought political asylum in the US. Despite new Village Council elections in March 2014, Village Council leaders and regular villagers have expressed dismay at their continued inability to resolve the land issue.[36] Further, a number of former village Party leaders have been re-named to the village Party committee.[37]

Experiences such as this have had a varied impact on farmers' political views. Even though beneficent national laws and pronouncements have given farmers the perception that top regime leaders are sympathetic to farmers' concerns, when farmers' efforts to appeal to high-level authorities have been ignored or rebuffed, farmers have become disillusioned with the political system as a whole. This attitude is poignantly expressed in the words of a disheartened petitioner who was detained after attempting to submit a petition in Beijing: "It's useless to seek justice. Opposing graft and corruption means time in prison."[38] Some farmers have given up in despair. Much more commonly, they have engaged in further contentious collective actions.[39]

The problem of land acquisitions – and the protests and often critical political views that have emerged among farmers as a result – have not abated. This is true even though central authorities have been well aware of the problem for at least a decade – both through their review of data collected by "letters and visits" offices, as well as via news of protests that has reached them via traditional and social media. This is because top CCP leaders have yet to address the problem's basic causes: the dearth of resources to fulfill local government responsibilities, the focus on economic growth in cadre evaluations, and the reliance on rural land development to satisfy these needs. As long as this incentive structure remains in place, land acquisitions will continue, and farmers will protest.

CONCLUSION

Between the 1980s and the present, hundreds of thousands of China's farmers have engaged in collective contentious actions – first around excessive local fees, fines and taxes, and more recently around unfair land requisitions. In both cases, central authorities have responded sympathetically to the farmers' grievances, engendering a view among farmers that top political leaders are on their side, and that their protest efforts might result in positive change. In the case of fees, fines, and taxes, this view was borne out. In the case of land acquisitions, the results have been mixed at best.

The overall consequence of these developments is that today, China's rural population is easily mobilized and volatile. Many rural residents either have participated in protests themselves, or know people who have. Their successes have further propelled their belief that such actions are worthwhile. Simultaneously, when they have met with intransigence on the part of political officials, or have suffered further abuses as a result of their collective protests, most have become only further enraged and determined. Until central government leaders resolve the land acquisition problems that continue to fuel farmer unrest, farmers' trust in the CCP-led political system may be expected to wane, and their protests are unlikely to subside.

3 | Labor Protest

China's urban workers also have been restive in the late post-Mao period. In 2015, there were 2,700 strikes in China (nearly doubling the number in 2014) and in 2016 there were another roughly 2,600.[1] Some of the largest worker protests have been undertaken by public-sector workers, but more frequently private-sector workers have been at the fore. Activism of both types has garnered the attention of Party-state leaders, as private-sector workers have been the lifeblood of China's growing economy, and public-sector workers labor in key industries viewed as essential to China's security.

Like farmers, urban workers have not criticized China's overall governing system or called for an end to CCP rule. Instead, they have focused on economic issues, targeting employers and occasionally local political elites. At the same time, since China's public enterprises are formally affiliated with the ruling Party-state, protests by their former employees have had more political overtones than has been the case with private-sector worker activism. Also in contrast to private-sector workers, who often have engaged in strikes to express their grievances, because public-sector workers typically have protested only after being laid off or forced into retirement, they rarely have been able to use strikes as a protest method. In addition, unlike farmer and private-sector worker protests, which have occurred with great frequency from the 1990s through the present, public-sector worker protests have arisen only in certain periods, in the context of widespread layoffs. Relatedly, private-sector protests generally have been small-scale and localized, whereas public-sector unrest has been large in scale and has evidenced connections among factories, even spanning entire cities and industries.

Moreover, unlike in the private sector, where protesting workers have focused on violations of the law (such as unpaid/underpaid wages), restive state sector workers have placed little emphasis on what is legal or illegal, and instead have expressed the more "communist" belief that the CCP has a duty to live up to its claim of representing and protecting the interests of the working class. Similarly, the latter have evidenced a sense of entitlement to good jobs and a secure standard of living due to the fact that for decades they enjoyed both, and were told that – as rank-and-file workers living in a community country – they were the "masters" of society.

In general, the government response to urban worker protests has followed a common pattern: delay and intimidate; harshly punish protest leaders; offer some material concessions to the "rank-and-file" protesters; and punish corrupt local political and/or economic elites. At the same time, central political authorities have on occasion stepped in to support the aggrieved workers. In the public sector, CCP leaders offered displaced state sector workers aid and benefits that were not provided to migrant workers. In the private sector, when protests have become sufficiently large and long-lasting that they have attracted the attention of central authorities, higher-level political leaders have in several notable cases sided with the workers. In addition, similar to farmer protests, CCP leaders have reviewed information collected by the Party-state regarding the major grievances expressed by restive private-sector workers, and have created new policies and laws and made official pronouncements designed to address these concerns.

At the same time, however, and also paralleling the situation with farmers, official stipulations regularly have been ignored or violated at the local level, with the result that private-sector contention has not abated. Further, the experience of protest often has left participants scarred and disaffected, yet simultaneously empowered. Moreover, younger generations of private-sector workers have been not only more prone to protest than their predecessors, but also more likely to press for more extensive rights and benefits. Simultaneously, since the 2012 ascension of Xi Jinping to China's top Party-state posts, political authorities have shown a greater propensity to repress labor activists. Coupled with the popular mentality that only a "big disturbance" will catch the attention of higher-level authorities and thus result in protest success, the overall result has been a volatile mixture that has the potential to lead to more regime-threatening protest behavior on the part of private-sector workers.

OPPORTUNITY STRUCTURES IN THE POST-MAO PERIOD

Collective contention by urban workers has been shaped by – and has shaped – their "opportunity structures." From the early post-Mao period through the present, most private-sector workers have been rural *hukou*-holders who have moved to urban areas to pursue wage work. Meanwhile, virtually all public-sector jobs have been allotted to urban *hukou*-holders.

Early Post-Mao Period: Public-sector Workers

In the early post-Mao period, public-sector employees had few material complaints. They enjoyed job security and "iron rice bowl" benefits (including subsidized housing, transportation, health care, and food), as well as increased wages and expanded bonus pay. On average, only about 5 percent of their family budget was spent on necessities. Concomitantly, the emergence of the private sector dramatically increased the number and quality of goods and services available to urban public-sector workers, as farmers now had the ability to grow and sell their own crops via the "household responsibility system," and private enterprises began to produce and sell consumer goods. Further, the private sector provided new employment opportunities for public-sector workers who felt "stuck" in their job and believed that they would benefit from finding a private-sector position, or from starting their own business.

Nonetheless, other developments during this time period led to dissatisfaction among urban state sector workers, leading many of them to support, and even join, the massive student-led demonstrations that started in Beijing in the spring of 1989. The main grievance expressed by public-sector workers during this period was political corruption. Specifically, they were outraged by their perception that the relative wealth of new private entrepreneurs had been gained unfairly through their political connections, and that Party-state cadres had used their own connections to make financial gains. Concomitantly, CCP leaders had declared that their main priority in recruiting new Party members was no longer the "working class;" instead, the Party sought out younger, more educated, and more technically oriented applicants. In addition, in the late 1980s inflation flared into the double-digits, resulting in a decline in the financial well-being of urban public-sector workers.

In late 1988 and early 1989, dissatisfaction with this situation led some urban SOE workers to engage in work slowdowns and even some wildcat strikes. When university students took to the streets in the spring of 1989, and their protests appeared to be greeted with sympathy among some top CCP leaders as well as other Party-state officials, the opportunity structure appeared to open, and some state sector workers joined in the protests. As discussed in chapter 1, the student protests began in mid-April and continued until the Party's violent crackdown on June 4. Many urban workers came out to show their support during student marches. In addition, some SOE workers in Beijing met to discuss their grievances, and secretly began to organize and distribute handbills and posters calling on other workers to join them. In mid-May, these Beijing SOE workers announced the formation of the "Beijing Workers Autonomous Federation" (BWAF). Subsequently, they attempted, unsuccessfully, to register with the official CCP-affiliated union, the All-China Federation of Trade Unions (ACFTU). On May 20, the BWAF called for a general strike among workers, and began a public registration drive at Tiananmen Square. By early June, WAFs had been established in over 20 major Chinese cities, with an estimated 20,000 SOE workers as members.

The WAFs were led by workers with limited formal education, though a few university students also worked with the organizations. Steel workers, builders, bus drivers, machinists, railway workers, and office staff made up the bulk of the membership. None of the leaders had any prior protest experience. BWAF activists also sought and maintained contact with SOE worker contingents who had engaged in public marches to Tiananmen Square, typically with the name of their SOE on a banner at their lead. Many CCP-affiliated cadres from various SOEs and the ACFTU also offered advice and support to BWAF leaders. In this context, despite official warnings from above, public-sector workers perceived an opening in the opportunity structure that encouraged their feelings of efficacy.

These protesting public-sector workers did not call for an end to CCP rule. To the contrary, they implored CCP leaders to be true to the Party's alleged communist ideals. Along with a clear commitment to values such as economic justice and worker rights, they expressed indignation at the economic disparities that had emerged and at the diminished standing of urban workers. For example, one WAF handbill stated that "we have calculated carefully, based on Marx's Capital, the rate of exploitation of workers. We discovered that the 'servants of the people' swallow all the surplus value produced by the people's blood and sweat."[2] Another WAF document asserted "the workers" should be "the real masters of the enterprise."[3] At the same time, WAF statements showed an awareness of, and attraction to, political values such as democracy, freedom of association, and the rule of law. Some also linked China's socioeconomic inequality to the corrupt and "dictatorial" nature of the regime.[4]

CCP leaders viewed the establishment of WAFs as a grave threat to their rule. Although no student leaders were arrested prior to the regime's bloody crackdown on the movement in early June, in late May three BWAF leaders were secretly arrested and detained. The next day, a few dozen BWAF members, led by 26-year-old railway worker Han Dongfang, protested in front of the Beijing Bureau of Public Security. Foreign reporters caught the scene on film, including an interlude when an overweight cadre emerged from the Public Security building and "loudly berated the workers," saying, "What law do you know; I am the law!" In the following days, tensions mounted as the BWAF and students continued to protest. On June 3–4, when military troops marched into central Beijing, shooting any who stood in their way, numerous BWAF members remained at the Square. Subsequently, Han was among the 21 "most wanted" who appeared on official handbills that blanketed official media outlets and public spaces. After turning himself in to the authorities, he was jailed for nearly two years. He was released only after being near death due to untreated tuberculosis contracted while caged in a small cell with other prisoners who had the disease. Other WAF leaders were arrested as well. The remainder went into hiding and ceased their protest activities.

For the next few years, public-sector workers were quiescent. As inflation subsided, and these workers' "iron rice bowl" benefits and job security remained intact, the intensity of their grievances declined. Further, the harsh end of the "Tiananmen" protests signaled that central political authorities would not tolerate contentious behavior, thus diminishing workers' (and other citizens') sense of efficacy.

Early Post-Mao Period: Private-sector Workers

Meanwhile, in the early post-Mao period private-sector workers were almost entirely quiescent. In part, this was because their conditions were improved relative to the Maoist era. Concomitantly, they had little sense of empowerment and efficacy. As noted above, most rank-and-file private-sector workers have been rural *hukou*-holders. Although through the early 1980s they were forbidden to move to the city, beginning in the late 1970s, some did so anyway. In part, this was possible because (as discussed in chapter 2) in the late 1970s, rural agricultural collectives were dismantled and rural land was leased to rural households. This new system freed rural residents from required agricultural work for the collective, and enabled members of households with "surplus" labor to pursue other economic options. Initially, there were few city jobs available, as state sector positions were reserved for urban *hukou*-holders, and the few private businesses in existence were mostly small-scale. Thus, in the late 1970s and early 1980s, many migrants to the city eked out a living as individual entrepreneurs – doing odd jobs (*dagong*), and engaging in street-side sales and services.[5] Some also found temporary work in construction, housework, or textile production – working for low wages and with no labor protections.

In the latter half of the 1980s, national political leaders eased restrictions on the geographic mobility of rural *hukou*-holders. However, central authorities made no attempt to help those who moved away from their home village. Indeed, in most urban areas local officials punished rural migrants as law-breakers – for example, taking them into custody and forcing them to do hard labor before being returned to their home village, and demolishing their makeshift shelters. Migrants also were forced to pay a variety of taxes (both legal and not), and those seeking legal registration typically faced subjective official treatment and arbitrary charges. Further, many migrants suffered "delayed payments and denial of wages, harassment, physical aggression, and petty theft" at the hands of employers and other city residents, yet received no sympathy or aid from local authorities. To the contrary, public security cadres themselves often were complicit in the mistreatment of rural migrants.[6] In this context, the number of (predominantly male) rural migrants engaged in private-sector work remained relatively small through the early 1990s.[7] Further, private-sector workers had no leverage over their employers, as there were more rural men willing to take their chances in the city than there were private-sector jobs. These aspects of the opportunity structure gave these workers little expectation that their situation might be improved through any sort of collective contentious action.

In addition, migrant private-sector workers in the early post-Mao period tended to feel less aggrieved than one might imagine. For, they compared their situation with that of the Maoist era, when many lived on the edge of survival. Further, most migrant workers in the early post-Mao period did not view the city as their ultimate residential location. Instead, most saw their work in the urban private sector as a temporary engagement wherein they could save money and then return to the countryside and live in relative plenty back on their household responsibility system land.[8]

Thus, from the late 1970s through the early 1990s, the opportunity structures surrounding private-sector workers worked against the emergence of feelings of both grievance and efficacy among private-sector workers. As a result, there were almost no private-sector worker protests during this period.

LATE POST-MAO PERIOD

In the late post-Mao period, in contrast, both public and private-sector workers have been restive. As noted earlier, public-sector protests have been sporadic, but large-scale, whereas private-sector protests have been persistent and small-scale.

Public Sector

The first wave of public-sector activism arose in the late 1990s and early years of the new millennium, in response to massive layoffs and forced early retirements due to the privatization of most of China's public-sector enterprises. In 1998, top CCP leaders announced that all SOEs would have three years to become profitable. Given that labor (and its associated "iron rice bowl" benefits) constituted the major expense of SOEs, enterprise managers were instructed to lay off or force into early retirement staff and workers, and to merge enterprises and let them go bankrupt.[9] Although reliable statistics are hard to come by, scholars agree that tens of millions of SOE employees – mostly middle-aged and older – were let go. In 2001 alone, official sources acknowledged that the number of lost SOE jobs totaled 15 percent of urban unemployment.[10] Another nearly ten million were required to retire early – in most cases 5–10 years in advance of the legal retirement age.[11] Moreover, many of them did not receive their pensions on time or in full. In a not inconsequential number of firms that were privatized, the new owners declared bankruptcy. In many cases, unscrupulous managers and Party leaders absconded with whatever resources were left at the factory prior to its closing. By 2002, nearly 74 percent of former SOE workers were not formally employed.[12] These workers certainly had reason to feel aggrieved. On top of their outrage at the corrupt behavior of their former managers and Party cadres in their firms, these individuals suddenly had moved from a privileged status to having to compete with unskilled migrant workers for undesirable jobs.

Simultaneously, the communist history and continued identity of the ruling regime led former employees of large SOEs to feel both entitled and betrayed. In interviews conducted around the time of SOE privatization, these individuals expressed a "'class-based' sense of entitlement, rights, and dignity" that derived from their official categorization as "masters of the enterprise" in the Mao era.[13] Further, they asserted that, because they had "contributed their entire working li[ves] to the factory,"[14] "the factory was not simply 'theirs' (the managers') but also 'ours.' "[15] In the words of one interviewee, "every inch of grass and every piece of steel in the factory belonged to us workers. They were our sweat and labor."[16] Moreover, in response to public-sector worker involvement in the protests of 1989, CCP elites in the 1990s had publicly stressed the importance of SOE workers to the Party, and had continued to emphasize the Party's socialist focus.

These developments made the "opportunity structure" more favorable to public-sector worker protest. Even so, whether and when actual protest activity emerged depended on the particular opportunity structure encountered by workers in a given firm. In enterprises that laid off workers or forced workers into retirement, but subsequently remained solvent, protests were rare, as former employees feared that protesting might lead the owners to reduce or cut their severance and/or retirement pay. In addition, in some cases former employees were warned that if they protested, they would not be allowed to return to the factory if its situation improved. Similarly, still-employed SOE workers generally did not join their former co-workers who took to the streets in protest, for fear of losing their own jobs.[17]

The opportunity structure also varied by location. In areas where private enterprises were more numerous and vibrant, former SOE workers had more economic options, and were less likely to protest. In regions where the state sector was the "only game in town" for unskilled workers, protests were large-scale and often highly conflictual. Relatedly, in locations where many large SOEs were concentrated and all or most simultaneously implemented layoffs and forced retirements, protests were particularly widespread. Layering on top of these factors, in areas that were more economically prosperous, officials had more resources to provide compensation to protesting workers, with the result that protests in such areas were relatively short-lived and amicably resolved. Conversely, in economically strapped localities where authorities lacked the means to "buy off" former SOE workers, confrontations were more tense.[18]

In at least ten provinces, the factors described above came together to spur large-scale and protracted protests. The biggest were in the cities of Daqing and Liaoyang – both in China's northeastern "industrial belt," where many large SOEs were concentrated, and few private-sector opportunities were available. At the same time, in both areas, SOE managers and local Party-state officials had enriched themselves as local SOEs were privatized and subjected to mass layoffs. Further, workers in both areas had a long-developed self-conception as exalted laborers serving the communist cause, but also one of having been abandoned.

Daqing was home to China's most important oil-producing enterprises, and its workers had long been hailed as heroes of the communist cause. Following the central CCP directive ordering all SOEs to become profitable, the Daqing Petroleum Administration Bureau was supplanted by the Daqing Oil Company Ltd, a subsidiary of the publicly-offered PetroChina. Enterprise managers warned workers that the company would go bankrupt as a result of its bloated workforce, and that workers would be let go with little or no compensation. Among the firm's more than 200,000 employees, an estimated 80,000 were pressured to accept pre-set severance packages. Many followed the company's advice and used the money to set up small businesses. But, most of these failed, leaving the workers with virtually nothing. With no other job opportunities in the area, nearly all remained unemployed. The official union claimed to have no responsibility to the workers, as they were no longer employed by the firm. Subsequently, the laid-off workers' expenses rose, resulting from what in their perception were unilateral changes to their severance terms made by their former employer. The final straw broke when Daqing Oil announced that if former employees wanted to retain their medical and old-age insurance, they would be required to make large annual payments. In addition, former employees were told that the enterprise would no longer subsidize their heating bills.

Led by a few individuals who were able to read and write well, and were knowledgeable about the law, some of the former workers formed an independent union. In March 2002, 3,000 workers gathered in front of the company's headquarters with the union banner unfurled. Demonstrations continued on a daily basis for the next month, on some days with tens of thousands of workers participating. Along with gathering in front of the company headquarters, workers protested at Daqing's "Iron Man Square." An estimated 800 public security troops monitored the protest sites, and dozens of suspected protest leaders were detained. Concurrently, authorities warned still-employed friends and family members of the demonstrators that their bonuses and even their jobs would be endangered if the protests continued.

Demonstrations persisted more intermittently through May. As time passed, local authorities became more forceful in their attempts to quash the protests, including surrounding the Square with troops and dogs and checking demonstrators' identification. But none were formally charged with any crimes, and violence was never employed by the authorities. Overall, managers and governing elites waited out the protests, while increasing the pressure on still-employed oil workers to convince the protestors that their efforts were not only for naught (because restructuring was economically unavoidable), but were also threatening to undermine the financial well-being of their friends and family members who still had jobs. In the end, this strategy was successful; no major concessions were offered to the protesters, and the protests lost steam and ceased.[19]

In Liaoyang, a similar storyline unfolded. Also an industrial city with a large concentration of SOEs that employed most residents, its workers had flourished during much of the Maoist and early post-Mao eras. In the late 1990s, this period of prosperity came to an end, as privatization, bankruptcy, and mass layoffs swept through the state sector. At Liaoyang Ferraloy, workers complained of corrupt behavior on the part of company mangers in collective letters and petitions to more than ten different Party and government offices from the central to the city level. After more than a year with no satisfactory response, in May 2000 Ferraloy workers blocked the main road from Liaoyang to the provincial capital. Subsequently, they moved to the factory, where they were met by 700 police and paramilitary officers. Approximately 50 protesters were beaten, and three of the protest's leaders – most prominently, Yao Fuxin – were detained. When this spurred further protest, the authorities released the leaders and agreed to address the workers' concerns. Over the next year, worker representatives met periodically with company and Party-state officials, who agreed to work on the problem, but never did. In May 2001 workers again protested when they discovered that trucks had secretly come to the factory one night to remove key assets. The Liaoyang city government promised to investigate the matter, but still no action was taken. In October 2001, workers were told that the factory was going bankrupt. Although technically the matter was put to an employee vote, on the day of the poll, workers were closely monitored by security forces, and "no" votes allegedly were destroyed. Workers renewed their protests, and company and city officials agreed to negotiate about the future status of the factory and its employees.

In the spring of 2002, the conflict spiked. In early March, workers issued a variety of open letters, decrying the corrupt practices of factory managers and local political leaders, and demanding justice. The letters were addressed to CCP General Secretary and PRC President Jiang Zemin, the governor of the province, city Party and government officials, Ferraloy employees, and former employees and their family members. When a local official being interviewed in Beijing told a television reporter that there were "no unemployed" in Liaoyang and that the economic transition had been free of serious problems, nearly

20,000 workers and former workers – not only from Ferraloy, but also from at least five other factories – participated in street demonstrations. As in the past, Party-state authorities met with worker representatives, and stated that they would address the protestors' concerns. A few days later, Yao Fuxin was kidnapped off the streets and secretly detained. City workers erupted, with an estimated 30,000 from 20 different factories, as well as taxi drivers, joining the demonstrations. For the next few days, protests continued, while police forces attempted to block them. Three additional worker representatives were captured by security forces and disappeared. As March drew to a close, the city government announced workers would be given half of their back wages, as well as their severance pay. However, the protest leaders were not released. In April, workers on at least three occasions applied for permits to demonstrate, but each time were denied. In May, workers protested without permission, and security forces violently beat protesters and seized their banners.

The conflict dissipated in the following months. From the perspective of the protesting workers, their efforts had some positive results: most received at least a portion of the payments that they had been owed, and the former manager of Ferraloy was arrested and sentenced to 13 years in prison. However, key leaders of the protests also were punished, including Yao Fuxin, who was imprisoned for seven years.[20] Subsequently, most of the workers who had been affected by the layoffs and forced retirements have turned their focus to looking for work, often making ends meet by doing odd jobs.

At the same time, CCP leaders undertook broader efforts to help displaced state sector workers, offering them aid and benefits that were not provided to migrant workers. Most importantly, when the housing units that state sector workers previously had been allocated through their work unit (at nearly no cost) were privatized, existing tenants were allowed to purchase the units at far-below-market prices – prices that were so low that most were able to buy their homes with cash.

Consequently, although many public-sector workers lost their jobs in the mid-to-late 1990s, virtually none had to worry about housing. In addition, political authorities made available to former state-sector workers some minimal forms of aid.[21] Further, since the early years of the new millennium, Party leaders have worked to put in place a new pension system to replace the earlier SOE-provided system. And, most urban *hukou*-holders have expressed satisfaction with the results. Together, these policies sufficiently alleviated the most severe grievances of state sector workers, such that they had less reason to feel propelled to protest.

From late 2014 through the time of this writing, renewed lay-offs and work reductions in the state sector precipitated a new uptick in unrest. Beginning in 2014, central Party leaders pushed for a new round of SOE restructuring, and many firms reduced employee hours and pay. In early 2016, central authorities announced that nearly two million coal and steel workers (roughly 15 percent of the workforce in those industries) would be laid off. Between October 2014 and early June of 2016, state sector workers initiated 50 separate collective contentious actions.[22] Like their predecessors, they employed "communist" language to justify their actions. For example, a protesting coal miner declared, "My parents and grandparents worked at the mine. The workers built the mine with their hands. It is where Mao Zedong led the Great Strike, and that's how the Communist Party rose – and now this?"[23] Since April 2016, local authorities have halted the planned layoffs, and the protests have all but disappeared.[24]

Late Post-Mao Period: Private-sector Workers

For private-sector workers, changes in opportunity structures in the late post-Mao period have led to more persistent, but relatively small-scale, protests. First, beginning in 1992 CCP leaders decisively embraced experimentation with free markets, expanding the "Special Economic

Zones" that had been established earlier in the post-Mao era, and allowing greater opening to foreign investment. This led to a boom in private enterprise (both domestic and foreign-invested), and an exponential rise in the number of private-sector employees – from nearly 22 million in 1989 to more than 200 million in 2006.[25] As in the early post-Mao period, most of these workers have been rural migrants.[26] Unlike the early post-Mao era, however, the largest portion of relatively recent migrant private-sector workers has been young, unskilled women from rural inland regions who have taken jobs in manufacturing, textile, and garment firms in coastal areas.[27]

Official laws and pronouncements

Central and local authorities have encouraged this rise in private-sector employment through new laws, practices, and pronouncements. As local city authorities increasingly recognized the economic benefits of migration, incidences of bullying on the part of public security and other Party-state officials declined.[28] In addition, central leaders attempted to regulate the employment conditions of those in the private sector such that – at least on paper – they enjoyed protection and aid. In 1994, a new Labor Law stipulated that laborers in state, private, and foreign enterprises were subject to the same employment standards in terms of hours, rest periods, overtime, and minimum pay. Simultaneously, the law required that private-sector workers sign contracts delineating their terms of employment and job termination. Further, beginning in the late 1990s, central political elites became more willing to pressure foreign-invested firms to comply with Chinese labor laws.[29]

In the first decade of the 2000s, government rhetoric and policies more explicitly addressed the economic grievances of private-sector employees. In 2003, central authorities demanded that migrant workers be paid more regularly. In 2004, city government officials in Beijing guaranteed legal rights to timely pay and improved working conditions for migrant workers.[30] Also in 2004, the CCP Central Committee voiced a new and sympathetic assessment of worker protests, acknowledging that they "were not necessarily anti-government or politically motivated," but rather occurred because "the masses believe their rights have been violated."[31] In 2005, national political leaders demanded that employers pay their workers "fully and on time," and instructed local governments to set aside contingency funds to prevent wage arrears.[32] In 2006, the State Council issued a document calling for "'fair and equal treatment without discrimination' for migrant workers," and outlining "specific solutions to the problems of low wages, wages in arrears, long work days, poor safety conditions, lack of social security, high rates of work-related illness and accidents, and the need for employment training, housing as well as schooling for the children of migrant workers."[33] In 2008, central authorities passed a new Labor Contract Law, which stipulated that workers completing two short-term contracts be granted full-time status and permanent benefits; empowered workers to bargain collectively with employers; and required that dismissed workers be given one month's severance pay for each year worked. The same year, a new Labor Dispute Mediation and Arbitration Law simplified labor dispute settlement procedures, extended the statute of limitations for labor violations, and reduced labor dispute settlement fees.[34] Taken together, if one brackets off the prohibition on forming independent unions, since the end of the first decade of the 2000s, China's labor laws have been among the most progressive in the world.

These changes were not the result of ideas that came to China's political leaders "out of the blue." Rather, they were responses to worker protests that had emerged throughout the period. As noted by Gallagher, "the 1994 Labor Law, the first labor law in the history of the People's Republic of China, was passed hurriedly after several years of discussion following a spate of wildcat strikes in development zones in China's coastal cities."[35] Similarly, government pronouncements and laws in the first decade of the 2000s were a reaction to workers' collective contentious actions. Like farmer protests, even when the specific grievances articulated in a particular strike or labor action were not addressed, central political authorities reviewed data collected by lower-level offices on the frequency, type, and demands of worker protests, and then based on this information formulated policies and laws and made public statements designed to ameliorate the causes of worker dissatisfaction and protest.

Law versus reality

The proximate cause of most private-sector worker protest in the late post-Mao period has been the disjuncture between official laws and statements, and the reality of workers' employment experiences. In surveys conducted in 2006, for example, only about half of private enterprise workers had signed job contracts, and a substantial portion had never heard of a job contract. Moreover, even those who had signed contracts often were not allowed to see the terms stipulated in the document.[36] A 2001 survey of migrant workers in Guangdong province found that 80 percent worked more than ten hours per day, and more than 50 percent worked 12–14 hours. Nearly half rarely had a day off.[37] In two extreme cases that occurred in 2006, a 25-year-old employee at a Shenzhen factory "collapsed and died from multiple organ failure" "after working repeated overtime shifts for an entire month," and a 35-year-old employee of a Guangzhou clothing factory died after working 54 hours and 25 minutes over four days.[38] These violations have remained prevalent despite the passage of the 2008 Labor Contract Law. Indeed, since the passage of that law, private businesses increasingly have hired employees through short-term subcontracting, which has enabled employers to avoid many of the Labor Contract Law's stipulations. Amendments to the law that took effect in July 2014 were designed to limit the use of subcontractors, but have had little apparent effect.[39]

Private-sector factory workers also have faced stringent workplace regulations and steep fines. At one Shenzhen company, for example, 200 workers "had just one temporary pass between them to leave their post. Workers had to carry such a pass to use the bathroom or drink water; otherwise they would be deemed to be skipping work and would be fined."[40] As of the first decade of the 2000s, an estimated 75–80 percent of private-sector factory workers lived in crowded dorms (the average room measuring 26 square meters, shared by roughly 12 people) and ate at cafeterias that were provided by their employers, with the cost deducted from the employee's wages.[41] These facilities usually have been located within the (typically gated and locked) factory compound, and often have been attached to the shop floor. In 1993, close to 200 young women workers burned to death at the Zhili toy factory in Shenzhen because the steel-mesh doors of their dormitory had been sealed.[42] When employees have been allowed to leave the factory grounds, they commonly have been searched by security guards possessing handcuffs and electric batons.[43]

Concomitantly, private-sector employers regularly have withheld worker pay for long periods, have not paid extra for overtime, and/or have failed to provide wages at previously stipulated rates. According to a 2003 survey conducted by the official Chinese news agency, more than 72 percent of migrants reported wage defaults.[44] Similarly, a 2006 survey by China's National Bureau of Statistics found that over 50 percent of migrant laborers worked overtime with no overtime compensation.[45] Evidence in recent years suggests little change in this situation.

To the degree that private-sector workers have been aware of relevant laws, they have felt that their legal rights have been violated. Further, they have believed that since higher-level authorities passed the laws, those authorities are likely to side with workers in cases where workers protest against the violation of the law. Moreover, inasmuch as workers have been aware that higher-level authorities have done so in the past, workers have been more likely to feel that their protest has some likelihood of success.

The disjuncture between the law and reality with regard to private-sector workers has led workers to focus their ire on their employers, and on occasion on local political authorities who support employers, but almost never on China's national leaders or overall political system. Because of this focus, nearly all private-sector worker protests have been small-scale and localized in nature. Further, workers' complaints have been almost entirely material, focusing on compensation, wage arrears, pay increases, social insurance, overtime, management practices, and working conditions.[46]

Fluctuations in the labor market

Another important aspect of the opportunity structure for private-sector workers has been fluctuations in the labor market. The most important variable in this regard has been the level of competition among private-sector workers. Generally speaking, when there has been a shortage of unskilled private-sector workers, they have been more prone to protest. From the early 1990s through the early years of the new millennium, the number of private-sector jobs rose exponentially as a result of changes in central government policy. Yet, the number of unskilled workers seeking private-sector jobs also skyrocketed as migration restrictions were loosened. Further, in the late 1990s, tens of millions of former public-sector workers were laid off or forced into early retirement, as scores of SOEs were privatized when central Party-state leaders declared that all SOEs would have to privatize or become profitable. As a result, the ratio of job seekers to jobs worsened. Generally speaking, this situation decreased private-sector workers' sense of efficacy. Meanwhile, in certain years – particularly 2001, 2008, 2010, and 2015 through the time of this writing – labor market fluctuations have contributed to spikes in private-sector worker protest.

Generational differences

Another changing aspect of the opportunity structure generally has made private-sector workers more likely to protest over time: whereas earlier generations of private-sector workers looked to the Maoist period as a comparative reference point and had no intention of settling permanently in the city, later generations have had a very different mentality. Many younger rural *hukou*-holding private-sector workers did not leave farming in the countryside, but instead migrated after ending their schooling. A majority of them has had no intention of moving back to the countryside. Also, rural *hukou*-holders who are parents increasingly have brought their children with them to the city. Thus, as time has passed, new generations of rural *hukou*-holders have emerged that have no experience of living in the countryside. These developments have coincided with the extension of legal rights to rural *hukou*-holders and private-sector workers since the early years of the new millennium.

In surveys, younger workers have demonstrated more awareness of China's current labor laws than have older workers. As a result, the former have been more "rights conscious" and "legally aware," and more demanding of social justice.[47] This mentality has made them not only more prone to engage in collective contentious action, but also more proactive in calling for better living and working conditions – even beyond what is legally required. Indeed, in contrast to farmer protests, which have tended to be led by older individuals in the community, a preponderance of private-sector worker protests has been spearheaded by relatively young workers. At the same time, as with farmer protests, the leaders of private-sector worker protests generally have held a position of some standing among the employees in the factory prior to organizing workers to collectively act.[48]

Labor NGOs

Coinciding with these generational shifts has been the establishment of non-governmental organizations (NGOs) devoted to workers' rights. As of 2008, there were estimated to be more than 30 of them in the Pearl River Delta area of Guangdong province alone.[49] Labor NGOs also have emerged and operated in virtually every other area of China that has large numbers of migrant workers. These groups have been key in educating private-sector workers about relevant laws, and in providing them with advice regarding strategies that have been used to effectively advocate for workers' interests.

The legal status of labor NGOs has varied by group, and by location. Although official Party-state policy forbids the establishment of labor unions that are not affiliated with the ACFTU, there is no national law expressly banning the creation of NGOs devoted to labor issues. In order to have official legal status, such a group must register with the government. If the group wishes to be designated a "social organization" (*shehui tuanti*), it must find a government-affiliated department (such as Human Resources and Social Security) or "mass" organization (such as the ACFTU, the All-China Women's Federation, or the Communist Youth League) to sponsor it. In addition, the group must register with the local Civil Affairs office. Few labor NGOs have been able to succeed at these tasks. Consequently, most have either foregone registration altogether, or have registered as for-profit enterprises with the departments of industry and commerce. Those that have taken the former path in many cases have been tolerated by local authorities, and in some instances have been quite active and open in their activities. However, their lack of legal status has put them in a vulnerable position. Studies of labor NGOs in the 2000s have found that although the core service of these groups has been to assist migrant workers in labor disputes with their employers, the groups have been careful to portray their actions as law-abiding and intended to help local officials achieve their policy goals. In the words of one labor NGO leader, "the government...wants to see migrant workers being equipped with more knowledge about the law because it realizes that if workers are able to defend their rights via lawful means, it will become unlikely that they will resort to radical ways such as strikes, demonstrations, or blockades. So, in fact, we are helping the government to maintain social stability."[50] Through the first decade of the 2000s, labor NGOs that were seen in this light by political authorities generally did not face any official harassment; to the contrary, many enjoyed positive relationships with local officials, and regularly visited government offices to report on and discuss their activities. During this period, typically only groups that overtly violated the law (such as by trying to establish independent labor unions) faced punishment.[51]

Since 2015, however, Party-state authorities have demonstrated much less tolerance toward labor NGOs and their leaders; in contrast with earlier years, dozens of labor activists have been arrested, detained, and/or harassed. In December 2015, 18 labor activists were detained and nearly 24 more were interrogated in Guangdong province alone, "contributing to an overall climate of fear" in the region. The charges against them included "inciting crowds to disrupt public order." As of early 2016, "many [labor] NGOs have found it almost impossible to carry out their work."[52] Overall, this shift in official attitudes toward labor NGOs has incited both fear and outrage among private-sector workers, and has made for a volatile situation in which previously economic grievances have the potential to become more political.

Elite responses

Almost without exception, private business owners and managers have responded to workers' collective actions with threats and harassment, and not infrequently physical violence. The response of local political officials has varied. In some geographic regions (such as Guangzhou), local authorities have learned over time that worker protests end best when police intervention is avoided. However, even in these localities, public security forces have been known to use strong-arm tactics when local officials believe that worker protests are "disrupting social order." In a China Labour Bulletin study spanning 2012–2013, in roughly 20 percent of all strikes and protests, local police had intervened.[53] Further, in some cases this intervention resulted in violent conflicts between police and protesters, and the arrest of protest leaders. However, when national political authorities have become involved in resolving labor disputes (something that has occurred only when protests have grown sufficiently in size, intensity, and duration), central elites usually have sided with the protestors.

In 2008, as private-sector protests spiked in the lead-up to the Beijing Olympics, political authorities increasingly began to provide restive workers with financial compensation. Officials even coined a slogan to describe this practice: "buying peace with money."[54] Private-sector strike activity increased again in 2010. These protest actions occurred in the context of a tightening labor market as export growth surged and domestic demand increased. In order to attract labor, Guangdong political authorities raised the minimum wage by over 20 percent. At the same time, working conditions in most private-sector businesses did not improve. To the contrary, conditions in many cases worsened as workers faced higher production demands. When reports emerged of worker suicides at a Foxconn factory (a major supplier to Apple, Hewlett Packard, Nintendo and Sony), Chinese government officials publicly criticized Foxconn management, and Prime Minister Wen Jiabao told a group of young private-sector factory workers that "migrant workers are the mainstay of China's industrial workforce. Our society's wealth [is a] distillation[] of your hard work and sweat. Your labor is glorious and should be respected by society at large."[55]

Since late 2014, private-sector worker strikes again have increased. This development has been spurred by a significant slowdown in the

Chinese economy, which has led many private employers to lay off workers, withhold their wages and benefits, or shut down entirely.[56] In the numerous labor disputes that have arisen during this period, workers have highlighted the illegal nature of employer practices.[57] Chinese political authorities have responded to this rise in worker protests with a mixture of repression and concession. As discussed above, much more than in the past, national leaders have condoned and even pressed for the arrest of labor activists, and have publicized their punishment.[58] In addition, in early 2016 some central Party-state officials publicly expressed the view that China's labor laws are over-protective of workers, and should be reconsidered.[59] Simultaneously, however, political elites have pressured private employers to settle disputes through labor concessions.[60] Thus, as of the time of this writing, the overall attitude of top Party-state leaders toward private-sector worker protest has become ambivalent and unclear.

CONCLUSION

Overall, urban worker protests have shown some basic similarities with those launched by farmers: all have looked to central authorities as benevolent protectors against corrupt behavior on the part of local political and economic elites, and national leaders have made some efforts to address protest grievances. A key difference with public-sector workers, however, is that they and central leaders exhibit a shared belief that public-sector workers should be privileged relative to farmers and migrant workers. As a result, current and former state sector workers have been more effectively coopted by the CCP-led political system than have these other groups. In addition, public-sector workers have not perceived their interests as being connected with aggrieved rural *hukou*-holding farmers or with rural *hukou*-holding urban-based labor-ers. As long as this remains the case, public-sector workers are unlikely to join with these other groups in any kind of unified protest.

Meanwhile, somewhat unique dynamics have emerged among private-sector workers. For them, protest has come to be viewed as their best hope for individual redress and improvement. And, at least through 2012, protests also have benefited private-sector workers more broadly to the degree that Party-state elites have passed new laws and made official pronouncements designed to address the more fundamental causes of workers' grievances. From the perspective of central Party-state leaders, private-sector worker protests have served as a "fire alarm" alerting authorities to the most egregious violations of worker rights. By intervening only in cases of extreme abuses that have resulted in protests of such a magnitude that they capture the attention of higher-level authorities, this has been a relatively low-cost way of managing worker grievances – without having to grant broader rights (such as the right to form independent unions) that the regime views as a potential threat to its power.[61] Similarly, protests have allowed aggrieved workers to "let off steam" without challenging CCP rule. Indeed, when national Party-state leaders have stepped in on the side of protesting workers, protest actually has helped to enhance the legitimacy of the central political system.

However, even when private-sector protests have been successful, they almost invariably have involved serious conflict, and even violence. For, the immediate targets of private-sector worker protests – employers – typically have responded to workers' collective actions with intransigence, threats, and physical force. Indeed, it generally has been only after workers have met with a negative response to their initial demands that they have engaged in more public and contentious collective actions designed to attract the attention of outside authorities. This experience often has been scarring for participants, with the result that even when they ultimately have been "paid off" in response to their protests, workers' gains have come only through a stress-laden process involving much fear, pain, and suffering. As noted by Lee, even successful protests have left participants feeling embittered, indignant, disappointed, and resentful.[62] Thus, as a means for conflict resolution, this "fire alarm" system has had serious collateral damage for those involved.

Moreover, the perception that only a "big disturbance" will get the attention of higher-level political leaders has encouraged more extreme behavior on the part of private-sector workers. As a result, such actions have become fairly commonplace. Although to date private-sector worker protests have remained localized and focused on economic grievances, the more large-scale and intense a protest action becomes, the greater the possibility that it might spin out of the central regime's control. Further, the actual practice of protest has given private-sector workers a feeling of empowerment and efficacy that has made them more likely to engage in collective contentious action in the future, and to demand more than simply the enforcement of their legal rights. Coupled with the psychological and physical wounds inflicted by their prior experiences of protest, this has made for a potentially volatile situation for Chinese Party-state authorities.

In this context, increased efforts to repress labor activism since the fall 2012 ascension of top CCP leader Xi Jinping have the potential to backfire. If Xi's repressive measures stifle the ability of workers to collectively voice their grievances, popular protest may no longer be allowed to act as a crucial social outlet. And if aggrieved workers come to view central political leaders as repressors rather than as allies, the legitimacy of China's CCP-led regime may decline. Further, because younger private-sector workers have been empowered by their prior protest experiences, and also have more ambitious goals than did earlier generations of private-sector workers, as time passes this segment of the population may be more inclined to engage in regime-challenging confrontations.

4 | Homeowner Protest ──────────

Urban *hukou*-holders also have engaged in collective contention related to their homeownership. As noted in chapter 3, along with the privatization of most state-owned enterprises (SOEs) in the 1990s, virtually all of the housing that previously had been leased to public-sector workers through the Party-state was sold to them. Thus, for at least the last decade, over 75 percent of all urban Chinese households have owned their own homes.[1] Because they were able to purchase their units at far below market prices, and typically with cash, most were happy with this development. However, other changes have bred discontent among many urban homeowners. The base cause has been the construction of new housing tracts. On the one hand, this construction has displaced existing residents. Initially, relocated households were satisfactorily compensated. But since the late 1990s, this has ceased to be the case, eliciting great outrage. On the other hand, the relatively affluent urbanites that have purchased units in newly-constructed tracts often have become aggrieved by perceived wrongdoing on the part of developers, the private management companies that manage the daily operation of the tract, and/or local government officials who support actions that harm homeowner interests.

Many disgruntled homeowners have felt empowered to act on their complaints. Those that purchased the homes that previously were rented to them by their work units have felt entitled to continue to live in these homes, or at least to live in the same vicinity. For the relatively affluent homeowners that have bought units in new tracts, feelings of efficacy have arisen from their privileged socioeconomic status, and their resultant connections and resources. In both cases, these perceptions have been further fueled by laws and regulations that in some ways have protected homeowner rights, but in other respects have left them vulnerable. As a result, since the late 1990s, homeowner protests have become a regular occurrence in China's cities.

These protests have exhibited a number of similarities with those undertaken by farmers and urban workers. In all of these cases, participants and leaders have referenced the law to justify their protest and to condemn the local economic and political elites that have violated official policies. Relatedly, central leaders have been portrayed as benevolent and well-intentioned. In addition, disgruntled homeowners initially have attempted to go through legal, institutionalized channels to voice their concerns, and have engaged in collective street actions only when their more moderate efforts have been thwarted. Finally, like farmer and worker protests, central authorities have responded to homeowner activism with the passage of new laws and regulations that address homeowner concerns. At the same time, however, top political leaders steadfastly have worked to ensure that homeowner protests stay within boundaries defined by the Party-state and do not threaten the stability of the political system as a whole.

Homeowner protests also have displayed some unique features. To begin with, unlike farmers and rank-and-file private-sector workers, virtually all urban homeowners are privileged by the fact that they hold an urban *hukou*. Beyond this, it is important to distinguish between protests undertaken by the relatively low-income urbanites that have been faced with housing demolition, and the relatively high-income residents of new housing developments that have had complaints related to the administration of their tract.

The former typically have not had an education beyond the high school level, and have been unskilled public-sector workers for most of their adult lives. Many were laid off or forced into early retirement when SOEs were privatized, and have since been unemployed or underemployed. Their homes, which tend to be small and old, but in most cases were purchased at a low price from their work units and are owned free-and-clear of debt, represent their only real financial asset and security. When this has been threatened and they have not been compensated adequately and fairly, many have fought fiercely to protect their home – sometimes even to the point of death. When they have done so, their protests have tended to be more individual than collective, and to not involve cross-community networking.

Protest on the part of urbanites that have purchased units in new housing developments has been quite different. These homeowners usually have a college education, and are affluent "white-collar" professionals, such as lawyers, engineers, and mid- to upper-level private-sector employees. As such, they often have connections with elites in academia, the media, and the government. Further, they have more financial freedom than do farmers and rank-and-file workers to devote their time to activism. Some well-to-do homeowner groups even have paid successful leaders of other homeowner groups to act as consultants. In addition, owners of new housing units have easy and regular Internet access. Indeed, virtually all residential complexes that have been constructed since the turn of the millennium have been wired with high-speed Internet connections. Overall, when these homeowners have engaged in collective contentious actions, they have had more resources available to them for communication and government lobbying than has been the case for farmers and rank-and-file workers. In part for this reason, the collective actions of these homeowners have moved further in the direction of cross-community networking than has been the case for farmers, workers, and evictees.

Political authorities' responses to homeowner protests generally have been similar to those regarding farmer and labor protests: local political and economic elites have stonewalled and at times have repressed demonstrators and particularly protest leaders, while central authorities have been relatively sympathetic. Yet the response to homeowner protests also exhibits some unique characteristics. First, although many evictees have been subjected to violence and outright repression, these have been much less prevalent among the relatively affluent owners of units in new housing tracts. Perhaps due to the privileged position and relatively expansive resources enjoyed by the latter, they rarely have been detained, arrested, or violently repressed. Further, central and local authorities in some notable cases have accepted the input of affluent homeowners in shaping new laws that relate to them. Overall, the activism of these urban homeowners stands as a relatively successful example of interest articulation and government response in China's current CCP-led political system.

LATE 1970s–MID-1990s

At the beginning of the post-Mao era, there were very few homeowners in China. At that time, nearly all urban housing units were owned and managed by affiliates of the Party-state. Most of these were provided to public-sector workers by their work unit; others were once-private homes that had been confiscated by political authorities and then rented to urban *hukou*-holders. By the late 1980s, clear problems with urban housing had emerged: with tenants paying exceedingly low rents and government entities putting little investment into housing, there was both a shortage of units and a dire need for basic repairs and maintenance. Party-state authorities decided that the solution was to privatize housing and turn it into a commodity available to consumers for purchase. Some previously confiscated housing units were returned to the families of the original owners, and some new housing complexes were built. Through the mid-1990s, these reforms moved slowly, with the rate of homeownership moving from 10 percent in the 1980s, to 30 percent in 1995.[2]

Many urban *hukou*-holders were required to relocate as part of these reforms. However, most were not upset by this, as they typically were provided with an appealing home elsewhere, and/or were given a new home in their old neighborhood after the new housing construction was complete. Some also received cash compensation, based on family size, sufficient to purchase a desirable new home.[3]

LATE 1990s–PRESENT

From the late 1990s through the present, the situation has been different. New housing construction has skyrocketed, encouraged by local political leaders that: (i) have been evaluated based on local economic growth, (ii) have depended on land deals to shore up their local budget, and (iii) have been able to personally gain from kickbacks from real estate deals. This development has had negative effects on both low-income owners of older units and high-income owners of units in new residential tracts.

HOUSING DEMOLITION

Opportunity Structures and Grievances

With regard to the former, since the late 1990s, hundreds of thousands have been evicted from their homes to make way for new construction. Unlike in earlier years, many have not been given a desirable home elsewhere or a new home in their old neighborhood. Instead, cash compensation has become the norm. Further, in Beijing, the amount has been calculated based on prior floor area rather than family size. As many families' existing units have been quite small but have housed large extended families, this change in compensation has been a serious blow. In addition, the amount of compensation typically has been calculated by local political authorities or the developer – both of whom have an interest in keeping compensation low. Relatedly, although the central Ministry of Construction (MOC) repeatedly has encouraged local officials to build low-income housing, few have done so. For, this has not been seen as a source of profit, or as an investment that will boost local economic figures in a way that will lead to favorable reviews for local political cadres. As relatively expensive new tracts have been built and affordable urban housing has disappeared, housing prices have risen dramatically. Consequently, from the late 1990s through the present, the amount of compensation offered often has been inadequate to purchase appealing alternative housing. Moreover, moving to a more affordable location has meant losing access to good schools and employment and business opportunities, such as renting out rooms or running a retail business from home.[4]

These threats to homeowner security and quality of life have bred serious grievances – particularly in cities such as Beijing and Shanghai, which have been the sites of massive new construction and old housing demolition. At the same time, official laws and regulations in some ways have seemed to protect displaced homeowners' rights, but in other ways have fallen short of doing so. This reality has fueled feelings of both efficacy and indignation among the relocated. Legally, urban homeowners do not have perpetual ownership of their units; instead, the unit is owned for a fixed term, with a typical maximum of 70 years. The land beneath the unit remains owned by the state. Political authorities may force residents to vacate their homes for demolition only for the construction of public projects, and only if the transfer follows legal procedures and "reasonable" compensation is provided. If a new commercial project is proposed, it cannot legally proceed without a prior agreement between the developer and the affected homeowners. In reality, however, local leaders frequently have violated these stipulations. According to one estimate, 80 percent of all housing demolition in the late 1990s/early 2000s was undertaken for commercial development, even though a large proportion of these were categorized as public projects by local authorities.[5]

Protest Rhetoric and Actions

For current and former public-sector workers that have resided in their units for many years, this situation has been outrageous and unjust – and illegal. Consequently, between 1997 and 2000, the number of housing-related conflicts rose by over 40 percent, to an estimated 166,000. By 2001, the problem was so pervasive that the popular press dubbed it the "year of the high-rise disputes."[6] In Beijing and other cities holding Olympic events in the summer of 2008, housing demolition and related conflicts spiked again in 2006–8 due to massive construction projects.[7]

Most aggrieved evictees have expressed their concerns first through legal, institutionalized channels. Typically, they have begun by submitting a collective petition to relevant government "letters and visits" offices – making reference to the law in justifying their appeal. In the first eight months of 2002, homeowners upset about planned demolitions submitted nearly 1,400 letters of complaint and made over 1,200 personal visits to the MOC. In 2003, residents of the cities of Hangzhou and Nanjing submitted collective requests to the Standing Committee of the National People's Congress, asking it to review the constitutionality of their cities' regulations on housing demolition.[8]

Some also have attempted to go through the courts. As noted in the Introduction, since the early 1990s, Chinese citizens have had the right to sue the government for abuse of power or malfeasance. Taking advantage of this opportunity, in the late 1990s and early 2000s, aggrieved homeowners filed hundreds of collective claims. In Zhejiang province, one-fourth of all lawsuits were related to housing; nationwide, government offices with power over land management and city construction were two of the most frequently sued. In just one district of

Beijing, disgruntled homeowners submitted 53 collective lawsuits between 1995 and 2000. In one of these cases, over 600 residents facing forced housing demolition sued the district's land and housing management bureau, claiming that the government illegally was allowing commercial development on the land upon which their homes were located. When the case was rebuffed by the intermediate high court, they came back with a new lawsuit on behalf of over 10,000 residents. In another case in Shanghai, over 2,000 sued the land management bureau. However, litigants such as these rarely have won in the courts. And even when they have, enforcement has been difficult. More ominously, in Shanghai, the lawyers representing the aggrieved residents were arrested and imprisoned.[9]

Frustrated with legal channels, many have pursued other means of resistance, leading to more heated conflicts. Some have been violent, and even deadly. Usually, homeowners have employed a mixed strategy that employs both legal/institutionalized and less clearly legal and/or non-institutionalized actions. Many have attempted to physically block developers from accessing planned demolition sites – such as forming citizen patrols to guard against the entry of non-residents. In addition, evictees have simply refused to vacate their units. This has led to the emergence of what are known as "nail houses" – a lone unit still standing amidst a site that otherwise has been razed for new construction. In many cases, this has been a single individual or household's protest, and has not involved collective contentious action. To publicize their case, evictees not infrequently have used the Internet to post the details of their conflict, highlighting legal violations on the part of local authorities and developers.[10]

The most famous such case is that of Wu Ping, an evictee who contested the amount of compensation offered for the demolition of her building. After three years of conflict, a court gave Wu and her husband three days to vacate. Wu refused, standing outside the building with a copy of the Constitution, and affixing a banner with a quote from the Constitution: "The citizens' legal private property rights must not be violated!" An amateur blogger took interest, posting online photos and interviews with residents, and his own commentary. When traditional domestic Chinese media outlets picked up the story, discussion exploded online. Within a few days, Wu was offered a compensation package that she found to be acceptable. The blogger, however, was subjected to restrictions on his activities both online and off.[11]

Responses

The response to homeowner protests has varied widely. In many "nail house" cases, developers and local authorities have resorted to physical coercion and even violence to force residents to evacuate. A common tactic has been to cut off utilities to the unit, such as water and electricity, in an attempt to drive the owner out. When this has failed, developers and demolition companies – and in some cases, local political authorities – have hired thugs or paid migrant workers to kidnap and/ or beat up recalcitrant owners. In 2003, a group broke into the condemned home of a family who was asleep inside, tied them up, dragged them outside, and demolished their unit. In a number of instances, evictees have engaged in self-immolation and suicide. In 2010, for example, three homeowners set themselves on fire on their roof when their electricity was shut off.[12]

The contentious actions of displaced homeowners have led central authorities to promulgate an array of new policies. In 2003, the MOC detailed the proper method for calculating and providing compensation – specifically addressing concerns that had been raised by protestors. The MOC also clarified the required documents that displaced residents need in order to seek administrative judgments regarding planned demolitions. In addition, the State Council made public an "urgent notification" that attributed the rise in housing demolition-related unrest to the failure of local authorities to provide proper compensation and relocation, as well as to the "inappropriate working style of government agencies." It also directed relevant local governments and departments to "attend to the people's interests" and "act in accordance with the law." Further, the notice stipulated that political officials would be held responsible if it were to be found that "a large number of collective appeals are due to the work of government agencies." Importantly, the notice also stated that in cases of disputes over compensation, demolitions can be carried out only after a formal government decision has been issued. The Supreme Court reiterated this directive, and also asserted that compensation should be no less than 90 percent of the price of existing homes in the area. In addition, the Court required that evictees should be given an inexpensive rental home in cases where compensation is not enough for them to purchase a unit.[13]

Local courts and government offices have followed suit, issuing regulations that attempt to resolve the problems expressed by disgruntled evictees. In particular, they have stated that demolitions cannot proceed until after the residents have been compensated; that utilities cannot be cut off prior to demolition; and that the police may not be used to enforce evictions. Following a homeowner's death by self-immolation, the Jiangsu provincial government and Nanjing city government stipulated that homeowners should be allowed to choose among options other than cash compensation, such as buying or renting affordable units. City officials also increased the amount of compensation, requiring that it be enough for the evictee to buy a modest unit in the city. Further, the city canceled 49 construction projects that would have affected over 20,000 homes. In some localities, legal action has been taken against officials engaged in corrupt activities related to evictions and demolitions. Most notably, in 2006–7, two Beijing officials were arrested and sentenced to death on charges related to gaining personal profit from real estate deals.[14]

However, local officials' incentives to pursue new housing construction and to provide minimal compensation for evictees have remained strong, and the problem has not abated. Faced with continued protests, in 2011 the Supreme Court issued another "urgent notification," alarmed that evictees have "incinerated themselves, jumped off buildings to kill themselves, or adopted similarly barbarous measures as resistance" and that "some security cadres and police... inappropriately used weapons resulting in deaths." To address these problems, the directive calls on courts at all levels to increase their supervision of housing demolition and resident relocation.[15]

Consequences

Yet, as with rural land expropriation, until such central pronouncements are enforced and/or the incentive structure of local leaders is changed, conflicts over housing demolition are likely to persist – and to involve violence. Like farmer and worker protests, this experience has been scarring for those who have faced punishment and abuse in the process of trying to protect their rights. In the case of housing demolitions, however, many protest actions have been undertaken on an individual basis, wherein only one or a very small number of affected evictees has held out while their neighbors have accepted buyouts and departed. Further, protests by evictees have been something of a "one-shot" game that has ended after the demolition has occurred or the compensation has been made.[16] Thus, these protests have not posed an expansive, organized or sustained threat to the stability of the political system. Nonetheless, many evictees effectively have used the Internet to publicize their plight and elicit public sympathy and support. To the extent that higher-level authorities have stepped in to sanction malfeasant local officials and developers and have issued new policies to address the grievances of the complainants, the protests have been successful, and the overall legitimacy of CCP rule has not been undermined. Even so, to the degree that reports of the mistreatment of low-income urban homeowners continue to circulate, cynicism regarding local leaders can be expected to grow.

NEW HOUSING DEVELOPMENTS

Opportunities and Grievances

The hastened construction of residential tracts also has created new opportunities and grievances that have made collective contention more likely among the affluent owners of these homes. The vast majority of these sites are exclusive/gated, with security guards to ensure that outsiders are denied entrance. The tracts typically include community amenities such as parks and recreational centers. As noted above, the private developers that build the tracts, the private management companies that manage the site once completed, and local political officials share a common goal: to profit from the newly-constructed developments. This focus not infrequently has led them to promise home buyers many desirable features and services, but to subsequently fail to deliver them, or to take them away when a new opportunity for profit emerges. Further, in disputes between residents and developers and/or private management companies, local authorities often have sided with the latter. Especially in cases where one or more of these entities has violated the law, homeowners have engaged in collective contention.

Official directives and regulations have helped to spur these homeowners to protest, but also have been changed in response to their activism. These changes are related to local governing structures in urban areas. The lowest formal government body in urban neighborhoods is the Residents' Committee (RC), which since 1989 officially has been designated as an elected body, but in reality, typically has been chosen and controlled by higher-level political leaders. One step up from the RC is the Street Office, which oversees multiple RCs. In 1994, the central MOC directed the owners and residents of urban residential tracts to elect "homeowner associations" (*yezhu weiyuanhui*; hereafter HOA) with the rights to establish a "management charter," and to represent and "uphold the legal rights and interests" of the owners and occupants. The HOA also was given the power to hire and fire the private management company that oversees the daily operation of the tract.[17] However, the directive left unclear the relationship among HOAs, RCs, and Street Offices.

Beginning in the late 1990s, homeowner activism increased dramatically. By the early years of the millennium it had become common. Between 2003 and 2008, domestic newspapers reported 600 homeowner-related "incidents" in Beijing and over 1,200 in Guangzhou.[18]

Among the best-known examples occurred in a complex known as Lijiang Gardens (LG), near Guangzhou. Between the early 1990s and 2004, over 10,000 units were constructed in LG – by a developer backed by the provincial and city district governments. A first dispute arose in 1999, when the LG management company announced that the bus fare to Guangzhou would increase. In response, several hundred residents protested in front of the company's offices, marched through LG, petitioned the provincial government and People's Congress, and boycotted the bus. The company subsequently agreed to offer tickets in bulk for the original price. A longer and more conflictual dispute began in late 2002, when the developer began to clear parkland on the periphery of LG to make way for a wide road. Again, several hundred residents protested – camping out on the road and planting saplings in the razed ground. They also contacted media outlets – gaining sympathetic coverage in the newspaper, *Southern Metropolis* – and petitioned the provincial People's Congress. In the end, the developer agreed to reduce the width of the road and move it a greater distance away from LG housing units.[19]

As with other kinds of protests, when high-level authorities came to see homeowner discontent in new housing tracts as a threat to social stability, they announced new guidelines designed to address the underlying problem so as to ensure that protests by these residents would not undermine Party-state control. In 2003, the central State Council updated the 1994 MOC regulations, attempting to draw clear boundaries around the power of the HOAs, and to re-assert the primacy of Party-state bodies (particularly RCs and Street Offices) in overseeing private housing tracts. The 2003 stipulations refer to HOAs as "executive" rather than "representative" bodies, and lay out their "responsibilities" rather than their "rights." The regulations also suggest that HOA powers "should be confined to the hiring and firing of a management company," and "reiterate[] in several places that [HOAs] are to be subordinate to government authorities."[20] Further, the document requires that any action or decision undertaken by an HOA must first be approved by a homeowner assembly (*yezhu dahui*) that includes all residents/owners. Moreover, the regulations stipulate that dismissing a management company requires a two-thirds vote of the homeowner assembly – a very high bar that is difficult to meet, particularly in large tracts with thousands of residents, and also given that most residents work full time and some owners do not reside in the tract.[21]

Simultaneously, central authorities demonstrated support for the interests of urban homeowners. Most importantly, in 2007, a new law was issued that for the first time in the history of the PRC protects private property rights. In addition, the law formally recognizes the "collective property rights of homeowners to common areas in their communities" and the "right of collective governance either through general meetings... or by forming a homeowners' association with a corresponding board of directors." Thus, the law provides "strong legal support for homeowners who seek to litigate against the infringement of their property rights."[22] The law is much more clear and specific than is that regarding rural collective land.[23] As will be discussed in more detail below, homeowner activists actively participated in the consultation process that preceded the promulgation of this law. Meanwhile, lower-level authorities have issued regulations that have both shaped and been influenced by homeowner activism.

While the opportunity structures related to official laws and policies have shifted over time and by location, other opportunity structures have been more internal to the new residential community. In developments where a problem or violation has affected all or most owners and has been seen as a serious or grave matter, collective protest has been more likely. Relatedly, in cases where there is a relatively high percentage of residents that are both the actual unit owners and Chinese nationals (as opposed to expatriate foreigners), protest has been more likely. In addition, protest has been more frequent in smaller or moderately-sized tracts than in large developments. For, in smaller tracts, communication and mobilization are easier, and the prevalence of "free-riding" (not participating but gaining the benefits from others' collective action) is lower. Given that the average new residential compound houses 2,000–3,000 families that do not know one another before moving in, these problems are common.[24]

Finally, homeowner protest in new housing developments has arisen only when one or more residents have taken the lead in mobilizing the community. In contrast to farmers, rank-and-file workers, and evictees, activist leaders that have purchased units in new developments typically have a college education and work in "white-collar" jobs. Indeed, their employment has tended to be stable, flexible, and well-paid, such that they have had the ability to invest substantial amounts of time in their activism – including hiring domestic help for their family members' basic needs. Also in contrast to farmer and worker activists, the leaders of homeowner protest in new tracts have been relatively young, and a notably high proportion have been women – including stay-at-home wives/mothers who do not need to work for pay outside the home.

Also, many have had experience living abroad.[25] At the same time, homeowners in new developments rarely have been acquainted with their neighbors when they first move in. As a result, unlike in rural villages, private and public-sector enterprises, and condemned neighborhoods – where community members know one another well, and protest leaders tend to already be of high standing within the group – those who come to be protest leaders in new housing tracts typically have not had any prior distinguished status in the community. Instead, they have become leaders only after a problem has arisen and neighborhood discussions have propelled them into an activist role.[26]

This relates to the question of why these homeowners have become protest leaders, and what has motivated them to sustain their leadership throughout a conflict. Initially, affluent homeowners in new tracts have become activists because they have suffered some personal harm, and have come to the conclusion that it is only through collective action that the problem might be resolved. Concomitant with this, however, most homeowner activists in new tracts have displayed "value-driven" behavior: they have become leaders because they feel that it is the "right" thing to do. Indeed, most were born in the 1960s and went to college in the 1980s – both periods of high youth activism in China. In the words of one leader, "I belong to the generation that experienced the 1989 movement and that has a very strong sense of social responsibility."[27] According to a study conducted around 2007–9, a growing number of homeowner activists have been motivated by broader values than simply personal interest, and have shifted from narrow economic demands (such as stopping construction on community parkland) to broader political demands (such as improving and strengthening legal and regulatory government institutions). These individuals have not been satisfied with simply the resolution of the particular problem that is plaguing their residential tract; increasingly, they have constituted a group of dedicated leaders focused on broader homeowner rights.

However, this has not been true of all leaders in new housing tracts. Some quit after becoming disillusioned and frustrated by their neighbors' lack of commitment or by their inability to succeed in resolving the problem at hand. Others have used their leadership status to make money or otherwise enjoy personal gain. In some cases, this had led their community to lose trust in them and oust them from their position. Some activists have tried to manipulate the HOA election and/ or the private management company selection process in their personal favor, and some have embezzled HOA funds. Others have used their leadership position to cultivate profitable contacts and business opportunities with other homeowners, and with outside businesses (such as travel companies) seeking access to the (typically gated) community. Still others have become professional homeowner activist consultants, charging fees for their services.[28]

As noted earlier, the grievances expressed by homeowners in new housing developments typically have revolved around issues related to the quality of their individual and community property, arising from perceived wrongdoing on the part of the developer, private management company, and/or local political authorities. In some cases, the developer has failed to fulfill its contractual obligations. For example, the project may not be completed on time and move-in dates may be delayed; the property may not match the quality portrayed in promotional materials; or the floor space of the unit may be smaller than specified in blueprints. In other cases, the public space associated with the property may be altered or compromised – such as views being blocked, parkland being converted, or a community center being sold, rented, or made open to people from outside the residential tract. Further, complaints have arisen when the private management company has provided poor service (such as failing to maintain the property or ensure its security) or has engaged in unreasonable actions (such as charging exorbitant fees). Finally, when aggrieved homeowners have met with intransigence on the part of local political officials to whom they have voiced their concerns, homeowners have expressed complaints about poor local governance. In addition, conflicts have arisen when local government authorities (typically RCs and Street Offices) have attempted to intervene in the HOA selection and/or decision-making process.[29]

Protest Rhetoric and Actions

Like other kinds of protestors, homeowners in new residential communities have referenced the law in their collective actions, and have portrayed themselves as being loyal to the central Party-state. Yet, affluent homeowners also have employed a somewhat distinctive rhetoric. In many cases, they have portrayed themselves as "high quality" (gao suzhi) citizens acting in defense of their consumer rights. More broadly, they have emphasized their role in advancing China's modernization, and have cast their opponents – greedy developers, management companies, and local officials – as impediments to this modernization.[30]

In terms of taking action, like other kinds of protestors, homeowners in new housing tracts typically have begun by voicing their grievances through legal, institutionalized channels, such as filing collective lawsuits and submitting collective petitions to "letters and visits" offices. Since the late 1990s, such actions have been common. Yet as with other lawsuits, in the vast majority of these cases the litigants have not been successful.[31] And even when homeowners have won court cases, the ruling often has been weakly enforced at best.

Also, similar to other kinds of protests, when legal channels have failed, disgruntled homeowners in new tracts have turned to non-institutionalized methods. Some of these actions have been physical, including both non-violent hunger strikes and occasionally more violent acts, such as destroying buildings whose construction they oppose.[32] Other tactics employed by affluent homeowners have capitalized on their privileged socioeconomic status. As with evictees and rank-and-file workers, homeowners in new tracts have used the Internet as a tool for communication and mobilization. However, the specific ways in which they have done so have been somewhat unique. As noted above, most residents of new housing tracts do not know one another before they move in. Further, most have work commitments that require commuting and long hours away from the residential site. As a result, community-building can be a challenge. Because all units in the tract have Internet connections, residents in many developments have established listservs and blog sites for the community, thus enabling virtual discussion of common issues as well as mobilization for potential collective actions. Indeed, HOA blogs are among the largest on the Chinese Internet.[33] Another tactic distinctive to these communities is simply refusing to pay management company fees until the issue is resolved. In addition, some disgruntled residents have skirted official prohibitions on street gatherings by engaging in "driving" or "parking" protests in their cars, with banners and/or broadcasted messages voicing their displeasure. This method of protest displays the affluence of these homeowners; it is not available to farmers, rank-and-file workers, and evictees, as few are wealthy enough to own their own vehicles. Further, some homeowners in new residential communities have used their connections with academic institutions to procure data to support their claims.

A final unique – and significant – feature of homeowner activism in new residential communities has been the rise of cross-community organization. Illustrating how opportunity structures can both give rise to collective action and be shaped by it, these associations have used existing laws to justify their formation, and then have worked to further change the law to better protect their interests. United groups of HOAs have emerged in a number of cities, including Beijing, Shanghai, Shenzhen, and Guangzhou. They have arisen due to homeowner activists' perception that concerted action will give them more strength vis-à-vis their opponents, and to their belief that the only way to resolve the many specific problems facing individual communities is to modify the law.[34] Most have not been officially approved as "legal" organizations. Yet in a number of cases, they have operated relatively openly, and have maintained regular communication with local officials. At the same time, the leaders of the various HOAs that are part of these alliances have shared information and provided advice to one another. Further, in some instances they have worked together to formulate and submit suggestions to government agencies, in a form of political lobbying.[35] In addition, they have worked to mobilize and advise homeowner groups and cross-city associations in other locations, such as Xian and Anhui. In some cases, they have received advice from local scholars. Some also have created websites, and have successfully worked with local media outlets to publicize homeowner mistreatment by management companies. Finally, some of these activists have been elected to district-level government bodies. In Guangzhou, a group leader quit his job in order to devote his time to the cause.[36]

Responses

Although the official response to protests by homeowners in new residential communities has been varied, it has shared some basic similarities with that in other kinds of protests: intransigence and at times the use of force by local economic and political elites, and sympathetic treatment from central authorities. In some cases, developers and private management companies have threatened homeowner activists, and have hired thugs to beat them. Local political leaders, who have tended to see their interests as being intertwined with those of the companies, often have worked in tandem with them to tamp down homeowner activism. RC leaders have contacted residents who are CCP members, pressuring them to oppose homeowner activists; have prevented activists from contacting residents (e.g., tearing down posters, removing material from mailboxes, refusing to provide contact lists); and have meddled in HOA elections to ensure that the HOA will be obedient to the RC. Overall, however, local economic and political elites have been less prone to use violence toward affluent homeowners than they have been with regard to other kinds of protestors. Further, activist HOA leaders generally have not been subjected to detention, arrest, or other kinds of legal punishment.[37]

When protests among residents of new housing tracts have become so widespread and serious that they have come to the attention of higher-level authorities, central leaders have issued new laws and policies designed to address the underlying problem. Moreover, in some important instances – such as the lengthy consultation process that preceded the passage of the 2007 private property law – governing officials have incorporated the input of HOA activists. In this respect, political elites have been receptive to a form of political lobbying on the part of affluent homeowners – a phenomenon that has not been seen with regard to other, less privileged, socioeconomic groups. Simultaneously, however, as with other kinds of protests, officials at all levels have worked to constrain any potential organized threats to their political control by circumscribing the autonomy and power of HOAs and cross-community HOA networks.

Consequences

As a result of collective contentious action on the part of homeowners in new residential communities, the quality of private and collective property in new tracts has been enhanced. According to one study, between 1998 and 2008, management fees in residential developments were significantly reduced, while service provision increased and improved.[38] Further, because affluent homeowner activists generally have not been subjected to physical violence or legal charges, their participation in contentious collective action typically has not been scarring. To the contrary, the relative openness of political authorities to the input of HOA activists has further increased their incorporation into the CCP-led political system.

CONCLUSION

Overall, the grievances that have led urban homeowners to undertake contentious collective action have been similar to those that have propelled farmers and workers to protest: homeowners generally have expressed narrowly-focused material concerns related to perceived mistreatment by local businesses and government officials. For homeowners, such grievances first arose in the late 1990s, and they have continued through the present. Although local elites typically have responded with intransigence and attempts at suppression, when these protests have come to the attention of central authorities, they have issued new regulations that have attempted to address the underlying problems.

For low-income homeowners that have been faced with housing demolition, protests often have been highly conflictual, and not infrequently have involved violence. At the same time, they have been more individual in nature, as in the many high-profile "nail house" cases that have emerged. They also have focused on a single issue – the demolition of their home – wherein the parties in conflict typically end their relationship once the dispute is resolved. As such, protests by evictees have not represented an organized, expansive, or sustained threat to the political status quo. Nonetheless, they have attracted a great deal of public sympathy, and in this sense have increased popular disenchantment with perceived political corruption. As long as the current incentive structure for local officials remains in place, conflicts over housing demolition should be expected to continue.

For affluent homeowners in new residential tracts, the situation has been quite different, but also has not worked to undermine the existing political system. The privileged socioeconomic status of these homeowners has given them much greater resources when it comes to protest – including the financial freedom to devote more time to collective action; and connections with academic institutions, media outlets, and government officials. In addition, as the owners and residents of new housing units, they are in a long-term relationship with local political and economic elites, which allows them to adjust their tactics over time, and to capitalize on opportune moments for resistance.[39] As a result, they have been able to effectively pressure developers and management companies to accede to their demands, and to lobby government officials and offices to revise flawed laws and create new ones that serve their interests. They also have developed cross-community networks wherein they have shared information and provided support. This stands in marked contrast to collective action on the part of farmers, workers, and evictees, which have tended to be confined to a single village, factory, or neighborhood. Further, affluent HOA leaders increasingly have evidenced more value-driven behavior – acting not simply out of a motivation to correct the material wrongs that they have suffered, but rather to represent their broader interests as a social group. To the extent that they have been successful, and continue to be, they are not likely to oppose the political status quo. Instead, they are likely to become further embedded in it. At the same time, there is little probability that they will join forces with less affluent socioeconomic groups that do not enjoy similar privileges.

5 | Environmental Protest ————————

As illustrated in chapters 2–4, in the post-Mao period, farmers, urban workers, and homeowners have protested around specific material grievances. Simultaneously, widespread and prevalent acts of collective contention have arisen in reaction to the severe environmental degradation and disruption that have arisen alongside China's dramatic economic growth. As with the unrest chronicled in preceding chapters, citizens with grievances related to environmental issues have been encouraged to protest by (mostly national) laws, policies, and pronouncements that appear to favor their cause. Relatedly, like other popular actions, those related to the environment initially have sought redress through institutionalized channels. When legal methods have failed, the aggrieved have undertaken more contentious acts that at times have involved violent conflict.

Still, environmental protests have not posed an existential threat to CCP rule; generally speaking, they have only called on ruling elites to abide by existing laws and official statements. And central political leaders – and in some cases local officials – have expressed sympathy with and support for environmental protests. Indeed, collective actions related to the environment have been more successful than have protests by particular socioeconomic groups. At the same time, environmental protests undertaken by more resource-rich urban residents have had more positive outcomes than have those in poorer rural areas. Protests related to environmental issues also have exhibited some unique characteristics. Most notably, they have included fairly substantial involvement by NGOs, and they have involved participants from an array of demographic groups.

GRIEVANCES

The grievances expressed in environmental protests in China have their roots in the country's fantastic economic growth of the past few decades. According to the World Bank, since 1978, China's "GDP growth has averaged nearly 10 percent a year – the fastest sustained expansion by a major economy in history."[1] Alongside this achievement, in 2008, China became the "world's largest emitter of greenhouse gases," and in 2010 it became "the world's biggest energy consumer."[2] These developments have imperiled China's natural environment to such a degree that its pollution problems are described as "postapocalyptic," "terrifying," and "beyond belief."[3] Over a quarter of China's land is "desertified;" virtually every major body of water is polluted; over 60 percent of all groundwater is rated between "bad" and "very bad;" and one-tenth to one-fifth of all cropland is contaminated with heavy metals. In almost every major city, drinking water contains arsenic and other toxic chemicals, and air particulate levels regularly – and often substantially – exceed levels considered safe for humans.[4]

Citizen grievances associated with these forms of contamination have included crop and fish deaths. As a farmer in Sichuan lamented, due to effluents from a nearby coal-washing plant, "the whole river turns black. We don't want to irrigate our crops with it, and the animals can't drink from it." As a result, he and his neighbors' livelihood had been destroyed.[5] In addition, pollution-related disease and illnesses have become widespread. Perhaps the most stark illustration of this phenomenon has been the emergence of "cancer villages," wherein cancer rates are far above the national average. As of the time of this writing, there are estimated to be roughly 500 such localities in China.[6] Concerns about the damage caused by polluting factories also have sparked large-scale citizen actions to prevent the construction of paraxylene (PX) and other kinds of chemical plants, particularly in urban areas.

To combat these growing pollution problems while still satisfying the ever-increasing energy demands that have accompanied China's frenetic pace of economic growth, political authorities at various levels have embraced clean and renewable energy sources, such as wind and water. Although the construction of wind power facilities has not generated any significant popular resistance, hydropower has. This is because dams displace people and submerge farmland – and typically extensively so. Numerous massive hydropower projects have been approved since the turn of the new millennium. As of 2008, about half of the large-scale dams in the world were in China, and still more were either in progress or planned for the future.[7]

Concomitantly, the increased consumption that has resulted from China's economic development has caused an exponential rise in waste. This problem has been exacerbated by China's urbanization over the course of the post-Mao period – and especially since the early 1990s, as internal migration restrictions have been relaxed. Between 1980 and 2008, China's urban population more than tripled, from 190 million to 600 million. By 2050, an estimated 75 percent of China's roughly 1.3 billion people will live in cities. With this comes increased waste: the average urbanite generates two-to-three times more waste than does the average rural resident. In 2009, official Chinese sources revealed that one-third of all cities were surrounded by waste, covering an area of over 500 million square meters. Seeking to address this growing problem, political authorities have turned to waste incineration. With an official goal of increasing incineration from one percent of waste in 2002 to 30 percent by 2030, between 2004 and 2015 nearly 250 new municipal incinerators were built, or were in the process of construction. From 2003 to 2013, the number of metric tons of incinerated waste went from close to zero to almost 50 million.[8] Although incineration is an efficient way to dispose of waste, it releases pungent and toxic fumes, thus contaminating the air in the incinerator's vicinity.

Grievances related to pollution, and to the construction of waste incinerators and dams, have sparked a multitude of popular protests across both rural and urban areas – particularly since the turn of the millennium. According to a study by the Chinese Academy of Social Sciences (CASS), between 2000 and 2015 half of all "mass incidents" with 10,000 or more participants were triggered by environmental pollution.[9] Another Chinese study found that from 1996 to 2010, "mass incidents" related to environmental issues increased by an average rate of 29 percent per year.[10] The first major anti-incineration protest occurred in the coastal city of Xiamen (in southeastern Fujian province) in 2007. Subsequently, over just the span of 2008–9, notable "anti-incinerator construction" demonstrations occurred in 30 cities.[11] Numerous large-scale protests related to dam construction also have arisen since the turn of the millennium, including demonstrations in Sichuan province that – with upwards of 100,000 protestors – constitute the largest in China since the student-led protests of 1989, and the biggest rural uprising since the founding of the PRC in 1949.[12]

OPPORTUNITIES AND EFFICACY

As emphasized in earlier chapters, grievances alone are insufficient to elicit collective contention; disgruntled citizens also must feel that they have some hope of redress. Similar to protests by particular socioeconomic groups, feelings of efficacy regarding environmental grievances have been fueled by official policies and pronouncements that have encouraged potential protestors to believe that their legal rights have been violated, and that by bringing this fact to the attention of the right political authorities, regime leaders will step in on the side of the aggrieved.

Government Rhetoric and Actions

In this respect, a number of central laws and statements have been key. Perhaps most notably, in 2003, a new Environmental Impact Assessment (EIA) law came into effect, requiring that all new construction projects "design, construct and put into use relevant environmental protection facilities along with the progress of the project itself."[13] To ensure that regular citizens were aware of the new law, its promulgation was accompanied by a publicity campaign launched by the State Environmental Protection Agency.[14] In early 2006, further provisions in the EIA law provided formal mechanisms for public input and consultation in the creation of EIAs, and in 2007, additional measures required the public disclosure of environmental information.[15] Specifically, political authorities must invite experts and the public to participate in the formulation of EIAs, with public hearings being a "desirable" form of public participation. Further, citizens have the right to express their preferences regarding new projects to their representatives in People's Congresses and the Chinese People's Political Consultative Conference (CPPCC).[16]

Meanwhile, official rhetoric and actions signaled central leaders' commitment to addressing environmental concerns. In 2007, CCP General Secretary Hu Jintao called environmental protection a "'vital interest' of the Chinese people." Concomitantly, the State Council announced that promotions and bonuses for provincial officials and key firms would depend in part on their success in meeting environmental targets. In addition, the Party-state's 11th Five-Year Plan (2006–10) stated that local officials would be held accountable for reducing pollution and energy use. Further, 18 government ministries signed an eight-year (2007–15) national action plan for the environment and health.[17] As discussed below, in response to the explosion of environment-related protests during the late years of the first decade of the new millennium, during the second decade of the 2000s, a new

Environmental Protection law with even more clear and strict stipulations was promulgated, and central leaders made further efforts to address environmental concerns.

Elite Disagreement

China's convoluted institutional structure related to environmental matters also has given aggrieved citizens the perception that they might have success in seeking redress. There are many official entities involved, and the authority relations among them often are unclear. Further, in many cases different offices have contrary interests that lead them to support or oppose a given project. These factors can give rise to disagreements among political elites that can be leveraged by citizens. For example, the EIA law was promulgated by China's State Environmental Protection Agency (SEPA), which was upgraded to the level of Ministry within the Chinese government in the late 1990s, and was renamed the Ministry of Environmental Protection (MEP) in 2008. Below the SEPA/MEP are province-level Environmental Protection Bureaus (EPBs). Lower-level EPBs exist as well, although their presence and functionality below the provincial level are spotty. But SEPA/MEP and sub-national EPBs are just some of the governmental entities that have power and influence over projects that might impact the environment. Others include: the National Development and Reform Commission (NDRC), which formulates national economic development plans; the national Ministry of Water Resources, regional Water Commissions, and state-owned power companies (all of which have the ability to approve projects); and bureaucracies related to seismology, construction, forestry, land resources, and "cultural relics."[18] This reality has provided openings for groups of citizens that wish to influence or block a proposed plan.

In addition, since the middle of the first decade of the millennium, numerous environmental courts have been established, giving citizens a further institutional avenue through which to attempt to adjudicate their environmental complaints. With the encouragement of some SEPA leaders, who viewed lawsuits as a mechanism to draw greater public and official attention to pollution, and to more effectively implement national policy, between 2007 and 2013, over 130 such courts were opened. In addition, the Supreme Court of China instructed lower courts to place the burden of proof on the defendant in civil environmental cases – a stipulation that also was written into China's 2004 solid waste law, 2008 water pollution law, and 2009 tort law.[19]

At the local governmental level, the varied attitudes of political elites also have contributed to feelings of efficacy among the environmentally aggrieved. In general, the changes in the evaluation criteria for local officials referenced above have given greater leverage to citizens with environment-related concerns. In some cases, local cadres even have taken the initiative to address environmental grievances. Indeed, Stern notes that environmental courts first appeared at the local level, established by political leaders looking for ways to show their "innovative" ways of approaching "social management" – catchwords that were emphasized in high-level Party-state documents and speeches beginning in the middle of the first decade of the millennium. Environmental courts served the dual function of helping local cadres to meet their environmental targets and to demonstrate their forward-thinking actions – with an eye to improving their chances of promotion.[20] Similarly, in some geographic areas local leaders have viewed environmental protection as way to attract investment and tourism.[21] Beyond instrumental incentives, researchers have found that some local officials simply care about the environment.[22]

Mass Media Coverage and ICTs

Mass media outlets and Information and Communication Technologies (ICTs) also have facilitated citizen protest by providing information about environment-related problems and enabling rapid communication among interested residents. From the early years of the millennium through the present, media outlets and the Internet have been key sources of information about environment-related issues.[23] In some cases, investigative journalists – often after being contacted by local residents affected by or fearful of being affected by environmental harm – have provided television and print coverage that effectively has pressured the government.[24] As noted by Turner and Mertha, since the turn of the millennium, environmental journalists in China have had more freedom than have reporters with other "beats," and as a result they have become "a force pushing environmental awareness and investigations of local problems."[25] Overall, this has given participants in environment-related protests greater leverage than has been the case in other types of contentious collective actions.

Nonetheless, in many instances, media outlets either have not shown interest in covering citizen discontent with environment-related problems, or have sided with the target of the citizens' ire. In these cases, the Internet and cell phones have been valuable mechanisms for information collection and dissemination, and for popular discussion and mobilization – including locating and attracting external allies.[26] Because most government offices now post online official policies, laws, and procedures, the Internet has facilitated access to such information. Also, aggrieved citizens can use the Internet to report their concerns and submit their demands via government websites. According to Wang, the number of environment-related citizen complaints conveyed in this manner began to rise in 2006, and has since continued to increase. Moreover, cadres relate that the weekly meetings of local EPBs emphasize the importance of handling these public submissions.[27]

In most instances of popular protest, some combination of mass media and ICTs has been employed by participants. At the same time, as noted in earlier chapters, urban residents are roughly twice as likely as rural residents to have access to computers and hand-held devices.[28] Moreover, ruralites have less access to laptops and desktop computers – which are easier to use to find information and document evidence.

In addition, many rural residents have limited literacy, such that communication modes like texting are constrained, as is the ability to use the Internet to search for information.[29]

Non-governmental Organizations (NGOs)

Beginning around 2010, political officials became more tolerant of civic groups focused on pollution-related matters, and since then various such organizations have become active. Importantly, this relaxation also has applied to international funding from environmental groups – such as Friends of Nature, Greenpeace, the Institute for Public and Environmental Affairs, and the Centre for Legal Assistance to Pollution Victims. In addition to nationally-focused organizations, many smaller environmental entities have blossomed at the provincial and local levels. Adding to their potential influence, many of the officers and staff members in these NGOs have been trained journalists or editors.[30] As described by Holdaway, these groups' "efforts have included publishing reports on pollution's impacts on health, pursuing accountability regarding public information about pollution ..., representing citizens in court cases, and reporting violating enterprises to the MEP [Ministry of Environmental Protection] or media." Indeed, the MEP publicly has acknowledged its incapacity to fully monitor pollution – "especially in rural areas" – and has "welcom[ed] the participation of NGOs in enforcement."[31] Overall, official tolerance of environmental NGOs has provided aggrieved citizens with valuable resources that generally have not been available in other types of protests.

WHEN DOES ENVIRONMENT-RELATED PROTEST OCCUR?

Within this general context, a number of particular factors may lead citizens to engage in collective contentious action. Conversely, even in a situation characterized by severe harm and a favorable legal and political atmosphere, citizens often do not rise up in protest. One factor that can work against the emergence of collective contention related to the environment is that pollution and its ill effects can be seen by the public as unavoidable in the pursuit of higher priorities – such as financial security and gain. Especially in poor rural areas where residents have few economic opportunities, polluters can be viewed as a necessary source of jobs, and as providers of much-needed infrastructure and funds for other public goods and services. In these situations, both residents and local political elites tend to be in agreement, such that nobody takes the initiative to oppose the polluter. Relatedly, if villagers have friends or family members whose livelihood depends on an occupation that damages the natural environment, these human relationships may undercut villagers' motivation to protest. Also, migrant workers that are employed by a polluting factory do not have a long-term stake in the environmental condition of their work location. Further, in cases of disease related to environmental degradation, it typically is difficult to demonstrate a clear causal connection with pollution.[32]

Popular protest related to the environment is most likely to occur when local residents do not clearly benefit from the source of environmental harm. Perhaps the best example is the construction of waste incineration and paraxylene (PX) plants, which contaminate the area in their vicinity, but usually provide no direct material gain to local residents. Oftentimes, these plants have been slated for areas near relatively well-off urban homeowners who are financially secure. These individuals tend to be uninterested in any employment opportunities that might be provided by the plant, and they also are relatively educated, and have free time, resources, and connections that lower-income citizens do not.[33] This helps to explain why many of the largest environmental protests that have occurred in China have been related to incinerators and PX plants – including in Xiamen (Fujian province,

2007), Beijing (in the localities of Liulitun and Asuwei, 2007), Guangzhou (Guangdong province, district of Panyu, 2009), Wujiang (Jiangsu province, 2009), Pinghu (Zhejiang province, 2009), Kunming (2013), and Shanghai (2015). In Xiamen, most participants were housewives, freelance workers, and white-collar private-sector workers. In Panyu as well, middle-class activists were key. Indeed, in this case, the relatively poor residents of a village that was most affected by the project were quiescent until more resource-rich homeowners reached out to them and offered assistance through the Internet. In all of these cases, protest organizers have had convenient Internet access, and foreign language skills that have allowed them to understand and incorporate information from international sources. Further, they have had contact with experts in their urban vicinity, including both academics and NGOs. Finally, many have had connections with media outlets.[34]

Further, as noted in earlier chapters, collective contention typically arises only when one or more protest leaders emerge. Generally speaking, those who have spearheaded protests around environmental issues have been similar to the leaders of other kinds of protests: they have some prior standing in the community, and are relatively educated and resource-rich. In Huaxi (Zhejiang province), for example, a protest against the relocation of a pesticide factory was initiated by the Party secretary of a village in the area.[35] Similarly, in rural Xiping village (in Fujian province), protests were sparked by the work of a local doctor, Zhang Changjian, who observed a significant increase in various ailments, including a rise in cancer, that he was able to trace back to the opening of a chemical plant in the area. With supporting evidence in hand, Zhang enlisted community members to start a letter-writing campaign that transformed over time into a lawsuit that the villagers won.[36] In Xiamen, the initiator and main leader of anti-PX efforts was a professor.[37]

Unlike other kinds of protests, however, some of the leaders of environment-related protests have not been propelled to act in response to their own personal harm. Instead, these leaders have been motivated by more idealistic commitments to environmental health and the well-being of their fellow citizens. One example is Green Watershed founder Yu Xiaogang, an anthropologist who developed an interest in environmental protection in poor rural communities while conducting his academic fieldwork.[38] Similarly, in Panyu, an activist stated, "we are not simply asking the government to move the project out of Panyu. Wherever it is located, burning garbage harms people's health and the environment, and we will protest."[39]

Perhaps in part for this reason, although many environmental protests have been responsive in nature – i.e., they have been a reaction to some harm that already has been suffered – quite a few have been preemptive – i.e., designed to prevent some future harm. As awareness of the ill effects of dams, waste incinerators, and chemical plants has spread, citizens have been more likely to engage in collective opposition to stop the completion of such projects. Preventive protests also have been undertaken by urban homeowners whose property values have been threatened by planned changes in the vicinity. But it is not just urban homeowners that have engaged in preemptive opposition to projects that will negatively impact their environment; relatively poor rural residents also have engaged in this kind of opposition. Further, to the extent that environmental protestors are not motivated simply by their desire to remedy or prevent their own personal harm, but instead are driven by a broader idealistic desire to protect the environment, protests of this nature are likely to be more widespread and frequent than are protests of other types.

HOW DO ENVIRONMENTAL PROTESTORS ACT?

When citizens have risen up around environmental issues, they generally have employed the same kind of tactics and discourses that have characterized the protests discussed in the preceding chapters: they

have begun with petitions, have made an effort to follow legal procedures, and have referenced the law and other official statements to
justify their demands. The government's promulgation of the various
policies and directives outlined above has provided protestors with
ample points of reference in this regard. Particularly in the case of
urban-based environmental protests, organizers and participants have
used the Internet and cell phones to spread information and mobilize
the public. Finally, as with other kinds of protests, environmental activists have engaged in more aggressive actions (such as street marches,
sit-ins and blockades) only when their efforts to work through legal
channels have failed.

Relatedly, environmental protestors consciously have framed their
arguments and demands around themes that are more likely to elicit
a supportive government response. For example, when it has proven
difficult to definitively prove a connection between pollution and health
issues, the aggrieved have articulated their claims in other ways. In
the case of Huaxi, when villagers' environmental complaints fell deaf
on official ears, they changed their focus to land-related grievances –
which at the time were being emphasized by central leaders.[40] In protests
against a planned pipeline in Qidong (Jiangsu province), even though
the real target of the residents' complaints was the Nantong municipal
government, activists framed their complaints around anti-Japan sentiments, as the pipeline originally was designed for a Japanese company.
Explaining this choice of language, one Qidong protest leader said, "It
is terrible to chant the 'down with the Nantong government' slogan,
as they would say it is counter-revolutionary rebellion. The Communist
party has always propagandized that small little Japanese invaded
us in the past, so we are provoked to say that the Japanese invaded us
with pollution now."[41]

At the same time, one somewhat unique aspect of many environmental collective actions is that organizers have conducted independent
research and have used these findings to inform and pressure

government officials – many of whom have only limited scientific or technical knowledge related to the issue at hand. This also has been seen in some of the homeowner protests discussed in chapter 4, and largely is enabled by the privileged position of urban homeowners in terms of education, social connections (such as with academics) and Internet access. Another factor that has made independent research possible for environmental protestors has been their ability to work with domestic and international NGOs that have the resources and expertise to provide compelling data to back protestors' claims and demands. These groups also have helped activists to formulate proposed solutions to problems – such as waste sorting and alternatives to incineration – that provide officials with a way out of the conflict.[42]

EXAMPLES

Urban: Anti-PX and Anti-Incinerator Protests

A brief synopsis of some prominent environment-related protests helps to illustrate the points made above. One general type includes urban-based opposition to the construction of chemical and waste incineration plants. As noted earlier, the first large-scale action of this kind arose in Xiamen (Fujian province) in 2007, in opposition to the construction of a paraxylene (PX) plant. The key initiator of the protest was Zhao Yufen – a female professor at Xiamen University who also was a member of the CPPCC and was affiliated with the government-affiliated Chinese Academy of Sciences. In March 2007, Zhao collected 105 CPPCC member signatures on a petition calling for the plant to be suspended and relocated due to health risks.

Subsequently, other intellectuals publicized the issue via blogs and posted recommended measures for residents to take. Many joined in Internet discussions of the topic, and also spread anti-incinerator messages via e-mail and instant messages. Along with focusing on health concerns, participants emphasized Xiamen's reputation as a "garden city." Meanwhile, local media outlets ran continual stories touting the economic benefits and safety of the planned project. In late May, a key instant message reportedly reached 1.5 million people in Xiamen, warning:

> The Taiwan-funded Xianglu Group has begun building a PX plant. It is like an atomic bomb in Xiamen. Many people will suffer leukemia and more babies will be born with congenital defects. A paraxylene project should be at least 100 km from a major urban settlement, but we are only 16 km from the project. For the sake of our future generation, please forward the message to all your friends to demonstrate in the streets on 1 June 2007.

Heeding this call, on June 1–2 an estimated 10,000 residents "took a stroll" to demonstrate their opposition to the plant, reporting their actions via text and Internet posts. In December, a public hearing was held, and government officials announced that the plant would be relocated to another city. However, one participant who wore a gas mask while protesting was detained for nearly two months.[43]

Importantly, coverage of this episode via media outlets, the Internet, and cell phones reached citizens in other cities faced with proposed chemical and incinerator plant construction. Drawing on the information and protest tactics employed by the Xiamen protestors, activists in numerous other cities have engaged in similar actions. These include significant demonstrations in Chengdu (2008), Dalian (2011), Ningbo (2012), Jiangmen (2013), Maoming (2014), Heyuan (2015), and Shanghai (2015). In all of these cases, large numbers of residents from all walks of life mobilized to prevent threats to the whole community.[44]

In Dalian (Liaoning province), protests arose when residents became concerned about the threat of future environmental damage caused by a PX factory jointly owned by the city and a private company. When a film crew from the government-affiliated China Central Television (CCTV) that had come to investigate the safety of the plant was beaten and the crew's news report was pulled, outraged online discussion spread. Following an anonymous Internet call for citizens to gather in the city's central square, more than 10,000 demonstrators appeared. By the end of the day, local officials had announced that the factory would cease production and be moved out of the city. However, the plant reportedly renewed production in early 2012. Further, in early 2013 six of the organizers of the protests were put on trial for "libel," and for "concocting false information to terrorize the public."[45]

Overall, most urban-based environmental protests have not involved violence, and have not resulted in serious punishment for the organizers. Nonetheless, the Dalian case shows that even in urban-based protests, leaders have faced risk. Further, in some urban protests – such as those that arose in Ningbo in late 2012 – violent conflicts have emerged. Relatedly, although urban-based environmental protests largely have been undertaken by relatively well-to-do homeowners, because the plants in question have threatened the health of all residents in the vicinity, people of all socioeconomic levels have participated in them. In this respect, urban environmental protests have differed from the farmer, worker, and homeowner protests chronicled in earlier chapters. Because urban environmental protests thus have the potential to become large-scale, they also may be perceived as a threat by political authorities.

Rural: Anti-Dam and Anti-Chemical Plant Protests

Among rural residents, two general categories of environmental protest have arisen: those in opposition to the construction of dams, and those in opposition to chemical plants and other sources of pollution. The former includes the Pugubou (Sichuan province) anti-dam demonstrations that began in 2004. Unlike most urban-based anti-PX and anti-incinerator actions, the Pugubou protests involved violent conflict and did not achieve the demonstrators' aims. In this sense, the Pugubou protests are representative of a significant portion of rural-based environmental protests. Although there also have been many rural environmental protests that have enjoyed at least partial success, even in these cases, violence has been common.

The Pugubou protests did not have a clear initiator or organizer; they emerged slowly as villagers in various localities were told to relocate and were offered compensation and new residences that they found unacceptable. In this respect, their actions mirror those seen in other cases of rural land acquisitions. Yet because the relocation was related to dam construction, the focus of the protests was somewhat different. Aggrieved farmers petitioned the county, municipal, and provincial governments, but were rebuffed at all levels. Subsequently, they traveled twice to Beijing to submit their petition – now with 20,000 signatures. Meanwhile, earthmoving equipment broke ground on the dam. In response, 20,000 protestors occupied the site, halting the excavation. Roughly one month later, an estimated 50,000–100,000 protestors gathered at the site. During the occupation, an elderly woman was beaten, and the crowd attacked, setting cranes on fire and pushing two police vans into the Dadu River. By early November, 10,000 residents had built temporary shelters at the dam site, and skirmishes there and at government offices were commonplace. When news of these events reached central CCP leaders, General Secretary Hu Jintao and Premier Wen Jiabao issued an internal report directing officials to halt work on the dam until the protestors' concerns were resolved. Subsequently, a number of local officials were investigated and punished. However, up to 400 demonstrators were questioned by local authorities, and more than a dozen protest organizers were jailed. In the end, villagers received compensation packages that they found unsatisfactory, and the dam construction proceeded.[46]

A more positive sequence of events around dam opposition unfolded around the same time in Dujiangyan (also in Sichuan province). Unlike the Pugubou protests, the collective actions at Dujiangyan were carefully framed by organizers, who used language emphasizing the cultural heritage of the site, and in so doing successfully appealed to the general public as well as media outlets for support. Also, unlike at Pugubou, activists skillfully used the Internet to convey their message. Further, whereas the Pugubou protests were largely spontaneous actions undertaken by poor farmers with few resources or connections, the Dujiangyan demonstrations were initiated by two journalists that were sponsored by an international NGO. Through their efforts, the project ultimately was abandoned.[47]

An example of rural protest against polluting factories occurred in Huaxi village (Zhejiang province). The opposition was initiated by a Huaxi village Party secretary, who in 2001 wrote up and circulated a leaflet to oppose the relocation of a pesticide factory to the area. Upon receiving the leaflet, three villagers began a door-to-door campaign and circulated a "joint appeal" to the township Party secretary. When he responded that the factory was safe, villagers physically dragged him to the industrial park and forced him "to walk around it in bare feet and to smell the foul waste water." When village officials arrived and took the township Party secretary to the hospital, the protestors destroyed a fence, smashed doors and windows, and vandalized computers and telephones on the factory grounds. Those involved were harshly punished: twelve were charged with "disturbing social order" and ten were jailed, including the Huaxi village Party secretary, who was given a three year sentence. Moreover, the pesticide factory was still moved.[48]

In 2004, provincial authorities publicly announced that industrial parks that had not been established through proper legal procedures should be shut down, and included the Huaxi pesticide factory complex on the list. Seeing this is a positive sign, three of the now-freed activists decided to sue the county government and the factory owner. However, they found themselves unable to get legal representation, as local lawyers refused to take the case, and even with fund-raising efforts, they did not have enough money to hire a law firm. Still determined, they began a new petition effort. When multiple visits to the prefectural and provincial offices were rebuffed, they traveled on two occasions to Beijing. Throughout this period, the village Society of Senior Citizens (SSC) played a key role, holding almost daily meetings to study legal documents, strategize, and mobilize. Some of the larger meetings attracted roughly 500 residents. In the end, however, their efforts to gain redress through institutionalized procedures were unsuccessful.[49]

Frustrated, in 2005, elderly residents of the village decided to occupy the entrance to the site and disrupt its operation. When local authorities pulled down their tent, the villagers came back in larger numbers, and residents of around ten neighboring villages joined the occupation. With the SSC actively organizing schedules for tent-sitting, supplies, and even paying occupiers a small stipend for their work, the occupation persisted for two months. The protestors also shifted the way they framed their actions, this time focusing on the illegality of the factory's land acquisition rather than on the ill effects of the factory on the environment. In addition, the organizers capitalized on the fact that nearly all of the more than 1,000 workers at the industrial park were not from the area. Through their organization and persistent efforts, the occupiers also attracted sympathetic media attention. Ultimately, the protests were successful: 11 of the polluting factories were removed from the site.[50]

The success of this final round of protest was enabled by a variety of factors. To begin, the changed framing of the issue to focus on illegal land acquisition resonated with current concerns among high-level political leaders. In addition, the factories were not providing locals with jobs or other benefits; their effects were only negative. Further, the SSC mainly was made up of retired villagers with free time.

Moreover, because the Huaxi area is relatively rich, the SSC had substantial financial resources that could be used to supply and pay the occupiers. Overall, the confluence of these factors contributed to the protest's positive outcome.

CENTRAL GOVERNMENT RESPONSE

As with other grievances that have led to widespread and persistent protests, central authorities have attempted to address the root causes of citizens' dissatisfaction. In 2007, national leaders encouraged empirical study of environmental and health issues. In 2011, they called for increased funding for research, integrated monitoring and risk assessment, the development of standards, and public education. Simultaneously, the CCP's 12th Five-Year Plan "refer[red] explicitly...to public demand for environmental goods" and "to the threat that pollution presents to health and to social stability."[51] Also in 2011, the president of China's Supreme Court supported environmental initiatives in his annual report to the NPC.[52]

From 2011 to 2014, central authorities – with significant input from citizens, NGOs, and cadres at all governmental levels – crafted a new Environmental Protection Law (EPL) that took effect in 2015. When an initial draft of the law "angered" and "rallied opposition from environmental protection groups," the MEP "widely sought opinions from local Environmental Protection Bureaus (EPBs), experts, scholars, environmental NGOs, and corporate representatives." The final draft dramatically strengthened the public's legal rights on environmental matters. Specifically, it allowed public interest groups to file environmental lawsuits (increasing the number of eligible groups from roughly 12 to more than 700); required EPBs at all levels to provide environmental information to the public via official websites; and stipulated that government offices at all levels must provide a yearly report on their environmental work to the NPC. In addition, the new law significantly ratcheted up enforcement and punishment mechanisms, including giving EPBs the power to confiscate equipment, order production limits, suspend production, and entirely shut down polluter operations. In addition, the law required that EPBs note environmental violations on companies' credit records.[53] Meanwhile, central bodies have permitted criminal prosecution for pollution, including the possibility of the death penalty. Shortly after the EPL was promulgated, Premier Li Keqiang declared "war on pollution" at the opening session of NPC and CCP General Secretary Xi Jinping stressed the importance of building an "ecological civilization."[54]

If these CCP efforts are effective, one may expect a decrease in massive street protests related to the environment and an increase in redress through institutionalized channels. However, at the time of this writing, change has been minimal. Most notably, this is because environmental issues continue to be handled by a fragmented organizational structure wherein various bodies have dissimilar concerns and interests; the MEP relies on local government officials to oversee local EPBs; and both local and national leaders are loathe to sacrifice short-term economic gains for environmental protection.[55]

CONCLUSION

Overall, protests related to the environment have resulted in some notable successes – including both specific cases where planned projects have been scrapped or moved, and a more general central government commitment to addressing the public's environmental concerns. In part, these achievements have been aided by the greater latitude given to environmental NGOs operating in China, as these groups have provided information, advice, and support to communities facing harm, or the threat of it. Relatedly, environmental protests undertaken by relatively resource-rich urbanites generally have been more successful than have those in poorer rural areas. And, violent conflict has been much more prevalent in rural-based environmental protests than in affluent urban locations. Moreover, in some cases, when incinerators or chemical plants have been moved in response to protests, they have been relocated to places where the resource-poor residents have been less likely to engage in collective opposition. Thus, the results of environment-related protest have been unequal, and have benefited already resource-rich communities more than others. In addition, in many cases political leaders have responded to environmental protests with "superficial, tokenistic" measures that successfully defuse popular unrest, but have no meaningful long-term impact.[56]

In comparison with the other types of popular protests discussed in earlier chapters, environmental protests evidence both similarities and differences. In all of the collective acts of contention discussed thus far, participants have focused on the law, and they initially have attempted to follow institutionalized processes to seek redress – such as petition efforts and the courts. In virtually every case, the aggrieved have undertaken more conflictual actions – such as street marches and occupations – only when these earlier efforts have failed. Protests related to the environment also have been facilitated by the Internet and cell phones, which have been used to gather and disseminate information about environmental issues and relevant laws and policies, as well as to mobilize the public to act. In this respect, as in other types of protest, relatively well-off urban residents that enjoy greater access to the Internet and cell phones (and that tend to be more literate) have had an advantage over their rural counterparts. Most environmental protests – like other kinds of protests – also have been locally focused on grievances specific to a particular community.

However, collective contention related to the environment also has displayed some unique aspects. First, it has featured much broader protest constituencies – including persons from a wide array of socio-economic groups. Second, it has focused not just on the protection of material goods (such as wages or land) but collective goods – a healthy natural environment. Third, protestors have voiced concerns about both short-term, immediate issues, and broad, long-term goals. Fourth, collective action around environmental issues has been not only reactive, but proactive. And finally, environmental activists increasingly have become involved in advocating for overarching policy change rather than simply redress for particular problems. In these respects, protests related to the environment have shown the most potential for improved state–society relations in China. However, as with other types of collective contention, the Xi administration's efforts to constrict the activities of journalists, academics, and NGOs have threatened to undermine this positive development.[57]

6 | Nationalist Protest ────────────

Mainland Chinese also have participated in nationalistic protests that defend China and criticize foreign governments. While not as frequent as the types of collective contention discussed in chapters 2–5, when nationalistic protests have arisen, they have in numerous cases included tens of millions of participants, and have appeared simultaneously in cities across China. The most consistent focus of nationalistic protesters' ire has been Japan, but the United States has been a target as well.

As with the protests chronicled in earlier chapters, nationalistic collective contention has arisen only when grievances and perceptions of efficacy have been capitalized upon by activist leaders. Further, nationalistic protests have featured petitions and some attempts to use China's legal system to seek redress. Yet in many important ways, nationalistic collective actions have exhibited distinctive features. First, their petitions generally have been online only, and have not been submitted to various levels of governmental "letters and visits" offices over a sustained period of time. Relatedly, their complaints have been more expressive and general – typically without the specific material focus that the protest types discussed in earlier chapters have displayed. Instead, their focus has been on the behavior of foreign governments and/or the foreign policy of the Chinese government.

In terms of participants and leaders, the vast majority of nationalist activists have been urban, relatively young, fairly educated, and apt to use the Internet. In many cases, college students have been at the forefront. However, many nationalistic protesters have come from less privileged social strata, such as migrant workers, unemployed urbanites (including unemployed college graduates), and older veterans and retirees. In this respect, nationalistic protests have been somewhat akin to urban environmental protests – they have involved city dwellers from virtually all walks of life. Unlike other kinds of protests, however, overseas Chinese also have had significant involvement in nationalistic protests.

Finally, nationalistic protests have been fairly successful in achieving their aims. In large part, this is because they have been permitted and tolerated only when top political leaders have agreed with the sentiments expressed by the participants, and have felt that such protests would serve the government's foreign policy aims. At the same time, it is important to emphasize that nationalistic protests have been spontaneous, bottom-up phenomenon instigated by regular citizens. Because of this, central authorities have viewed nationalistic collective contention with caution and some concern.

GRIEVANCES

The grievances expressed by nationalistic protestors are quite different than those articulated by the activists discussed in earlier chapters. By and large, the protesters discussed thus far have focused on specific, material issues that directly affect them. Those who engage in nationalistic collective contention, in contrast, are spurred into action by their anger at foreign governments that engage in behavior that threatens China's dignity and/or territory, and at times also at the Chinese government for not taking stronger action against such provocations. Although many who have participated in nationalistic collective actions harbor negative feelings about the foreign country in question (typically Japan or the US), it is only when the government of a foreign country undertakes a specific action that nationalistic protest is sparked. As detailed below, examples include the 1999 US bombing of the Chinese embassy in Belgrade; Japan's 2005 bid to gain a permanent seat on the UN Security Council and revision of its history textbooks; and Japan's 2012 decision to buy three of the contested Diaoyu (Chinese name)/ Senkaku (Japanese name) islands.

OPPORTUNITIES AND EFFICACY

Negative feelings about Japan and other foreign countries stem in part from the lived experience of many Chinese, but also from the portrayal of these countries in China's educational system, museums and other commemorative sites and events, and mass media. To the extent that this portrayal has been publicly sanctioned by the ruling CCP, nationalist activists have felt that governing authorities will (or should) support activists' "patriotic" actions. In other words, potential protestors have felt a sense of efficacy.

With regard to Japan, the experience of the Japanese invasion and occupation of China preceding and during World War II left a lasting impression on many Chinese. Between 1937 and 1945, Japanese troops swept through large swaths of China, leaving much destruction in their wake. In the most extreme example, in December 1937 an estimated 200,000 Chinese were killed and 20,000 Chinese women raped by Japanese soldiers in and around city of Nanjing. Although few Chinese are still alive who personally witnessed events such as these, the memories have been passed down over the years.

Government Rhetoric and Actions

Of equal importance, the Chinese government – especially since 1989 – has made a concerted effort to instill these memories in Chinese citizens. Chinese authorities have undertaken wide-ranging efforts to promote nationalism and "selective anti-foreignism" in domestic mass media outlets and the Chinese educational system. Since the early 1990s, the CCP has invested in patriotic monuments and museums, and has emphasized "patriotic education" in China's schools, with a focus on historical harms suffered by China at the hands of foreign powers.

From the founding of the PRC through the 1970s, ruling authorities in China focused educational efforts on class conflict and the division between the CCP and the Kuomintang (KMT). In the 1970s, most young Chinese had only minimal knowledge of Japanese war atrocities, as government-approved schoolbooks rarely mentioned the topic, and academic research on the subject was banned. Further, mass media outlets in China during this period were tightly controlled by the state, and the Internet did not exist. In the 1980s, the CCP slowly began to shift toward teaching China's history of resisting foreign aggression, and began to establish museums and allow scholarly research on the issue. Some popular books also appeared, including Zhigeng Xu's *The Great Nanjing Massacre (Datusha)* in 1987.[1]

Following the massive student-led protests of 1989, CCP leaders markedly ramped up these efforts, seeing nationalism (and the idea that the CCP is the only true protector of the Chinese nation) as a new foundation to buttress the regime's weakened legitimacy. By the early 1990s, a new "patriotic education campaign" focusing on Chinese tradition, history, national unity, and territorial integrity was in full swing. Primary and middle school students were shown patriotic films approved by the state education commission, and many high schools and colleges added required courses on the "state of the nation" (*guoqing*) and "lectures on patriotism." In addition, Zhao relates, "forums to discuss patriotism were organized in government agencies, enterprises, research institutes, neighborhood committees, and villages;" "all tourist spots, such as museums, memorials, historical (especially revolutionary) sites, cultural relics, conservation units, popular architecture sites and even local community (town and village) centers were ordered to highlight their patriotic identities;" and "one hundred movies glorifying the CCP were nominated and distributed to the public."[2]

Although studies have not been able to definitively demonstrate that these government actions have increased feelings of patriotism and anti-foreignism among the Chinese citizenry, there can be no doubt that since the early 1990s regular Chinese have been significantly exposed to negative information regarding the historical actions of Japan and Western nation-states, and that the Chinese Party-state has promoted this narrative.[3] In this context, when a country with "tainted" past relations with China has engaged in a new act that has been seen to threaten or diminish China's dignity or interests, the Chinese public has felt that government authorities will understand and support the people's anger.

Mass Media Coverage and ICTs

These perceptions have been furthered by developments in mass media and electronic communication technology from the 1990s through the present. As Chinese media outlets have become commercialized – i.e., focused on profit – they have pursued more sensationalistic stories in order to attract a wider audience. Fertile ground in this respect has been provided by incidents that show Japan/Japanese or other "suspect" foreign countries engaging in actions that slight or threaten China. Indeed, scholars that have compared the coverage of Japan in official "propaganda" outlets [such as the *People's Daily* (*Renmin Ribao*)] with commercial outlets have found much more negative reportage in the latter.[4] Another example is the publication of the bestselling, *China Can Say No*, in 1996. Written in "vulgar street slang" intended to "shock" readers, the book is "a collection of impassioned essays decrying Western disdain for China, and the importance of China being able to defend its interests against Western attempts at containment."

Seeing the book's argument as beneficial to the state's interests, top CCP leaders and institutions initially endorsed it. Subsequently, the commercial media took the idea and ran with it, publishing a plethora of "say no" stories. By December 1996, top CCP leaders had become sufficiently concerned that they were "losing control over nationalist discourse" that they "clamped down on 'say no' writings," including banning the even more critical follow-up book, *China Can Still Say No*.[5]

Meanwhile, from the mid-1990s through the present, the Internet has become much more widely available, providing an additional platform for the collection and dissemination of news, and for organizing collective actions surrounding nationalistic issues. This development has overlapped with the increased use of cell phones, which further has facilitated Internet access and group communication. Some of the most popular websites on the Chinese Internet have been related to nationalism, as have been some of the most notable online items that have "gone viral." A prime example of the latter is the video, "2008! China Stand Up!" (*Zhongguo Zhanqilai*), which appeared on April 15, 2008, on Sina.com. In the first ten days after its initial posting, the six-minute film drew more than one million hits and tens of thousands of positive comments. As described by Evan Osnos, the film opens "with a Technicolor portrait of Chairman Mao, sunbeams radiating from his head," followed by Mao's mantra, "Imperialism will never abandon its intention to destroy us." After warning that "the West intends to 'make the Chinese people foot the bill' for America's financial woes," the film shows ostensibly Tibetan "rioters looting stores and brawling" in Lhasa, flashing the words, "so-called peaceful protest!" Displaying foreign press clippings and the logos of CNN and the BBC, the film decries these "reports from distorted Western media," saying blatantly, "they lie, they lie, lie…lie again and again." The film calls on viewers to "Wake up! Wake up!" asking, "What are objective, justice, freedom, and democracy so-claimed by the Western media?" The film responds with Mao's words: they are "all reactionaries, paper tigers." As described by Osnos, "the film ends with the image of a Chinese flag, aglow in the sunlight, and a solemn promise: 'We will stand up and hold together always as one family in harmony.'" The film was not created by government-affiliated propaganda units; it was made by a 28-year-old graduate student studying Western philosophy at one of China's top universities.[6]

Similar views frequently have been expressed on a wide array of websites. Around 2008, the site "Anti-CNN" was extremely popular. Founded by a 24-year-old university graduate and successful Internet company owner, the site's focus was on "expos[ing] the lies and distortions in the Western media." In 2009, when "anti-CNN" posted a UN Human Rights Council report on China, a substantial majority of the user comments "criticized the West for meddling in China's affairs." Another site, "Fenqing.net" (angry/indignant youth), featured an "Angry Youth Forum" that included a "Fenqing Manifesto" presenting an account of Chinese history that emphasized its oppression by foreign nations such as Japan and the US; called on readers to expose the West's hypocrisy in calling for greater human rights and democracy in China; declared that "angry youth" should let the world know of China's strength (which is not necessarily belligerent, but can be if provoked); glorified the merits of nationalism; and urged readers to uphold their nationalism despite Western criticism of it.[7] Similarly, the Patriots Alliance Network (*Aiguozhe Tongmeng Wang*) was founded in 2002 by a group of college graduates with professional jobs in the tech industry. Since that time, it has spearheaded numerous online campaigns and public protests, mostly calling for the Chinese government to take a stronger stand against Japan, Taiwan, and the US.[8]

Nationalist activists also have been prominent on "Strong Nation Forum" (*qiangguo luntan*), an online site associated with the *People's*

Daily. One of the most popular sub-topics on the site is the China–Japan Forum, which regularly includes nationalistic postings that question or are in conflict with the official CCP "line." In 2005, for example, when protests arose surrounding Japan's history textbook revision and bid to become a permanent UN Security Council member, forum participants critiqued official domestic media statements and pointed out discrepancies between government-affiliated media outlets and what they considered to be more reliable news sources.[9]

With many websites such as these available, and cell phones at the ready, when an international event has occurred that has sparked the ire of nationalistic citizens, they quickly have been able to spread this information and mobilize. As is discussed in further detail below, a particularly popular approach has been the circulation of online petitions, some of which have attracted tens of millions of signatures in a short period of time. Online calls for boycotts and street protests also have been prominent.

WHEN AND WHERE DOES NATIONALISTIC PROTEST OCCUR?

As indicated above, nationalistic protests have occurred in China when potential participants have felt both aggrieved and efficacious, and when one or more citizens has attempted to initiate a collective response. In most cases, this action has begun online and/or through affixing "big character" posters on university campuses. When nationalist protests have moved offline and onto the streets, they have occurred only in urban areas. But, they have not arisen only in China's major cities; such protests have emerged in many of China's smaller cities as well. As noted by Weiss and Wallace, this is in large part due to the fact that the nationalistic grievances are not localized, and are readily spread through the Internet and cell phones, which are used by residents in all cities.[10]

HOW DO NATIONALISTIC PROTESTORS ACT?

When citizens have acted collectively to address what they perceive to be a threat or slight to China, their protest behavior has displayed some similarities with other kinds of protests. As noted above, they have undertaken petition efforts, and generally have tried to work within the boundaries of the law. Relatedly, they have stressed the legality of their behavior and goals. At the same time, rather than citing particular regulation, policies, and Constitutional provisions – as typically has been the case in the protests discussed in chapters 2–5 – nationalistic protestors have emphasized the patriotic nature of their demands and actions. Indeed, a common slogan among those engaged in nationalistic collective contention has been "patriotism is not a crime."[11]

Nationalistic protests also have displayed a number of unique characteristics. A major reason for this is that the nature of nationalistic protestors' grievances and goals has been fundamentally different. Whereas farmers', workers', and homeowners' protests have been motivated by specific material complaints that do not affect the wider population, nationalistic protestors have been propelled by more idealistic concerns about problems faced by the country as a whole. Even environmental protestors typically have been focused on issues that are more local in nature, such as PX plants or dams. Thus, nationalistic protestors typically have not attempted to go through the various levels of China's "letters and visits" system, and only infrequently have pursued cases in the courts. The only case of the latter has been some small-scale attempts to demand compensation for damage incurred during the Japanese invasion and occupation before and during World War II.

Typically, nationalistic activists have circulated petitions online, often collecting millions of signatures. Instead of submitting the petitions to "letters and visits" offices, activists more frequently have sent petitions to government-affiliated media outlets and national political institutions, such as the NPC and the CPPCC. At the same time, some online campaigns have not been directed at the Chinese government, but rather at the offending foreign government. Most often, these online campaigns have called for boycotting businesses and products associated with the country in question. In many instances, calls for collective action have begun on college campuses, with information circulating on university electronic bulletin boards, via e-mail and text, and in the more traditional form of "big-character" posters affixed in public locations on campus.

When nationalist protestors have engaged in more physical kinds of protests, they typically have marched to and gathered at the diplomatic buildings of the offending country, and/or to businesses associated with that country. Along with burning the country's flag, protestors have carried signs and shouted slogans criticizing the country in question. Although most nationalistic protests have been peaceful, in a number of instances, crowds have damaged diplomatic compounds and foreign businesses. Finally, in some cases individuals with other kinds of grievances – such as land acquisitions, layoffs, and unfair advantages given to those with political connections – have used the occasion of nationalistic street protests to voice their concerns.[12]

WHO HAS PARTICIPATED IN, AND WHO HAS LED NATIONALISTIC PROTESTS?

As mentioned earlier, nationalistic protests have been urban-based. Although some rural residents with access to the Internet have joined in online petition campaigns, because one's likelihood to use the Internet on a regular basis tracks with income, education, and urban residence, most of those who have undertaken collective nationalistic actions online have been urbanites. When street demonstrations have occurred, they have been centered on diplomatic buildings and foreign businesses in urban centers. By far the largest portion of participants in such street protests has been college students. Not infrequently, significant numbers of unemployed college graduates, migrant workers, and older retirees and veterans have joined as well. In some cases, such as the 1999 anti-US protests following the American bombing of the US embassy in Belgrade, participants have included people "of all generations and walks of life."[13] At the same time, many overseas Chinese – typically college students studying abroad – have demonstrated support for mainland nationalistic protests, either by staging demonstrations in their country of residence, or by joining online activities.

As noted above, citizen-created websites have played a key role in initiating nationalist protests. Almost universally, the individuals that have undertaken these efforts have been relatively young, urban-based college graduates – often with careers related to intercommunication technology – and typically male. For example, the main founder of the Patriots Alliance Network moved to Beijing after graduating from college and working at an Internet content company. In 2002, he became enraged when he read online postings regarding Japan, and convinced a group of friends to create a new website "to oppose what they saw as Japan's resurgent militarism." Along with posting information, the group has organized numerous online petitions, including one in 2004 that gathered nearly 90,000 signatures in ten days to prevent Japanese companies from building China's new bullet train. In addition, the website has spearheaded many public actions. Some of these have been very high-profile, such as the group's 2003 sponsorship of activists to sail to the Diaoyu/Senkaku islands.[14]

HOW HAS THE GOVERNMENT RESPONDED TO NATIONALISTIC PROTESTS?

The Chinese government's response to nationalistic protests has been varied. Scholars such as Weiss find that when an event occurs that might spark nationalist public actions, "the central leadership considers its diplomatic and domestic concerns and objectives, weighing the risk of instability and the cost of repression alongside its desire to show resolve or reassurance."[15] Based on this calculation, Party-state leaders decide on whether it is in their best interest to prevent, tolerate, and/ or suppress nationalistic collective public actions. Such protests typically have been allowed when they can be used to buttress the government's case vis-à-vis the "offending" foreign power, and/or when repressing the protests threatens to elicit public anger toward China's ruling regime. Conversely, nationalistic popular actions have been prevented or repressed if governing elites agree that popular expressions of nationalism will not (or will no longer) serve the Party-state's aims, and/or if public protests become violent and destabilizing. In some instances, authorities have proactively moved to prevent any potential public contention, detaining or placing under surveillance known activists; sending emissaries to universities to warn students against actions; stationing public security officers at potential protest locations; and issuing editorials in government-affiliated media outlets that make the government's stance clear. In other cases, nationalist contention has been allowed or even encouraged for a period, and then controlled and curtailed. As is discussed in more detail below, this progression was apparent in nationalistic unrest that emerged in 1999, 2005, 2008, and 2012. Finally, although some nationalist activists have been subjected to government scrutiny and questioning, and sites such as the Patriots Alliance Network periodically have been shut down, overall, nationalistic activist leaders have faced no serious punishment.

In terms of outcomes, nationalistic collective actions have a fairly impressive track record, particular in comparison with other kinds of protests. Most importantly, nationalistic protests successfully have conveyed to foreign leaders the potentially serious consequences of the country's "offense," resulting in a change of behavior on the part of the foreign government. In 1985, for example, popular protests in China in response to Japanese Prime Minister Nakasone's official visit to the

Yasukuni Shrine (where a number of Japanese war criminals are memorialized) convinced him to cancel a second planned visit. Similarly, student-led demonstrations following the 1999 US bombing of the Chinese embassy enabled the Chinese government to force the US to make a number of public apologies and also provide compensation. In addition, public unrest surrounding Japan's 2005 bid to gain a permanent Security Council seat in the UN contributed to its abandonment of this pursuit.[16]

EXAMPLES

A closer look at the initiation, progression, and conclusion of some of the major nationalistic protests that have occurred in the post-Mao period helps to illustrate these points.

1999 Anti-US Protests

One major wave of collective nationalistic contention arose in 1999, in response to the May 8 bombing of the Chinese embassy in Belgrade by American military planes, which killed three Chinese journalists and wounded 20 Chinese. That the bombs had been precision-guided and the embassy had been in that location for many years led many Chinese to believe that the destruction was intentional. Almost immediately after the news reached the mainland, "big-character" posters with anti-US slogans appeared on college campuses, and students requested permission to hold street demonstrations. A few hours later, central authorities strongly condemned the bombing through government-affiliated media outlets. Although students at most universities had not received permission to demonstrate, they did so regardless, marching from campus to the US embassy and other diplomatic buildings in dozens of cities across China. Tens of thousands participated. The protestors' slogans – such as "down with the Yankees" and "sovereignty and peace" – echoed the CCP-controlled media's castigation of the US and NATO. Though most of the demonstrators remained orderly and peaceful, in Beijing some in the crowd threw chunks of concrete and ink bottles at the US embassy, and other unidentified individuals attacked American businesses such as McDonald's and Kentucky Fried Chicken. In the city of Chengdu (Sichuan province), the residence of the US Consul-General was set on fire.[17]

Initially, central government authorities signaled their support of the protests. On the morning of May 9, the front page of the *People's Daily* included a photo of the Beijing protests, and stated that the demonstrations had been approved by the Public Security Bureau. The paper did not mention that the US had issued a "statement of regret" about the bombing. That evening, Chinese Vice President Hu Jintao expressed "firm support" for "legal protest activities," but emphasized that social stability must be ensured. Evidencing the desire to both facilitate and control the demonstrations, in several cities government authorities provided buses for transit to and from rallies. In Beijing, many students were wary of this government "assistance," and insisted on walking on their own.[18]

By May 10, central leaders were convinced that the usefulness of the protests had run its course, and instructed universities and work units to end their protests. On May 11, government-affiliated media outlets reported that formal US apologies had been made, and urged citizens to return to their normal duties. Protests persisted that day, but ended shortly thereafter.[19]

2005 Anti-Japan Protests

The anti-Japan protests of 2005 exhibited similar basic features. Their "patriotic" demands and actions spontaneously arose mainly on college campuses, and involved street protests at diplomatic buildings and foreign businesses. Initially, collective public actions were supported by governing authorities, but this shifted to efforts at control and constraint when ruling elites came to believe that the protests' benefits had become outweighed by their risks. At the same time, the protestors generally succeeded in their aims. The most significant difference with the demonstrations of 1999 was that by 2005, the Internet had become widely available to college students and other urban residents.

The 2005 demonstrations arose in the context of Japan's push for permanent membership on the UN Security Council, which was endorsed by the UN Secretary General in March. In conjunction with overseas Chinese associations, the Patriotic Alliance Network launched an online petition to oppose Japan's bid. The petition quickly spread to over 250 mainland websites and net portals. According to a news editor at Sina.com, seven additional servers had to be added to handle the traffic. Importantly, central authorities signaled their support. The petition effort was mentioned on the *People's Daily* website, and supported by the official Chinese news agency, Xinhua. Relatedly, Sina.com stated that the State Council had given the site permission to host the petition, and the spokesperson for China's Foreign Ministry reported favorably about the online effort. By early April, more than 40 million people had signed the petition. Over the weekend of April 2–3, street protests emerged in the cities of Chengdu and Shenzhen.

Further stoking Chinese anger, news spread that the Japanese government had approved a new middle school history textbook that diminished Japanese atrocities in China during World War II and portrayed Japan as a "benevolent liberator." University students across the country decried this action on campus electronic bulletin board systems (BBSs), and called for street demonstrations. Students publicized their plans online, including the protest routes in particular cities, slogans, and precautions. Public protests emerged on nearly 110 university campuses in at least 38 cities. The biggest were in Shenzhen and Guangzhou, with even more than the roughly 10,000 that participated in Beijing.

As in 1999, most of these acts of collective contention were law-abiding, orderly, and peaceful. Indeed, demonstrators made an effort to communicate and reach an agreement with local authorities with regard to the timing and location of planned protests. Along with marching to Japanese diplomatic buildings, in at least 14 cities "street petition" stations were set up (sponsored by the Patriots Alliance Network and another citizen organization) at parks and city squares to collect signatures and distribute leaflets. In some cases, violence emerged: in Chengdu, demonstrators smashed the windows of a Japanese supermarket; in Shenzhen, protestors threw garbage at police officers when the latter blocked the entrance to a Japanese supermarket; in Beijing and Shanghai, some threw bottles and rocks at the Japanese embassy; and in Shanghai a number of Japanese businesses were vandalized. Although the petition efforts widely were reported in Chinese media outlets, the protests received virtually no coverage.

By mid-April, it appeared that the protesters' demands would be fulfilled: both US and Chinese officials made public announcements indicating that Japan's UN bid was unlikely to succeed. Further, Japanese Prime Minister Koizumi stated that he would not ask for an apology for the damage done to Japanese diplomatic sites and businesses. Although several anti-Japanese websites called for mass demonstrations in early May, government officials made it clear that these would not be allowed, announcing that future "unauthorized marches" would be illegal, and warning that police "would mete out tough blows" to those caught damaging property. These threats were successful; no further demonstrations occurred.[20]

2012 Anti-Japan Protests

Exhibiting many of the same characteristics, another massive wave of anti-Japanese protests arose in 2012. In early July – on the 75th anniversary of Japan's 1937 invasion of China – the Japanese government announced that it would buy three of the disputed Diaoyu/Senkaku islands from their private Japanese owner. Shortly thereafter, activists from Hong Kong sailed to the islands, receiving "blanket Chinese media coverage" praising their patriotic action. When the activists were taken into custody by Japanese authorities, the Chinese government demanded their release. The Japanese agreed to do so immediately. Nonetheless, Chinese netizens announced plans for anti-Japan demonstrations the following weekend, providing details about protest locations, routes, and times. Although some of the postings quickly were deleted, many were not. On August 19, Japanese activists landed on the islands, and citizens in nearly 40 Chinese cities took to the streets. Over the next six weeks, approximately 400 protests occurred in 208 of China's 287 prefecture-level cities. As in earlier nationalist collective actions, most centered on diplomatic buildings and businesses associated with Japan. Protesters also met at sites commemorating World War II.[21]

By and large, the demonstrations were peaceful, but in a number of cases they involved violence and/or purposeful property damage. Indeed, when this occurred, the actions were more destructive than was the case in earlier nationalist protests. In the city of Qingdao, several Japanese factories were set on fire and a Toyota dealership was destroyed. In Shenzhen, Japanese cars (including a police vehicle) were overturned, and Japanese restaurants and department stores were vandalized. In Guangzhou, protesters broke into the hotel within which the Japanese consulate was located and smashed the window of a Japanese restaurant. Similar acts occurred in smaller cities as well. In some instances, bystanders were targeted; in Shanghai, "several Japanese nationals were harassed in the street," and in Xi'an, the owner of a Toyota car was "nearly beat to death."[22]

As with other nationalistic protest waves, the government's attitude and response shifted over time, and varied by location. Although initially, government-affiliated media outlets had praised the Hong Kong activists, political authorities – particularly in major cities such as

Beijing and Shanghai – clearly were concerned that protests might spin out of control, and thus worked to curtail them from the outset. In particular, university students in Beijing came under serious pressure to remain on campus. In many other cities as well, local authorities warned enrolled university students against participating in street demonstrations. In general, these efforts were successful at dissuading college students from participating. As a result, this wave of protests featured a smaller percentage of enrolled students, and a larger percentage of other urbanites (such as veterans, construction workers, auto club members, and white-collar employees) relative to earlier nationalistic collective contention.

In mid-September – as cases of violence increased, the number of protests peaked (at 128 on September 18), and the 18th National Party Congress drew near – political leaders stepped up their efforts to contain and curtail further demonstrations. On September 17, a high-level circular directed all government units to "properly manage" popular collective actions. Meanwhile, government-affiliated media outlet stories highlighted the punishment of unruly protestors that had engaged in unlawful behavior. At the same time, central officials tried to defuse the protesters' grievances by vowing "'zero tolerance' for Japan's provocations," pulling Japanese novels from state book stores, ordering the Chinese navy to expel Japanese vessels sailing near the disputed islands, and refusing to attend international meetings in Tokyo.[23] By the end of September, protests over this issue had ceased. Although the islands remained under dispute, this wave of citizen collective action can be seen as successful in that the Chinese government did not simply attempt to suppress them, but rather acted on protestors' demands for a tough stance against Japan.

CONCLUSION

Overall, nationalistic protests have been more successful than the other categories of collective contention discussed in earlier chapters. This is perhaps not surprising, given that the demonstrators' demands have echoed official narratives and rhetoric, and also that it has been relatively cost-free for central leaders to act responsively. Instead of calling for political reform (as in the student-led demonstrations of the late 1970s and 1980s) or for material redress (as demanded by farmers, workers, homeowners, and environmental activists), nationalistic protestors typically have pressed only for central authorities to take a "tough stance" toward foreign governments.

At the same time, as seen in the waves of nationalistic protests described above, these collective actions have been met with concern on the part of political authorities, and for good reason. Most importantly, unlike protests by farmers, workers, and homeowners, nationalistic protests have not been locally focused and small-scale. Instead, they have arisen simultaneously in cities across China, and have involved millions of participants. Even Chinese nationals living overseas have taken part. Further, although generally speaking, the demands of nationalistic protestors have not significantly diverged from the stance of China's national government, when nationalistic activists have become frustrated with what in their perception is weak or ineffective behavior on the part of central authorities vis-à-vis the offending foreign country, nationalistic activists have critiqued China's leaders. In addition, in nearly all of the nationalistic protest waves that have occurred in China's post-Mao period, a certain portion of protestors have voiced other kinds of grievances, such as those chronicled in earlier chapters. In this sense, any sort of large-scale and widespread protest has the potential to spill over into other issues. Similarly, protests that are widespread and large-scale are much more difficult to control and defuse than are localized instances of collective contention. In sum, although participants in nationalistic popular actions generally have acted to defend China and the Chinese government, they have been a potentially volatile political force that Chinese authorities have had to engage with caution.

7 | Political Protest ─────────

While nationalistic protests mainly have targeted foreign regimes, other protests in the late post-Mao period have focused on China's domestic political system. The latter have not taken the form of mass actions in the streets, but rather have appeared as collective petitions, lawsuits, and online satire and "storms." Although some of these efforts have come to a successful end, in many cases they have not. Indeed, a significant number of political activists – particularly since 2012 – have been subjected to severe punishment. In part, this is because, unlike the types of protest discussed in chapters 2–6, political protestors have expressed the desire for national-level political reforms that would move the polity in a more liberal democratic direction. At the same time, political protests since 1990 have been small-scale and undertaken mainly online and in the courts, and thus have not posed a serious threat to the stability of China's ruling regime. Nonetheless, the suppression of more moderate and reformist political activists in recent years has fueled a process of radicalization that has undercut their belief in the possibility of achieving satisfactory political reform, and ultimately may lead to the creation of a more sizeable political opposition in China.

TYPES OF POLITICAL PROTEST

Since 1989, political protests focused on China's domestic political system have taken three main forms. First, a small number of mostly middle-aged and older intellectuals have called for liberal democratic political reform. One of the most notable actions of this sort occurred in 1998, when some of the leaders of the political protests of the early post-Mao period publicly formed China's first true opposition party in the PRC – the China Democracy Party (CDP). The party was allowed to expand for roughly six months before its leaders were arrested and jailed. The party continues to exist underground in China, but its membership is exceedingly small. A second significant action of this type occurred in 2008, when a group of intellectuals led by writer Liu Xiaobo posted online a manifesto called "Charter 08" that called for fundamental liberal democratic political reform. Liu was jailed as a result, and remained in prison until his death (from untreated cancer) in 2017. Although this type of protest has received a great deal of coverage in Western media outlets, few mainland Chinese have joined or exhibited support for these actions.

Another type of political activism that has arisen since 1989 is known as "rights protection" (*weiquan*). Typically, these activists have been lawyers and journalists that have utilized China's legal system and mass media to press the Chinese government to redress wrongs perpetrated by local officials on individuals and groups of citizens. As with the categories of protest discussed in earlier chapters, "rights protection" activists have focused on violations of Chinese citizens' legal rights. Although most have started out as moderate lawyers seeking only individual justice in a given case, their negative experience with the legal system and inability to successfully engage the courts has led them to voice broader criticisms of the legal and governmental system as a whole. Participants in these actions generally have not engaged in street protest, and have not been organized beyond forming some loose networks. Despite a number of early successes, participants in "rights protection" activities increasingly have been harassed and punished by local authorities. In recent years, nearly all of them have been detained and jailed – and even academics who study them have been subjected to interrogation and harassment.

A third kind of political activism that has emerged in the post-1989 period includes Internet satire and mass "storms." The former is known in Chinese as *e'gao*, or satirical "punning," and it is a thriving sub-culture among Chinese bloggers, who use plays on Chinese words to avoid China's Internet censors and criticize official hypocrisy and governmental corruption. Thus far, this kind of protest has occurred only virtually, and has not resulted in any concrete actions. But its popularity indicates that there exists fairly widespread political frustration among mainland Chinese. Similarly, mass online "storms" have arisen when netizens have expressed outrage over cases of political corruption or abuse. They are similar to some of the mass online protests that have emerged regarding perceived foreign transgressions, yet they focus on the political misbehavior or shortcomings of China's domestic political regime. In recent years, governing authorities increasingly have restricted and repressed these modes of political expression. Should these government actions spark deeper outrage among Chinese netizens, online political criticisms have the potential to become more concrete.

OPPORTUNITIES AND EFFICACY

As emphasized in earlier chapters, potential participants must feel a sense of efficacy before they will engage in contentious public action – they have to feel some hope that their efforts might have a positive effect. In the case of political activism, a number of factors have contributed to a perception of efficacy among Chinese citizens that desire political reform and/or transformation.

Central Government Laws, Actions, and Rhetoric

Similar to the categories of popular protest discussed in prior chapters, central government laws, actions, and rhetoric have encouraged the emergence of the types of political protest described above. Most fundamentally, as discussed in the Introduction, China's state constitu-tion includes provisions protecting civil liberties such as freedom of speech, the press, assembly, association, and demonstration; the right to criticize and make suggestions to government bodies and officials; and "human rights." All three of the types of political protest mentioned above reference these provisions.

For activists associated with "rights protection," perceptions of effi-cacy also have grown out of central authorities' rejuvenation of the legal profession and rhetorical commitment to "rule by law" in the post-Mao period. As noted in the Introduction, beginning in the late 1970s, central authorities pushed for the creation of privately-employed lawyers with professional qualifications. This occurred in conjunction with CCP leaders' promotion of the ideal of "ruling the country in accordance with law (yifa zhiguo)." The overall result has been the emergence of "legal and litigative channels for defending civil rights" and the development of a professional legal community.[1] Further, inas-much as central officials have seen the law as a way to rein in local-level political abuses and to "channel conflict through legal procedures," CCP leaders have encouraged the phenomenon of "rights-protection" lawyering.[2]

Indeed, when in the early 2000s some lawyers successfully repre-sented aggrieved citizens in seemingly "unwinnable" cases concerning political corruption and abuse, the lawyers' victories were celebrated in official media outlets and honored by government leaders. The high point for this kind of positive public exposure was in 2003, when a number of contentious cases received a great deal of attention in the media and online, and the lawyers that successfully represented the wronged clients were hailed as heroes by both officials and regular citizens. In some of these cases, the lawyers moved beyond simply representing their client and called for broader policy changes that subsequently were enacted. The most famous was the trial of migrant worker Sun Zhigang, who had been detained when he was unable to provide police with a proper identity card. Along with winning in their defense of Sun, lawyers Teng Biao and Xu Zhiyong successfully petitioned the National People's Congress to abolish national regulations regarding the Custody and Repatriation system for rural migrants. In 2003, they were named in official media among China's "top ten 'rule of law figures.'" These developments fueled stronger feelings of efficacy among both active rights-protection lawyers and lawyers that previously had steered clear of cases with a political angle. In turn, successful rights-protection lawyers gained the confidence to take on more difficult cases, and other lawyers began to move into rights-protection activities.[3]

Media and Internet

Mass media outlets, the Internet, and cell phones also have been key contributors to perceptions of efficacy among the politically dissatisfied. As discussed in the Introduction and chapter 6, as China's mass media outlets have become increasingly commercialized, they have focused on more sensationalistic stories. In addition, some media outlets have become known for their relatively liberal viewpoint and willingness to cover stories highlighting the need for political reform. Knowing this, many rights-protection lawyers have developed relationships with like-minded journalists, who have provided media coverage for cases involving political abuse.

Similarly, the Internet and cell phones have provided democracy activists, rights-protection lawyers, and regular citizens with the means to spread their political complaints and demands. The Internet was particularly critical in the dissemination of the Charter 08 document. Very few of the signatories of the document met in person; nearly all of their communication was online. When the document was publicly posted in December 2008, it had just over 300 signatures. As word spread online, within one month the number of signatories had grown to 8,100.[4] Two years prior, Charter 08 initiator Liu Xiaobo described the Internet as "God's gift to China," saying, "The Internet was like a super engine. It ma[de] my writings burst out like an oil well."[5] Since the posting of Charter 08, websites devoted to the document and its ideals have disseminated like-minded statements and articles, and news of rights-protections actions across the country. Further, rights-protection and democracy activists have used social media – including the banned Twitter and Facebook – to share information. Indeed, rights-protection lawyer Teng Biao states that although only a small number of people actively use Twitter in China, it is widely used by rights-protection lawyers, liberal journalists, and democracy activists. Overall, Teng notes that the Internet has made communication among these individuals "extremely frequent and convenient," enabling the creation of a political community characterized by increasing "mutual support, cooperation, and collaboration."[6]

The Internet also has led to the development of a phenomenon known as the online "surrounding gaze" (weiguan), wherein virtual "crowds" gather around some kind of public spectacle. Rights protection lawyers have capitalized on this phenomenon by trying to focus the public gaze on the abuses suffered by their clients, as well as the larger policy wrongs that have precipitated such abuses. One of the upshots of the fact that China's judges are subjected to political pressures is that when the "court of public opinion" weighs in on an issue, this can sway the outcome of a case. In 2009, for example, when a female manicurist was put on trial for killing two officials with her manicuring shears as she tried to fend off their sexual assault, public support for her exploded online. The court ruled that she would not be given any criminal penalty.[7]

In some cases, this "surrounding gaze" has been initiated not by rights-protection lawyers seeking public attention to their case, but by regular netizens who have become aware of wrongdoing on the part of government officials and/or their family members. A particularly notable instance occurred in late 2010, when the son of high-ranking local public security officer Li Gang killed a pedestrian and critically injured another while driving drunk. When confronted after trying to escape the scene of the accident, the young man apparently yelled, "Sue me if you dare. My father is Li Gang!" News of the incident spread like wildfire online. Netizens quickly discovered and posted Li Gang's status and his son's name and other personal information. Ten days later, the *People's Daily* published an article calling for an official investigation. In early January 2011, the son was arrested, sentenced to six years in prison, and ordered to pay restitution to the victims' families.[8] Similarly, political dissatisfaction has been collectively voiced in online "anger-venting" "storms." For example, following the crash of two high-speed trains in the city of Wenzhou in 2011, Sina Weibo users expressed their outrage online, with at least ten million participating in the discussion. Overwhelmed by the number of posts, Weibo set up a specific page devoted to the train crash. In the posts, netizens expressed complaints about safety issues, corruption, the secretive handling of the crash, and prior official boasting about the high quality of the trains.[9]

Similarly, the Internet has made possible the development of online satire. Perhaps the most well-known example is the "grass-mud horse" (*caonima*) which is a homonym for "f— your mother." The term appeared as a protest against a 2009 government campaign to censor vulgar content online. Its meaning morphed to "f— the CCP" following an online posting of a music video depicting the grass-mud horse defeating a "river crab" (*hexie*) – a homonym for "social harmony" – a term official promoted by the CCP.[10] A plethora of other homonyms, symbols, and allusions circulate widely on the Internet, creatively subverting official discourses and criticizing political leaders' corruption and hypocrisy.

Foreign Governments and NGOs

The support of foreign governments and non-governmental organizations (NGOs) also has enhanced perceptions of efficacy among potential political protestors. When democracy activists and rights-protection lawyers and journalists have been jailed for their public political statements and actions, foreign governments (particularly those in the West) often have criticized Chinese leaders for disregarding basic human rights. In some cases, foreign governments have backed up this criticism with actual foreign policy pressure, such as the US government's prior tying of China's "Most Favored" trade status to human rights protections, including the treatment of specific political dissidents. Potential pressure from foreign governments also was key in the timing chosen by the activists who formed the China Democracy Party (CDP) in 1998; they purposely decided to publicly announce the CDP's existence (via posting an "open declaration" online) the day before US President Bill Clinton was due to arrive in China. Further, they hoped that their chances of avoiding immediate repression would be improved by the impending visit of the UN High Commissioner for Human Rights in September 1998. Indeed, this proved to be a wise strategy, as the group was allowed to develop and expand until December of that year, after international attention was no longer focused on Beijing.[11]

Similarly, when foreign NGOs have learned about the successes and punishment of rights-protection lawyers, they have invited them overseas and given them funding for their work. In this way, more well-known rights-protection lawyers have been able to secure greater resources to pursue their work, and have operated with greater confidence due to their knowledge that overseas organizations will publicize their situation and support them should Chinese authorities take repressive action against them. In addition, various domestic NGOs have promoted the work of rights-defense lawyers, both through providing staff support and financial resources, and by aiding in publicity efforts.[12]

GRIEVANCES

In the more materially-based protests covered in chapters 2–5, grievances were personally experienced by the participants. In contrast, and similar to nationalistic protests, for rights-protection and democracy activists, as well as online participants in mass "storms" and political satire, the motivation to protest is more ideational: the grievance arises from the regime's failure to abide by the principles that the person holds dear. For dissidents such as Liu Xiaobo, these are the ideals of liberal democracy: individual freedom and popular sovereignty as expressed and protected through competitive elections and expansive civil rights and liberties. Unlike in the 1980s, there has been no visible disagreement among top CCP leaders regarding the desirability of this kind of political reform. Instead, such advocacy universally has been viewed by Party elites as sedition. In this respect, the grievances and goals articulated by democracy activists have been viewed in a fundamentally different way than have those expressed by the protestors chronicled in earlier chapters.

For rights-protection lawyers, grievances have emerged when government officials have not followed their own laws, and/or when the laws themselves have resulted in the mistreatment of regular citizens. These cases have been brought to the attention of rights-protection lawyers by clients (such as farmers and migrant workers) that have suffered personal harm when officials have broken the law, or when the law itself has put them in an untenable situation. Having tried a multitude of other solutions, by the time these clients approach a lawyer, they often are desperate, angry, and frustrated. Typically, rights-protection lawyers start out with very moderate views vis-à-vis the government, seeing central leaders as benevolent, and seeking to find justice for their clients within the existing political system. When they hear the details of their clients' mistreatment, and subsequently find themselves unable to find justice for their clients due to the political interference of judges, police officers, and other political cadres, previously moderate lawyers not infrequently become more radical critics of the political system as a whole. Some then shift away from taking cases in order to resolve the individual grievance of their client, to taking cases in order to expose wider governmental abuses and flaws. At this point, rights-protection lawyers become like democracy activists such as the Charter 08 signatories, motivated by their commitment to liberal democratic ideals.[13]

The grievances expressed in online satire and mass "storms" include generalized opposition to censorship and political corruption. As noted above, the "grass-mud horse" appeared in the context of the government's 2009 anti-vulgarity campaign, which involved crackdowns on popular cultural content online – including the liberal cultural website Douban.com, which was forced to remove numerous intellectual, literary, and cultural discussion groups that it had hosted.[14] Rather than demanding particular changes, however, online satire and "storms" are best characterized as public venting of political dissatisfaction.

BEHAVIOR

The main thing that stands out regarding the behavior of the politically dissatisfied is that – unlike the other kinds of protests discussed in prior chapters – they have *not* (at least since 1989) taken to the streets to air their grievances. Virtually all of their protest actions have been online, through the media, or in the courts. Both democracy activists and *e'gao* pundits have worked almost entirely online. In large part, this is because they have recognized that if they attempt an in-person protest in a physical space, they will be rapidly and severely punished.

In other words, their choice of protest behavior has reflected the limitations of the "opportunity structure" that they face.

Right-protection activists also have worked extensively online, but – unlike other kinds of protestors – have focused their actions on the courts. Most right-protection lawyers have begun as individual attorneys representing aggrieved clients. Since 2003, however, rights-protection lawyers increasingly have collaborated on cases in teams. By 2011, this had become so common that the magazine *Southern Exposure* (based in Guangdong province) denoted 2011 "the year of collective legal action." Even so, rights-protection activists have avoided creating formal organizations or having regular meetings, so as to minimize their risk of repression. Concomitantly, rights-protection lawyers have established blogs that provide interested netizens and NGOs with up-to-date information on their cases.[15] All the while, those involved in rights-protection have tended to be politically savvy, deliberately highlighting the legality of their and their clients' actions, and making every effort to avoid direct confrontation with the government.

Even so, some have undertaken more contentious actions. Although none of these come close to the boldness of those who organized the CDP in 1998, a tiny few have gone beyond online dissent and protest via the courts. In March of 2012, for example, 12 democracy and rights-protection activists held up signs in pedestrian walkways in the southern city of Guangzhou, calling for liberal democratic political reforms. Five of them were detained, but later were released after concerned netizens decried their punishment. In addition, some rights-protection lawyers have run as candidates in People's Congress elections. Relatedly, rights-protection activists have written handbooks on topics such as independent candidacy, citizen rights defense, torture, and taxation. Finally, they have worked together to represent and support one another in cases where one or more has been detained or imprisoned.[16]

LEADERS AND PARTICIPANTS

Nearly all of those that have participated in political protest activities in the post-Mao period have been urban-based and relatively well-educated. The democracy activists that established the CDP in 1998, as well as those that were the initial signatories of Charter 08, were mainly intellectuals and university graduates, and a significant portion had participated in the 1989 student protests. Further, although the CDP developed some nascent organization before it was repressed and forced underground, it was very decentralized and had no agreed-upon leadership structure. Similarly, even though the Charter 08 document was spearheaded by Liu Xiaobo and a few other intellectuals, they and the other signatories were not connected by any organization, and their public statements and decisions have shown little evidence of collective decision-making.[17] This has been even more the case with participants in online satire and mass "storms" – they have engaged in these activities spontaneously as individuals.

Rights-protection activists share all of these general characteristics. In terms of when and how they initially began their political activism, one study finds that few of the lawyers that are now radical political critics were interested in this type of activity when they began their legal careers. Most were transformed over time as they heard of the mistreatment of their clients and experienced frustration with the unjust functioning of the politicized legal system. Others became involved in rights-protection actions after witnessing a particular event – such as the crushing of the 1989 student protests – or when they themselves were the victims of political corruption or abuse. An example of the latter is Zhao Lianhai, whose young son was one of roughly 300,000 children who were poisoned by contaminated milk in 2008. Subsequently, Zhao founded a website to provide information about the scandal and to organize collective legal action against the responsible parties.[18]

GOVERNMENT RESPONSES

In general, the government has responded to political dissent and protest in the late post-Mao period with harsh repression. Although rights-protection activists achieved some notable successes in the early years of the new millennium, many have been harassed and punished, and in recent years scores have been jailed. Meanwhile, online satirists and political critics have come under increased scrutiny, restrictions, and suppression.

The more overt political dissidents who founded the CDP or were leading participants in Charter 08 have been severely punished. The main leaders of the CDP were sentenced to lengthy prison terms, and/ or forced into exile overseas. Charter 08 initiator Liu Xiaobo was found guilty of "inciting subversion of state power," and given an 11-year jail term. When he was awarded the Nobel Peace Prize in 2010, he was not allowed to attend the ceremony. Another prominent Charter 08 signatory – Beijing University law professor He Weifang – was exiled to a remote area of Xinjiang province. At least 70 other well-known signatories have been harassed or detained. In addition, law students at Beijing University have been forbidden to sign Charter 08, and journalists have been banned from interviewing any signatories.[19]

In contrast, rights-protection activists initially were embraced and applauded by central authorities, but subsequently have been subjected to harsh treatment. As noted earlier, in the late 1990s and the early 2000s, top CCP leaders wishing to enhance social stability through the legal adjudication of citizen grievances welcomed the rise of rights-protection lawyers willing to represent the "weak and disadvantaged" in the face of local corruption, and even changed policies that were shown by these lawyers to be unjust.[20] By the middle of the first decade of the 2000s, however, national elites had become concerned that rights-protection activists were becoming a threat to the political system – particularly as lawyers took on more controversial cases and began to coordinate in legal teams. In 2006, central authorities "urged the adoption of 'forceful measures... against those who, under the pretext of rights-protection, carry out sabotage'" and "attack... our judicial system." Similarly, the Chinese bar issued instructions on the handling of collective cases involving ten or more litigants, requiring that lawyers in such cases notify their local bar association, accept "guidance and supervision," and refrain from using "non-legal" methods or encouraging their clients to petition or otherwise violate "the social order." Since then, most well-known rights-protection activists have been subjected to surveillance, harassment, threats, and physical violence. Many also have been barred from practicing law, and/or jailed.

Since the ascension of Xi Jinping to the CCP's top position in late 2012, the repression of rights-protection activists has dramatically escalated. From 2013 through the present, over 500 rights-protection activists have been detained and/or jailed. Some, such as female rights-protection activist Cao Shunli, have died in custody after being tortured. Indeed, it appears that central authorities' current goal is to entirely "wipe out" rights-protection activism. As a result, the already tiny number of practicing rights-protection lawyers has shrunk to nearly zero.[21] Similarly, as discussed in the Introduction, online satirists and political critics have been subjected to increased surveillance and punishment since late 2012.

CONCLUSION

Relative to the protest types chronicled in earlier chapters, political protest in its various forms has evidenced almost no organization, and has been characterized by its online activities and focus on the courts. True political dissent, as engaged in by the founders of the CDP and the signatories to Charter 08, has been undertaken by only a few citizens – at most a few hundred in the case of the former, and roughly 10,000 in the case of the latter. Similarly, there have been only perhaps a few thousand individuals that have participated in rights-protection activism. The number of online political satirists and critics is far larger, potentially including hundreds of thousands or even more. However, thus far these netizens have confined their activities almost entirely to virtual commentary.

Certainly, Chinese authorities' harsh repression of proclamations, organizations, and actions that they perceive as a threat to the CCP-led system has scared many politically dissatisfied citizens away from political protest of any kind. And perhaps the regime is rightly afraid of the goals advocated by democracy activists such as those involved in the CDP and Charter 08, as these activists desire an end to the CCP's monopoly on political power.

However, the regime's attempts to quash rights-protection activities and online satire and mass "storms" may backfire. Rather than solidifying CCP rule, such measures are likely to foment increased public dissatisfaction and political instability. Although few younger lawyers have been brave enough to take on rights-protection cases in the current high-risk environment, those lawyers that have remained or become involved in rights-protection have become only more radicalized and energized to challenge the political status quo. Had ruling authorities chosen to allow them to continue with rights-protection work, they likely would have remained reformist in orientation, *and* they would have been able to continue to aid the Party-state in its quest to resolve societal conflict and address political abuse via peaceful, legal methods. To the extent that rights-protection workers are no longer available to aggrieved citizens, those citizens will have no choice but to engage in more disruptive actions. Similarly, the censorship and punishment of online political satire and criticism likely will have negative repercussions for the regime, as affected netizens will develop even more critical political views as a result. Moreover, such repression will rob regime authorities of the opportunity to hear the complaints of regular citizens, thus rendering the government unable to satisfactorily respond to public dissatisfaction.

8 | Ethnic Minority Protest ──────────

Along with the forms of political protest chronicled in chapter 7, two additional categories of popular contention have called for transformational changes to China's political system – ethnic minority protest, and protest in Hong Kong. These actions have emanated from the "Autonomous Regions" that are part of China's domestic political system but are supposed to be granted more autonomy than regular provincial-level entities. Some of the activists from these regions have called for domestic political reform, but others have called for outright separation from the Chinese polity. Their protests have involved fundamental conflict between central Chinese political leaders and protestors, and have threatened to destabilize the governing regime in those regions. Yet, these actions have not posed a serious threat to the CCP-led political system outside of those regions. For, they have not been viewed with sympathy by members of China's majority Han ethnicity. To the contrary, especially when it comes to collective contention on the part of ethnic minorities, most Han Chinese have expressed fear and condemnation, and have supported strict measures to control and repress such actions.

This chapter focuses on the ethnic minority groups that have been the most active and contentious in China's post-Mao period – Tibetans (who mostly reside in China's Tibet Autonomous Region – TAR), Uighurs (who live mainly in China's Xinjiang Uighur Autonomous Region – XUAR), and Mongolians (who largely reside in China's Inner Mongolia Autonomous Region – IMAR). In all three cases, a major grievance has been the CCP-encouraged influx of Han Chinese into once ethnic minority-dominant regions. Causing particular ire have been the resultant economic and political dominance of Han Chinese in these regions, the diminution of local minority culture and lifestyles, and environmental degradation. In the case of Tibetans and Uighurs, a concomitant – and typically even more incendiary – source of anger has been the central Party-state's repression of religious practices (Tibetan Buddhism in the case of the former, and Islam in the latter). Protests on the part of ethnic minorities have at times involved violence. Further, in recent years protest actions by Uighurs have included attacks on civilians outside of the XUAR. The response of central CCP leaders to protests on the part of Tibetans and Uighurs has been harsh, violent, and unrepentant; political authorities have evidenced no disagreement over this stance. In turn, these repressive government actions seem to have exacerbated the anger and determination of ethnic minority activists. As a result, neither the frequency nor the volatility of these protests is likely to diminish in the near future. Meanwhile, protests by Mongolians have featured rhetoric and behavior that have been less threatening to CCP elites, and political authorities have evidenced more varied attitudes toward them. As a result, Mongolian activism has been much more successful.

Indeed, protests by Mongolians have been somewhat similar to the types of protests reviewed in chapters 2–5 – they have focused on localized, material grievances; they have emphasized central laws and policies to justify their demands; and they have not called for national-level political reforms. Activism by Tibetans and Uighurs has been quite different. First, Tibetan and Uighur activists explicitly have criticized central government policies and laws; they have not viewed national leaders as sympathetic allies, but rather as the source of oppression. Relatedly, they have not tried to play different levels of government against one another, as they have (for good reason) viewed the Chinese Party-state as a unified, repressive whole. Second, Tibetan and Uighur activists have voiced not just material concerns, but ideational ones, centered on their freedom of religious belief and practice, as well as political demands for independence from the PRC. Third, Tibetan and Uighur activists have been supported by foreign groups and nations, as well as by diaspora communities. Fourth, Tibetan and Uighur activists generally have not attempted to use domestic legal, institutionalized channels to resolve their grievances. Fifth, these activists have been united by their ethnic and religious identity rather than their socioeconomic status. For all of these reasons, Chinese government officials at all levels have viewed Tibetan and Uighur activism as a grave threat, and have responded with harsh repression. Concomitantly, Tibetan and Uighur protest actions often quickly have become violent, or have involved violent activist behavior from the start.

GRIEVANCES, OPPORTUNITIES, AND PROTEST: IMPERIAL CHINA THROUGH THE MAOIST ERA

China's ethnic minorities have operated within an "opportunity structure" that in part derives from China's geography. As of 2010 (the time of the last census), over 91 percent of Chinese on the mainland were of Han ethnicity. Yet Han Chinese are concentrated in the eastern, much more densely populated, half of China's territory. Among the roughly eight percent of China's populace that is identified as an ethnic minority, 55 different ethnic groups are officially recognized by the government.[1] Some of the largest are: Uighurs (approximately 11.5 million), Tibetans (6.2 million), and Mongolians (5.9 million). Though they constitute only a small portion of China's total population, the territory in which they reside is vast; the Autonomous Regions of Tibet, Xinjiang, and Inner Mongolia include over half of China's total land mass. Further, China's ethnic minorities live in areas of China that border other countries to the north, west, and south – locations that are perceived by CCP leaders to be of critical strategic importance.

Xinjiang, for example, abuts eight of China's 15 neighbors, and has a border of nearly 5,600 kilometers, the longest of any subnational region in China. In addition, the land within these three Autonomous Regions has immense energy resources, and includes an international pipeline that became active in 2005.[2] Consequently, Chinese authorities have been extremely fearful of unrest among the ethnic minorities living in Tibet, Xinjiang, and Inner Mongolia.

At the same time, ethnic Tibetans, Uighurs, and Mongolians have had a long history of conflict with Chinese authorities that has bred numerous still-unresolved grievances. What is now the XUAR was added to Chinese territory relatively late, under China's last dynasty, the Qing. From that time through the early 1900s, violent conflicts between Xinjiang residents and Chinese political leaders erupted almost every other year. Between 1944 and 1949, parts of Xinjiang were ruled by the Eastern Turkestan Republic. Xinjiang formally became a province of the PRC in 1949. Six years later, the area was re-categorized as the Xinjiang Uighur Autonomous Region. From the mid-1950s through the mid-1960s, unrest was relatively rare, but when it occurred, featured separatist demands. The most notable instances were in 1954 (when separatist activists in Karakash, Hotan, and Lop issued documents calling for the establishment of an Islamic Republic in the area, and attacked a prison camp), and in 1962 (when massive numbers of Uighurs and Kazakhs fled to Russia in response to CCP grain rationing and land acquisition, and Han migration). In the mid-1960s, Uighurs (allegedly with the help of the Russian Soviets, and/or Uighurs who had fled to Russia in 1962) established the clandestine Eastern Turkestan People's Revolutionary Party (ETPRP), which has remained active through the present, and has as its primary aim the establishment of a separate Muslim state in Xinjiang.[3] Meanwhile, when CCP leader Mao Zedong launched the Cultural Revolution in 1966, religious practice was deemed counter-revolutionary, and religious symbols, artifacts, and sites were destroyed.

Tibet's modern history is analogous. Like Xinjiang, Tibet was politically separate from China during long periods prior to the 1949 establishment of the PRC. In 1950, CCP leaders sent thousands of troops to Tibet to enforce their territorial claims over the region. Most of the area was placed in the PRC's Tibetan Autonomous Region (TAR), but a number of Tibetan-dominant locations were incorporated into adjacent provinces. From 1951 to 1959, an agreement was reached wherein the TAR would be given autonomy, but the Tibetan-dominant areas of other provinces were subjected to land reform that confiscated much of the land and property formerly owned by Tibetan Buddhist monasteries – at that time the largest landowners in all such localities. This sparked major revolts in the ethnic Tibetan regions of Kham and Amdo, to which the Chinese Party-state responded with a massive aerial bombardment of Tibetan monasteries believed to be sheltering the rebels. In 1959, large numbers of Tibetans rose up again against CCP rule and repression. In Lhasa, thousands of Tibetan women surrounded the Potala Palace, the main residence of the Dalai Lama. Within hours, Chinese soldiers were sent in, and violent conflict broke out. In danger of arrest, the Dalai Lama fled under pursuit of CCP troops, ultimately making it safely to India, where he set up a government in exile. Tibetans in New York and other cities around the world decried these developments. Back in the TAR and neighboring Tibetan areas, the CCP forbade the practice of Tibetan Buddhist monasticism and destroyed numerous monasteries. CCP-instigated violence and destruction became even more pervasive during the Cultural Revolution (1966–76); during this time, most of the remaining Tibetan Buddhist monasteries were destroyed, and those caught practicing religion were castigated and punished.[4] In sum, Tibetan and Uighur grievances with CCP authorities are long-standing and deep.

Inner Mongolia's history bears some similarities, but has involved less conflict with the Chinese Party-state. During the Qing dynasty, Han migration to the area increased substantially, dramatically changing the demographic composition of the region, and leading to disputes over land (largely due to the fact that Mongolians were nomadic herders whereas the Han were farmers). After the fall of the Qing in 1911, Outer Mongolia declared independence, but Inner Mongolian nobles chose to stay with China. While civil war raged between the CCP and KMT from 1945 to 1949, Inner Mongolian leaders sided with the CCP, and in 1947 the Inner Mongolia Autonomous Government was established, led by Mongolian leader Ulanhu. Ulanhu remained in power until the tumultuous Cultural Revolution of 1966–76, when he and hundreds of thousands of other Mongolians were accused by Han elites of forming a separatist political party – the Inner Mongolian People's Party (*Neirendang*) – to cut ties with the PRC and unite with the independent Mongolian state to the north. The accused rebels were treated ruthlessly – including torture to extract forced confessions. According to official statistics, nearly 350,000 people were labeled as *Neirendang* members, and over one million were affected by the campaign. According to unofficial estimates, roughly 100,000 people died either directly or indirectly during the course of the movement, and 350,000–500,000 were arrested.[5]

GRIEVANCES, OPPORTUNITIES, AND PROTEST:
LATE 1970s–EARLY 1990s

After Mao Zedong died in 1976 and reformist leader Deng Xiaoping assumed the helm of the CCP in 1978, the political opportunity structure for these ethnic minority groups loosened substantially. Restrictions on religious practice were relaxed, and religious sites were rebuilt, restored, and reopened. Universities were required to admit a quota of ethnic minorities, and the Party's strict new birth control policies were not applied to minority groups. Feeling a new sense of efficacy and optimism, Tibetans, Uighurs, and Mongolians voiced their grievances and pressed for resolution.

In Inner Mongolia in 1976, Mongolians put up "big-character posters" in public locations, describing their terrible suffering during the Cultural Revolution, and calling for redress; over 50,000 signed a petition calling for the arrest of the official who had led the anti-*Neirendang* campaign, the return of lost land, and a halt to the export of Inner Mongolia's mineral wealth. In 1981, thousands of Mongolian students went on strike, marched in the streets, and petitioned the central government to continue its affirmative action policies toward Mongolians (which most Han in Inner Mongolia opposed), punish those responsible for the abuse of Mongolians during the Cultural Revolution, and enact restrictions on the migration of Han farmers to the region. Han Chinese in the area vocally disagreed with these demands, criticizing the Mongolians for their "backwardness." Party-state authorities responded to the Mongolian activists with tolerance; no violence was used against them, and a number of their demands were partially fulfilled. Because the protestors' demands did not challenge the legitimacy of CCP rule, but rather asked for smaller policy changes, ruling elites did not view their actions as an existential threat, and found it acceptable to accede to at least some of the activists' requests.[6]

In both Xinjiang and Tibet, protests during the early post-Mao period were much more conflictual, and were ended with violence. In Xinjiang, as political authorities allowed some religious activities to resume in the late 1970s, pan-Islamism and pan-Turkism also arose. In 1980 and 1981, riots erupted in the city of Kashgar, and in 1985, 1988, and 1989, demonstrations broke out in Urumqi. All were repressed with force. In Tibet, protests calling for religious freedom and political independence emerged in the late 1980s, and also were violently suppressed. In late 1987, when the Dalai Lama addressed the US Congress, around 20 Tibetan monks marched in central Lhasa, calling for independence and holding the banned Tibetan flag. Police arrived swiftly, arresting and beating the monks. A few days later, another roughly two dozen monks took to the streets and were arrested. Subsequently, an angry crowd gathered near Tibetan Buddhism's most sacred site, Lhasa's Jokhang Temple, unfurling the Tibetan flag and shouting, "Free Tibet!" "Chinese Out of Tibet!" and "Dalai Lama, Come Back to Tibet!" Some also set a police station on fire. Police barricaded the protestors in the area and fired into the crowd; the demonstrators attempted to fight back with stones. According to Chinese authorities, six protestors and 19 police officers were killed, and dozens were arrested, including two Americans. Over the course of the next two years, more than 20 incidents of large-scale protest and repression occurred. In early 1988, Chinese authorities began to round up, arrest, and jail suspected activist monks. In one particularly notable case, military troops entered the Jokhang site, beating and arresting the monks therein. Some reportedly were killed. Those who were imprisoned were tortured. Such government responses provoked only further protests, and tensions continued to mount. In March 1989 (over a month before the massive student-led protests centered in Beijing began), Chinese authorities declared martial law in Tibet. Demonstrations broke out again in early 1990, and were met with further arrests and jail terms.[7]

GRIEVANCES, OPPORTUNITIES, AND PROTEST: EARLY 1990s–PRESENT

From the 1990s through the time of this writing, Chinese government policies and actions have brought pre-existing grievances to the surface, and also have engendered new complaints. Although protests have arisen in all three of the Autonomous Regions focused on in this chapter, earlier patterns have persisted; protest actions involving Uighurs and Tibetans have been violent, highly conflictual, and have received a harsh government response, whereas actions on the part of Mongolians have been relatively law-abiding and successful. One change in the opportunity structure that has affected all three of these minority groups has been the Party-state's "Open Up the West" campaign, which began in early 2000 and has encouraged new waves of Han migration to ethnic minority areas. Along with diluting the cultural dominance of ethnic minority groups, particularly in urban areas, the Han migrants have had a much higher standard of living. Many own and operate their own businesses (something that ethnic minority individuals typically lack the resources to do), and they also tend to get the best jobs due to their superior Mandarin language skills. This has spurred ethnic minority resentment toward the Han population. Concomitantly, most Han migrants have had a negative view of local ethnic minorities, seeing them as uneducated, ungrateful, and seeking special treatment. When protest actions by ethnic minorities have arisen in recent years, they have involved conflict between ethnic minority and Han residents. In a number of cases, Han businesses and individuals have been attacked.

Uighurs

Since 1990, the circumstances of Mongolians, Uighurs, and Tibetans have had some unique aspects as well. For Uighurs, a key development was the dissolution of the Soviet Union and the rise of independent Central Asian states in the early 1990s. This not only instilled Uighurs with renewed hope for the possibility of establishing an independent Eastern Turkestan, but also gave aggrieved Uighurs in China potential foreign allies and sources of support. Capitalizing on this new opportunity, between 1990 and 2001, "'East Turkistan' forces inside and outside China" were involved in more than 200 "bloody incidents," including "explosions, assassinations of government officials, poisoning, arson, attacking government buildings, riots and assaults."[8] The first of these occurred in 1990 in Baren, when "hundreds of armed Uighurs attacked local government offices and for several days fought off Chinese military sent to stop them." This "logistically complex" action had been planned for months in advance, during which training camps were set up and weapons and vehicles were stolen or seized." The rebels reportedly had planned to "secure Baren as strategic beachhead and from there build an 'East Turkestan Republic.'" In 1996, central authorities began a massive "Strike Hard" campaign against crime and portrayed "illegal religious activities and ethnic separatism as the two greatest threats to Xinjiang's stability."[9] This crackdown featured "mass roundups of Uighur suspects, quick trials (followed by quick executions), the breakup of dozens of organized cells and the seizure of their weapons."[10]

Another major conflict transpired in early 1997. In protest against the arrest of some Uighur activists, thousands of demonstrators in the city of Yining gathered to demand their release. After a few hours, police fired on the crowd. Incensed, "demonstrators went on a rampage, torching cars, looting [Han] Chinese stalls, burning flags, and shouting pro-independence slogans." Seven Han bystanders were killed. The protestors also reportedly "burned government-issued documents...and stripped off their 'Han style' clothes." The government responded with harsh punishment, arresting and executing numerous Uighurs, closing the airport, imposing a curfew, barring visitors to the city, and stationing armored troops in Yining's central park.[11]

Top CCP leaders also reacted by cultivating positive diplomatic relations with the Central Asian states, and by the turn of the millennium had succeeded in diminishing foreign support for Uighur activism. In addition, the September 2001 attacks on the US brought greater international attention to countering "Islamic terrorism," leading US government officials to seek greater cooperation with China on "counterterrorism" efforts and to show less interest in supporting Uighur activism. In 2002, the UN Security Council added the "East Turkistan Islamic Movement" to its sanctioned list of terrorist groups.[12]

From the turn of the millennium through the present, this more constricted opportunity structure for Uighur activists has led to "a dramatic decrease in Uighur-related violence in general, but also...the appearance of logistically creative attacks [requiring] little planning or materials."[13] Around the start of the Beijing Olympics in 2008, Uighur activists on at least two occasions used vehicles to engage in violent acts (including ramming a group of soldiers and throwing explosives at police vehicles and government buildings) that resulted in numerous fatalities and injuries.[14] In July and September of 2009, multi-day riots broke out between Uighurs and Han Chinese in Guangdong province and the city of Urumqi in Xinjiang, related to a dispute between Uighur and Han workers at a Guangdong factory. Altogether, nearly 200 were killed and over 1,700 were injured. Thousands of vehicles were destroyed, police barricades were overturned, and numerous government buildings were damaged.[15] The government response was harsh; large numbers of Uighurs were arrested, and many were sentenced to death. Government authorities also tried to block outside communications.[16]

Under Xi Jinping, tensions have only mounted. In 2014, eight Uighurs stabbed to death more than 30 Han civilians at a train station in the southwestern city of Kunming. Four of the assailants were killed by police, and the other four were arrested. Government authorities have since called for heightened restrictions on religious practice in Xinjiang, including a ban on wearing veils or beards, giving children "Islamic" or "splittist" names, or using religious procedures for marriage, divorce, and funerals. They also have sent "thousands of heavily armed police" to parade through Xinjiang's major cities. Further, government officials have outlawed not only group prayer services led by non-government-approved imams, but also prayer within the home. Cadres regularly have visited Uighur households to enforce these edicts, and those found to be in violation have been sentenced to up to 12 years in prison. These restrictions and punishments have only further angered Uighurs, engendering more violent attacks. In February 2017, for example, three Uighurs in the Xinjiang city of Hotan, who were angered by local officials' threats to punish their families for praying, attacked government cadres and passersby with knives, killing five and wounding five.[17] Han Chinese expressed virulently anti-Uighur views online in the aftermath of this incident, posting comments "equating Islam with terrorism, calling it an 'evil cult' and Muslims 'dogs' and 'leeches;'" "lament[ing] the authorities' 'preferential treatment towards minorities,' and complain[ing] that government censorship is unfairly protecting Muslims;" and calling for "collective punishment: 'Families of terrorists should all be killed!' wrote one, while another advocated for the eradication of 'the entire [Uighur] ethnic group.'"[18]

Tibetans

From the early 1990s through the present, the opportunities, grievances, and protest actions of Tibetans have been similar to those of Uighurs. To begin, central authorities put forth new policies to limit religious practice by Tibetans, seeing it as fomenting separatist sentiments and behavior. Tibetan Buddhist sites were required to register with the government, Buddhist curricula were restricted, and only a stipulated number of Buddhist monks and nuns were allowed to practice. Further, the Dalai Lama was castigated in official media outlets, his picture was banned, and "educational teams" were sent to monasteries to force monks and nuns to publicly denounce his religious authority. As a result, Tibetans' grievances mounted.[19]

However, it was not until 2007–8 that the opportunity structure opened such that protest emerged. In late 2007, the Dalai Lama was awarded a US Congressional Gold Medal, and publicly addressed then President George W. Bush and members of the US Congress. In Lhasa, several monks who reportedly celebrated this event were arrested. Meanwhile, the summer Beijing Olympics approached – the first Olympics ever held in China. According to researchers, Tibetans both within China and in exile believed that political authorities were less likely to forcibly repress protesters during this time. Thus, on March 10, 2008, the 49th anniversary of the 1959 Tibetan uprising (when the Dalai Lama was forced to flee), hundreds of monks gathered in Lhasa to commemorate the anniversary and call for the imprisoned monks' release. As police streamed in to quash the protests, riots erupted in Lhasa and other Tibetan areas, lasting for days. Hundreds of Han businesses in Lhasa were burned to the ground, and 18 people were killed. Central political leaders blamed the protests on the Tibetan community in exile, and took harsh measures to prevent any further public collective actions. Dozens were arrested and executed.[20] When the international community and some foreign governments criticized the Chinese government's use of force, Han Chinese both domestically and abroad vocally sided with their government, asserting online and in public demonstrations that the Tibetans had initiated the violence, and that their suppression was justified. When the French government allowed protestors to impede the progress of the Olympic torch relay in France, Han Chinese called for a boycott of French "Carrefour" stores in China.

As with Uighurs, since 2008–9 the opportunity structure for collective protest by Tibetans has been highly constricted due to central authorities' demonstrated resolve to violently suppress any such actions. As a result, in recent years large-scale demonstrations by Tibetans have been virtually non-existent. However, because Tibetan grievances have not been addressed, and in fact have only intensified, individual acts of protest have occurred. In the case of Uighurs, these have taken the form of sporadic attacks on government officials and Han civilians. In the case of Tibetans, the main form of protest since 2008 has been self-immolation; according to Radio Free Asia, 147 Tibetans have set themselves aflame since 2009. As with Uighurs, these acts have arisen in response to continued central government moves to further restrict and repress religious practice. In early 2017, such actions spiked again, as political officials announced that thousands of Tibetan Buddhist complexes would be demolished, and that the monks and nuns living therein would be expelled. Many of these religious figures have been forced to undergo "re-education" and have been forbidden to provide the religious services upon which they depend for their income. In

March of 2017, another Tibetan farmer set fire to himself, but survived. When his relatives attempted to see him, they were severely beaten by local police.[21]

Mongolians

From the early 1990s through the time of this writing, Mongolians also have developed new grievances. However, unlike Uighurs and Tibetans, their complaints and demands have been more material and less threatening to the political control of CCP elites, and political authorities have not demonstrated unified resolve to suppress them. As a result, Mongolian protests have been much more successful. Beginning in the late 1990s, central authorities – citing environmental concerns – began to ban the grazing of cattle in order to protect rangeland in Inner Mongolia, pressing hundreds of thousands of Mongolian herding families to instead raise their animals in stables or move to the city. Mongolians have resisted, arguing that they will be unable to make a living under these new conditions, and that the compensation they have been offered is inadequate. Meanwhile, as part of the central government's "Open Up the West" campaign, "Inner Mongolia was transformed almost overnight into one of China's most flourishing mining hubs."[22] As a result, more land has been removed from herding families, grasslands and wetlands have been destroyed, surface and ground water have been depleted, and the water, land, and air have been polluted.

Generally speaking, Mongolians have reacted in the same way as have the citizens chronicled in earlier chapters: they have petitioned the government at various levels, and have voiced specific, material demands. Further, as in the types of economically-based protests discussed previously, at least some government officials have responded sympathetically. The most notable collective actions on the part of Mongolians in recent years occurred in 2011. In one case, a Mongolian herder was killed while attempting to stop coal trucks from entering local grasslands. Subsequently, local residents and miners fought one another with metal rods and pickaxe handles, and another local resident was killed. Outraged, in at least three separate localities, Mongolian students from herding families that had been forced into the city when once-open pastures were fenced off marched to government offices. The government response included a mixture of repression and conciliation: on the one hand, it dispatched large numbers of armed police to the area, restricted citizens' freedom of movement and assembly, and closely monitored the activities of Mongolian university students and government employees; on the other, it gave harsh sentences to the four men allegedly involved in the deaths of the herders (including executing the main offender), ordered nearly 150 mines to shut down and/or change their practices, and offered compensation to those affected by the conflict and the mines.[23]

In a second case, protests were preceded by attempts to seek redress via formal methods of political participation. Although local authorities responded to the protests with force, central authorities reacted sympathetically. In June 2011, Mongolian herders in Inner Mongolia's Bayannuur region repeatedly submitted petitions to local political offices, requesting attention to a local mine that was polluting the area. Frustrated with the lack of an official response, the petitioners marched to the mine and shut down its water pump. The following day, local officials sent riot police to the mine, and numerous herders were severely beaten and detained. Concurrently, however, central authorities reportedly "launched a month-long overhaul of the lucrative coal mining industry, vowing to clean up or close polluters."[24]

CONCLUSION

In sum, although collective contention on the part of Mongolians has evidenced some of the features seen in protests undertaken by primarily Han farmers, workers, homeowners, and environmentalists, popular actions on the part of Uighurs and Tibetans have been fundamentally different. Inasmuch as these ethnic minority protests have directed their ire at central authorities and have voiced political demands, they have had more in common with the political activists discussed in chapter 7. Further, political leaders at all levels have been unified in their intolerance of such activities. However, compared with cases of political activism on the part of Han Chinese, Uighur and Tibetan actions have been much more organized, and have involved far more people and far greater violence. In part, this is because the history of CCP relations with these ethnic groups is replete with violent conflict centered on deep-seated feelings of ethnic identity and religious belief. Relatedly, many Uighurs and Tibetans desire political separation from the PRC – a demand that Communist Party leaders and most Han Chinese view as a mortal threat to China's national security. Further, because Uighur and Tibetan activists see central authorities as the source of their dissatisfaction, and do not view existing modes of popular input as efficacious, they have not attempted to follow legal procedures or to couch their demands in legal terms. Overall, these factors have engendered a vicious cycle of violent conflict that shows no sign of diminishing, and in recent years appears to have worsened.

9 | Protest in Hong Kong ─────────

In the post-Mao period, collective contention also has been frequent in China's Special Autonomous Region (SAR) of Hong Kong. And in recent years, these protests have shared some features with those by Uighurs and Tibetans. First, participants in collective contention in Hong Kong have not viewed China's central political leaders as being benevolent, or as potential allies in the struggle against ill-doing local elites. In addition, as with ethnic minorities, in Hong Kong calls for separatism have emerged, and concerns about the economic and cultural influence of immigrants from the mainland have grown. The biggest difference between protests in Hong Kong and those examined in earlier chapters is that in Hong Kong, residents have enjoyed meaning-ful, institutionalized channels for political input – including democratically-elected representatives within the territory's legislature. Consequently, local political elites have diverged dramatically in their views of and behavior regarding citizen protests. Perhaps relatedly, protestors in Hong Kong generally have been more law-abiding than those examined heretofore, and the government response to their pro-tests has involved far less violence. Protestors in Hong Kong have had some success in achieving their aims, but their more recent demands have been perceived by CCP leaders as a core threat, and have been met with official intransigence. At the time of this writing, this dynamic has bred a charged and volatile political environment in Hong Kong.

PRE-HANDOVER

At the beginning of China's post-Mao period, Hong Kong was a colony of Britain. In 1997, Hong Kong was due to revert to Chinese rule. To prepare for this shift, in the 1980s British and PRC officials negotiated a Joint Declaration stipulating that although after 1997 China and Hong Kong would be "one country," they would be governed according to "two systems." More specifically, CCP leaders agreed that Hong Kong's capitalist economy would be maintained, and that fundamental political freedoms (including freedom of speech, the press, academic research, and labor rights) would be protected. The Declaration stipulated that its content would be written into a Basic Law that would govern Hong Kong after the handover. By doing so, PRC authorities hoped to maintain Hong Kong's economic dynamism and political stability.[1]

The Basic Law was drafted by PRC officials in conjunction with representatives of Hong Kong's business elite and some liberal democratic activists; in 1990, it was approved by the PRC's National People's Congress. The Law states that for at least the first ten years following the handover, Hong Kong's Legislative Council (known as LegCo) would be elected by a mix of geographic and functional constituencies (the latter including disproportionate representation for business associations) and that its Chief Executive would be elected by a committee of Hong Kong political and economic elites. The Basic Law also affirms that subsequently, the region would move toward a democratic nomination process and universal suffrage in the overall vote for the Chief Executive, and direct election of the entire LegCo.[2]

While the Basic Law was still in draft form, the massive student-led protests of 1989 broke out in the PRC. Hong Kong residents quickly rose up in support. Over 100 groups formed the Alliance for Support of the Patriotic Democratic Movement in China, which sent representatives to Beijing and other cities and provided the mainland students with financial and material support. After the bloody crackdown of June 3–4, roughly one million Hong Kong residents marched in the streets, and the Alliance helped mainland student leaders escape the PRC. In response, CCP authorities announced a change to the Basic Law: through Article 23, the Hong Kong SAR government was granted the power to enact laws regarding treason and other forms of political subversion toward the central PRC government. Nonetheless, every year since 1989, the Alliance has held a candlelight vigil on the anniversary of June 4, "often with tens of thousands chanting, 'end one-party dictatorship in China.'"[3]

Beyond these protests, prior to the handover, Hong Kong residents engaged in other kinds of collective contention. Some were related to nationalist, "pan-Chinese" causes, such as actions to protect Chinese claims to the Diaoyu islands (as discussed in chapter 6). Other protests were organized by interest groups (such as labor and civic associations) raising material demands. Finally, as the handover approached in the 1990s and the Democratic Party became more powerful within LegCo, liberal democratic activists initiated popular actions around political issues such as the direct election of the Chief Executive and the number of directly-elected LegCo seats.[4]

1997–2002

For the first five years following Hong Kong's handover from British to Chinese rule, apart from the annual 1989 commemoration gathering, virtually no protests were directed toward the central PRC leadership. As during the pre-handover period, the political opportunity structure was much more open than was the case on the mainland: civil liberties were respected, the judiciary was allowed to act independently, and LegCo continued to hold a critical mass of democratically-elected representatives and liberal democratic activists. Moreover, mainland CCP leaders did not meddle in Hong Kong affairs. At the same time, workers and other socioeconomic sectors were both appeased and kept under political control through associations that were integrated into the political system.[5]

Protests did occur during this time, but they generally focused on economic issues. Coinciding almost exactly with the handover, the 1997 financial crisis that devastated much of Asia put Hong Kong into a recession. In this context, groups expressing material concerns – such as public and private-sector workers, the elderly, the unemployed, immigrants, and professionals – engaged in planned, government-approved, and scripted collective street actions to pressure the Hong Kong government to address their complaints.[6]

2003

This situation was relatively short-lived. In 2003, a new political grievance emerged: the Hong Kong SAR government's proposed "subversion" law based on Article 23 of the Basic Law. Hong Kong's first Chief Executive under Chinese rule – Tung Chee-hwa – had not acted on this issue during his first term. But after his second term was secured, in 2002 he was directed by high-level CCP leaders to move forward with this task.[7] Nonetheless, Tung was constrained by established quasi-democratic procedures and institutions, and by citizens that capitalized on their civil liberties to oppose the proposed law. In the end, a massive series of protests caused Tung to abort the process.

In late 2002, the Hong Kong SAR government made public the proposed law. According to established procedure, a three-month consultation period was to follow, whereupon the proposed law would be acted on by LegCo. Numerous groups immediately voiced their opposition to the proposal. In addition to concerns that key terms (including "subversion" and "theft of state secrets") were left vague, they opposed the document's restrictions on links with "foreign political organizations" and its requirement that Hong Kong-based groups actively report on their work in the mainland.

The opposition was widespread, but only loosely organized. By the summer of 2003, more than 40 groups had joined a Civil Human Rights Front, which formed in late 2002 to oppose the proposal. Members included human rights organizations, political parties, unions, lesbian, gay, bisexual, and transgender (LGBT) associations, religious groups, labor organizations, student associations, and democratic activist groups. The Front was a platform for information exchange and coordination, and had little formal organizational structure. Though member groups were apprised of the plans of the others, each set its own agenda, decided on its own actions, and created its own signs and slogans.[8]

Two groups were particularly active and effective in mobilizing the opposition: the Catholic Church (which was especially concerned about proposed controls on links with "foreign political organizations"), and legal professionals. Catholic leaders "called on believers to 'speak up loudly,'" held prayer sessions, and organized collective marches. Legal professionals worked to explain the proposed legislation to the public, including through printed pamphlets (which they distributed in person to passersby and protestors in the streets), online and mass media outlet commentaries, and working with various professional bodies and schools. [9]

Further, activists capitalized on Hong Kong's relatively free Internet and mass media system to promote collective actions against the bill. Online, Hong Kongers used e-mail and newsgroups, posting political jokes, commentaries, and information about the Article 23 proposal and encouraging their friends and families to participate.[10] Meanwhile, Hong Kong's most popular newspaper and weekly magazine – the *Apple Daily* and *Next Magazine* – which are owned by "maverick media tycoon" Jimmy Lai and have an "antigovernment" reputation, "relentless[ly]" attacked the proposal and "openly called on people" to join planned street marches. In addition, commercial radio phone-in programs featured the topic. Further the owners of Hong Kong's "most influential financial daily," the *Hong Kong Economic Journal*, declared that if the proposed legislation was passed, they might sell or close the paper.

At the same time, anti-proposal LegCo representatives worked within the legislature to block and/or change the bill. In addition, foreign governments and multinational businesses with economic ties to Hong Kong (including the US, UK, European Union, Canada, Australia, New Zealand, the US Chamber of Commerce, and the International Chamber of Commerce in Hong Kong) expressed concern about the proposed legislation. Meanwhile, pro-Beijing elites worked to use Hong Kong's civil liberties to their own advantage, mobilizing pro-Beijing groups to hold counter-demonstrations, and to lobby LegCo and submit supportive comments during the consultation period.[11]

From late 2002 through the summer of 2003, these actions crescendoed in a number of large-scale street rallies. Particularly prominent among the attendees were Catholics, Protestants, journalists, academics, librarians, social workers, lawyers, teachers, homeowners facing negative equity, and welfare recipients. In December 2002, a 60,000-person march in opposition to the legislation was followed by a 40,000-person demonstration in support. On July 1, 2003, after months of mobilizing activities and LegCo conflicts over the bill, the largest street protest to date in Hong Kong's post-handover era occurred. Despite high temperatures and humidity, approximately 500,000 marched for six hours to protest the legislation. Within LegCo, members of the opposition "immediately demanded that the government postpone or abrogate the bill." Keeping the pressure up, the Front announced a rally outside of LegCo on July 9.[12]

Evidencing the contrast between the political opportunity structure in Hong Kong and in the PRC mainland, Hong Kong's pro-Beijing leaders were constrained by Hong Kong's established quasi-democratic institutions and legislative processes. By July 6, it was clear that the law did not have the votes to gain LegCo approval. In response, on July 7 the SAR government announced that it would postpone further discussion of the bill.

With enhanced perceptions of efficacy on the heels of this success, on July 9 and 13 citizens again capitalized on Hong Kong's guarantees of freedom of speech and assembly by holding two additional rallies – the first attended by 50,000 and the second by 20,000. The protestors continued to voice opposition to the Article 23 legislation, but now also began to push for direct election of the Chief Executive by 2007, and of all of LegCo by 2008. In September, the Hong Kong government entirely withdrew the Article 23 legislation.[13] In November, pro-democracy parties enjoyed a "stunning win over major pro-China parties in district elections."[14]

2004–2013

CCP leaders on the mainland and pro-Beijing officials in Hong Kong reportedly were taken by surprise by this massive show of political activism. Determined to prevent further troubles of this nature, between 2004 and 2013 they attempted – through legal mechanisms – to assert greater control. Although the Basic Law affirms Hong Kong's quasi-democratic institutions and civil liberties, it also makes clear that the ultimate authority in Hong Kong is the PRC central government, as represented by China's CCP-dominated National People's Congress (NPC). Starting in 2004, the Standing Committee (SC) of the NPC issued a series of decisions designed to rein in moves toward greater democratization: it froze the existing electoral system for LegCo; reiterated that all political reform in Hong Kong must be approved by China's central government; and stated that there would be no direct election of the Chief Executive in 2007 or LegCo in 2008.[15] Simultaneously, between 2004 and 2013, the Hong Kong SAR government increasingly prosecuted the leaders of street protests.[16]

However, central CCP leaders and pro-Beijing Hong Kong officials also realized that various aspects of Hong Kong's political opportunity structure restrained their ability to simply assert their will. Pro-democracy representatives held a significant number of LegCo seats, and pro-Beijing representatives would need to win more LegCo seats in order to more effectively counter them. In 2005, under pressure from Beijing (allegedly for poor governance), Chief Executive Tung resigned from his post, again bringing the issue of Chief Executive election to the fore. Donald Tsang was chosen to serve out the rest of Tung's term, but a new term would begin in 2007. Further, a LegCo election was scheduled for 2008. In this context, in 2007 the SC of the NPC ruled that: (a) universal suffrage would be possible in the 2017 Chief Executive election; and (b) if this did indeed transpire, then the following 2020 LegCo election also would occur via universal suffrage.[17]

Concomitantly, pro-CCP leaders in Beijing and Hong Kong sought to foster further integration between Hong Kong and the mainland PRC. Through the Closer Economic Partnership Agreement in 2003, new high-speed rail links were built between the SAR and the mainland PRC, and cross-border trade and investment were encouraged. Also in 2003, restrictions on individual visits by mainland Chinese to Hong Kong were lifted. Consequently, factories and other businesses relocated to the mainland due to its cheaper labor and production costs, and mainland Chinese flooded into Hong Kong as tourists and investors (especially in real estate). Hong Kong's infrastructure was stretched, and its downtown area was "restructured to suit the needs of luxury hotels and shops." As the economy became more reliant on tourism, job growth mainly was in the "low-end, low-value-added service sector." Economic inequality grew significantly.[18]

These developments bred new grievances among Hong Kong residents. At the same time, dissatisfaction with the lack of democratic political reform remained widespread. Coupled with feelings of efficacy that had been reinforced by citizens' success in blocking the Article 23 legislation, between 2004 and 2013 Hong Kong residents engaged in a number of large-scale acts of collective contention. In 2006, the planned demolition of the Star Ferry and Queen's piers spurred opposition from a loosely-organized group of academics, journalists, and students.[19] In 2007, protesters opposed the demolition of "Wedding Card" street, seen as part of Hong Kong's unique cultural heritage. In 2009–10, similar concerns spurred demonstrations against the construction of a high-speed rail link between Hong Kong and the mainland PRC.

In these cases, as in the past, protestors took advantage of their legally-protected civil liberties and Hong Kong's semi-democratic political institutions – lodging petitions, marching, and staging sit-ins outside of government buildings. They also continued to use the Internet, developing sophisticated websites that frequently were updated, and using bulletin boards on sites such as People's Radio Hong Kong and Hong Kong In-Media to "clarify issues, plan, network, appeal for actions, and evaluate outcomes."[20] Yet in other respects, protests during this period differed from those that occurred prior to 2003. According to one activist, post-2004 protests were not carefully planned or organized; they generally were improvised on the spot, and did not follow clear rules or procedures. Further, participants were "not inclined to work with existing pressure groups, political parties, or other formal channels." In addition, they were "not afraid to engage in direct confrontation with the police."[21]

The biggest protests during this period arose when Chief Executive Tsang proposed a new National Education curriculum for Hong Kong students. Many residents viewed the proposal as a threat to Hong Kong's autonomy and democracy. Opposition to the plan was led by high school students (most prominent among them, Joshua Wong, who in late 2011 founded Scholarism to organize students around the issue), but included more than 20 other civic groups. As in the 2003 movement against the Article 23 legislation, Wong and many of the other movement leaders were Protestants and Catholics. Explaining the connection, Wong relates that "from the time I was in primary school, I realized that it was very difficult to have religious freedom under a Communist regime, and that quantifiable material things should not be the goal of our lives. Rather, we should be prepared to make sacrifices for values and beliefs." Wong also stresses that through his church, he developed his organizational and public speaking abilities.[22]

Anger at the proposed curriculum deepened in the context of the July 1, 2012 Chief Executive transition. The date also was the 15th anniversary of Hong Kong's handover to Chinese rule. Moreover, a LegCo election was slated for September. Led by Scholarism, a "team of 200 volunteers stood outside train stations in ten districts, six-to-eight hours a day in 30 degree [Centigrade] heat," collecting roughly 100,000 signatures on a petition to revoke the proposal. In addition, Scholarism and other organizations spearheaded a series of marches, occupations, and sit-ins.[23] The first was on July 1; after new (pro-Beijing) Chief Executive C.Y. Leung was sworn in, an estimated 400,000 citizens marched for four hours, voicing opposition to Leung; decrying the curriculum proposal; calling for greater democratization; and raising a variety of material concerns.[24] Later that month, opponents of the curriculum held another large-scale march to the Hong Kong government headquarters. On August 30, Scholarism and other groups began an occupation of the park below the headquarters, and three students began a hunger strike. On September 7, an estimated 120,000 gathered at the headquarters. With the LegCo election immanent, Leung announced that the curriculum plan would be put on hold. Thus, the opposition movement ended with success.

THE 2014 "UMBRELLA MOVEMENT" THROUGH 2017

These developments did not denote a diminution of conflict between pro-Beijing Hong Kong authorities and pro-democracy and pro-autonomy Hong Kong residents. To the contrary, from 2013 through the time of this writing, the combination of: (i) CCP resolve to halt further democratization in Hong Kong and increase its integration with the mainland PRC, and (ii) heightened feelings of grievance and efficacy on the part of Hong Kongers, has bred an increasingly volatile environment in Hong Kong. This dynamic peaked and accelerated in 2014, when central CCP leaders ruled that the Chief Executive election of 2017 would not feature universal suffrage – going against what the SC of the NPC had seemed to promise in 2007.

Prior to the new ruling, the established process for amending the Basic Law was followed, wherein the SAR government was to "consult" citizens for a roughly six-month period, beginning in December 2013. Afterwards, the Chief Executive would report the citizens' views to the NPC. During the consultation period, the Hong Kong Alliance for True Democracy (a group that included all of the pro-democracy LegCo members) demanded that there be a "civil nomination" process for Chief Executive, wherein the Nomination Committee would be required to include any nominee with a requisite number of citizen signatures.[25] Yet when Chief Executive Leung released his report, he highlighted only material from pro-government submissions. The SC of the NPC not only approved his report, but included additional restrictions on the nomination process, including a limit of three nominees and raising the threshold for consideration as a nominee.[26]

Led by student groups, academics, and Christian leaders, large numbers of Hong Kong residents rose up in protest. Their demonstrations persisted for nearly 80 days. Earlier, in March of 2013, Hong Kong University law professor Benny Tai, along with sociology professor Chan Kin-man and Baptist minister Chu Yiu-ming, proposed an "Occupy Central with Love and Peace" (OCLP) initiative, including a referendum on universal suffrage. Prior to the NPC ruling, it gained little traction. Immediately after the NPC ruling, a separate action was initiated by high school and university students: Scholarism and the Hong Kong University Federation of Students jointly called for a class boycott, to begin on September 22. A few days later, high school students staged a sit-in outside of the LegCo building. When some of the students broke into an area of the Civic Plaza that had been closed off, a number were detained and had their homes searched. As news of these developments spread via traditional media, online sites, and social media, many more joined the sit-in, including the three main OCLP leaders. When police tried to disperse the protestors, the demonstrators moved onto the streets, blocking traffic. The police deployed tear gas and pepper spray, while protestors tried to protect themselves with umbrellas and goggles. All of this was captured in pictures and on video, which spread rapidly via the Internet and cell phones, as well as traditional media outlets. The protest ranks swelled to upwards of 100,000, occupying the full width of an eight-lane road in the Admiralty district, the Causeway Bay shopping area, and Nathan Road in the Mongkok district. That night, Hong Kong's highest court ruled that the detained students would be released without charges – an indication of how the independence of the judiciary could work to the benefit of the protestors.[27]

The students made four demands: that the Civic Plaza be opened; that the Chief Executive and those involved in his plan for constitutional reform resign; that the NPC decision be revoked; and that a "civil nomination" process be adopted for the Chief Executive. Chief Executive Leung publicly refused to consider the demands, calling them "unconstitutional." In response, the students threatened to "storm" the Chief Executive offices on October 2. Just half an hour before midnight on October 1, the government agreed to talk with the

students. The meeting was postponed several times, both by the protestors and by government officials. When it finally took place on
October 21, no agreement was reached. However, the student representatives generally were perceived by the public as making a "calm,"
"rational," and "highly persuasive" case, evidencing a clear and in-depth
understanding of the NPC decision and the Basic Law. Public opinion
polls found that a plurality of Hong Kongers supported the "Occupy"
Movement, and that the Hong Kong Federation of Students was the
"most popular political organization in Hong Kong."[28]

Faced with this reality, in early October Leung and central CCP
leaders met multiple times, coming up with what proved to be an
effective strategy: "taking minimum action while maximizing incon-
venience to ordinary people's lives... [and] flooding the news with dire
warnings about the economic consequences for the city as a whole."
In other words, they would "wait out the protestors."[29] Though October
and November, the demonstrations blossomed, with artistic and creative symbols and actions proliferating, and a massive "tent city" in
operation. Still, there was no clear leadership or decision-making structure to the demonstrations. Nonetheless, the participants generally
were disciplined, orderly and polite, and made it a priority to keep
their protest areas clean. It helped that they were well-provisioned by
spontaneous citizen donations.[30]

ICTs played an important role in the movement. As Hui relates,
"whenever supplies ran low, calls for aid would go out via social media,
and scores of supporters would swiftly turn up with needed items."[31] In
addition, the Internet and social media were critical sources of information for movement participants. In the words of Scholarism founder
Wong, "Facebook was my library."[32] "Citizen journalists" also circulated
first-hand accounts of protest actions, along with pictures and video
footage. In addition, as in 2012, sophisticated websites were continuously
updated, and blogs about the movement proliferated. Further, ICTs
facilitated the growth of the organizations that were most prominent

in the movement. For example, the members of Scholarism began as "strangers who were rallied through Facebook and WhatsApp."[33]

Traditional media outlets were influential as well. Like in earlier movements, the *Apple Daily* and *Next Magazine* strongly supported the "Occupy" protestors, and even drew pro-Beijing counter-demonstrators at their offices.[34] In addition, despite the ownership of Hong Kong's traditional media outlets by pro-Beijing tycoons, their focus on profit led them to extensively cover the colorful, captivating, and sometimes violent developments that were occurring on the ground.[35]

As noted above, the movement was not entirely peaceful. In late September, police had used pepper spray and tear gas, and had detained some participants. In October, a number of protestors in Mongkok were beaten by other civilians – allegedly with triad gang connections. Also in October, police forcibly tried to move protestors from a tunnel in the Admiralty area, and a social worker was arrested, dragged into a corner, and beaten and kicked by police.

By late November, support for the continued occupation of public areas was wearing thin among Hong Kong residents, but many protestors persisted. Trying to use legal, peaceful means to disperse the participants, Hong Kong authorities pushed taxi and bus companies to ask for court injunctions to halt the occupations that were harming their livelihood. With injunctions in hand, bailiffs were accompanied by police to clear the areas in question. The protestors quickly adapted their tactics, moving to areas not covered by the injunction. When Leung publicly stated that Hong Kongers must be allowed to resume their normal shopping, demonstrators flooded Mongkok's shopping areas. The police responded with force – using pepper spray and beating with clubs many in the area, including reporters and bystanders. They also made arrests. Running out of options, on December 1 Wong and other student leaders began a hunger strike. Wong and two others also tried to surrender to the police, and on December 3 they succeeded in getting arrested. When (in mid-December) police made their final efforts to clear out the other major protest centers in Admiralty and Causeway Bay, they refrained from using force, and the remaining demonstrators did not resist.[36]

Overall, the government succeeded in waiting out the protests, and did not concede to any of their demands. However, the underlying causes of the "Occupy" or "Umbrella" Movement remain unresolved, and at the time of this writing, dissatisfaction with Beijing remains widespread. An estimated 1.2 million of Hong Kong's total population of 7.2 million participated in the protests in some way. Although the very wealthy in Hong Kong typically are loyal to Beijing, most in the upper middle class participated in the occupation, as did many middle- and working-class Hong Kong residents.[37] Further, the participants and leaders were relatively young; one study found that 85 percent were under 40 years of age.[38] Like Joshua Wong, many were high school students. Moreover, 60 percent of Hong Kongers between the ages of 18 and 29 self-identify as "pure Hong Kongers" rather than as "Chinese."[39] Thus, the issue cannot be expected to wane over time.

To the contrary, from 2015 through the time of this writing, tensions have been high and the political environment unsettled. After Wong and two other student activists (Nathan Law and Alex Chow) were convicted of unlawful assembly and sentenced to community service hours (Wong and Law) and a suspended jail sentence (Chow), prosecutors convinced Hong Kong's Court of Appeal to revisit the case. When it did, in August 2017, Wong, Chow, and Law were sentenced to six, seven, and eight months in jail (respectively). In late October 2017, Wong and Law were released on bail, pending a final appeal to be held in early 2018.[40]

Meanwhile, separatist sentiment has grown, especially among the young, and members of the "opposition" have continued to capitalize on Hong Kong's quasi-democratic political institutions and civil liberties to challenge the authority of the CCP/PRC over Hong Kong. Most prominently, six newly-elected pro-democracy LegCo representatives altered the required oath when being sworn into office. By July 2017, court rulings had removed all of them from their posts.[41]

CONCLUSION

Unlike Han protest in mainland PRC, in Hong Kong a real threat of collective contention challenging CCP rule has arisen over time. Yet, even pro-separatist activists in Hong Kong have been law-abiding and have avoided the use of violence – in contrast to the ethnic minority actions chronicled in chapter 8. Concomitantly, unlike in ethnic minority protest and farmer and worker unrest in the mainland, government authorities in Hong Kong also have exhibited generally law-abiding responses to popular protests in Hong Kong. Even in the relatively long-lived and expansive "Umbrella" Movement of 2014, wherein the police used more violent methods than had been the case in earlier post-handover demonstrations, political leaders opposed to the movement quickly decided that in Hong Kong's quasi-democratic environment, their best strategy would be to eschew further use of force and simply "wait out" the protests.

Conclusion

With the preceding pages in mind, we may now revisit the questions posed at the start of this book. What has caused Chinese citizens to protest? What has happened when they do? And how has protest affected the stability of CCP rule?

PROTEST CAUSES

Turning first to protest causes, the general elements in China have been the same as those that have spurred popular activism around the world: grievances, perceptions of a favorable opportunity structure (including a belief that at least some political power-holders are sympathetic to the protestors' cause), and citizen leaders that capitalize on both. In China's post-Mao era, citizen complaints have been varied and many. Most have been material, involving the concrete interests of a particular group: wages and working conditions for private-sector workers; layoffs and forced retirements for public-sector workers; taxes and land acquisitions for farmers; property demolition and degradation for homeowners; and local environmental destruction. In these cases, protestors have focused only on their specific concerns and have not spread beyond their particular locale; they have not attempted to forge connections with other socioeconomic groups or expand their protests to other locations. For some, however, the grievances motivating protest have involved general values that do not correlate with personal or group interests. This has been true of political dissidents, human rights lawyers, some environmental activists, and protestors motivated by nationalism. In turn, these actions have included participants from a wider array of socioeconomic groups. And in the case of nationalist activism, collective contention has spanned urban areas nationwide. For protestors in Hong Kong as well as Tibetans and Uighurs, grievances have been both material (e.g., economic changes due to mainland Han migration) and idealistic (most importantly, democratic values and religious beliefs).

Among the aggrieved, perceptions of a favorable opportunity structure have had a number of sources. Perhaps the most basic has been the disjuncture between what national political leaders state (both verbally and in written documents such as constitutions and laws) and what local political and economic elites do. To the extent that disgruntled citizens have believed that higher-level political officials have the people's interests at heart and that ill-intentioned local elites are violating the will of top leaders, Chinese citizens have felt encouraged to protest – they have felt that by collectively and publicly voicing their grievances, they may spur well-meaning central political elites to intervene on their behalf. When national authorities actually have done so (either in a particular case, such as a labor strike, or through general policy change to address the underlying problem that has fomented widespread protests), these feelings have been further reinforced. Relatedly, the fragmentation of the Chinese Party-state has provided aggrieved citizens with multiple points of contact in pressing their cause, and has enabled them to play different parts and levels of the regime against one another. At the same time, the ambiguity of many national-level documents, pronouncements, and practices has engendered in the citizenry a feeling that the opportunity structure is not entirely closed.

ICTs and mass media outlets constitute another key aspect of the opportunity structure that has enhanced perceptions of efficacy among disgruntled Chinese. Both have facilitated the dissemination of information, providing knowledge about relevant laws and policies that protestors can use to their advantage. In addition, both have circulated information about international and domestic developments that have fueled grievances (as in the case of nationalistic protests) and have provided information about successful protest tactics elsewhere (as in environmental, homeowner, and worker activism). In a number of cases (particularly affluent homeowner actions and environment-related protests), activists have capitalized on contacts with media personnel as well as the profit orientation of media outlets to gain publicity for their cause. ICTs such as the Internet and mobile devices also have stimulated feelings of efficacy by making it easier to mobilize large numbers of people around common concerns. With the "cost" of net-working made very low by social media and other electronic communication mechanisms, the perceived obstacles to rallying a crowd large enough to make an impact have all but disappeared. Nonetheless, ICTs have been much more available to aggrieved citizens that are relatively educated and affluent, and live in cities.

In most mainland protests by the majority Han population, protest leaders have had some prior standing in the community. In rural areas, some have been elected village council members or retired veterans. Across all types of protest, leaders have been relatively educated, with the ability to read relevant materials and write petitions and other protest-related documents. In a few cases – most significantly in environmental and private-sector worker protests and activism in Hong Kong – NGOs (including Christian churches in the latter) have played important leadership roles.

PROTEST FEATURES

Looking next at what happens when Chinese citizens protest, one finds a number of commonalities. Most prominently, activists almost always reference the law (or other official documents and statements), and first press their case via legal, institutionalized channels – typically by submitting a petition to relevant "letters and visits" offices. They also make a conscious effort to follow legal procedures. In the case of Hong Kong, where there are far more legal and institutionalized means of popular political participation, cases of illegal behavior on the part of protestors have been exceedingly rare. In the mainland PRC, citizens have resorted to illegal actions only when repeated legal efforts have failed. The only exception has been Tibetan and Uighur activists, for whom national laws and practices are themselves the source of grievances. For them, there are few options for protest other than illegal acts. As a result, their protests have involved far more violence than has been the case in all other types of collective contention.

In terms of protest demands, although in the 1980s student-led demonstrators called for political changes at the national level, from 1990 through the present very few Chinese have publicly and collectively voiced such concerns. Instead, the vast majority have called for adherence to existing laws or other official policies, or have asked for policy or legal changes within the existing political system. Even among the various types of mainland PRC political protest discussed in chapter 7, only political dissidents such as the China Democracy Party founders and the Charter 08 signatories have challenged the political dominance of the CCP and advocated for systemic political change. Apart from these mainland dissidents – whose numbers are tiny in comparison with the number of participants in other types of mainland PRC protests by predominantly Han Chinese – demands for fundamental political transformation have been voiced solely by Tibetans, Uighurs, and Hong Kong residents, all of whom have demanded greater self-determination and autonomy and have questioned the legitimacy of CCP control over the Special Autonomous Regions within which they live.

Government responses to protests have differed depending on the nature of citizen demands. When activists have asked for material redress, adherence to existing laws, or changes to policies, government officials – particularly at higher levels – have been more receptive, and protestors have been more likely to achieve their aims. However, even in these cases, success typically has been only partial, and has come only after protracted efforts and local-level harassment, repression, and outright violence. Further, protestors with more money, connections, education, and status have been the most successful, and the least likely to be subjected to violent treatment. This has been most notably the case with affluent urban homeowners, but also with relatively well-to-do environmental activists. Meanwhile, protestors that have demanded systemic political change that challenges CCP rule have met with official intransigence at best (as in Hong Kong, where the more democratic political structure limits the options of CCP authorities), but more often harsh and violent suppression (as with mainland political dissidents, Uighurs, Tibetans).

PROTEST CONSEQUENCES

With the exception of actions undertaken by political dissidents, Tibetans and Uighurs, the other types of mainland protests that have arisen from 1990 through the present have had a positive effect: they have led China's high-level leaders to adjust their policies and practices to address the concerns of the aggrieved. In this sense, popular contention has improved governance in China and enhanced regime legitimacy. Indeed, this is why top political elites have behaved in this manner – they wish to stay in power, and they know that it is much easier and less costly to do so if the public is happy. At the same time, however, popular protest in China has had a negative effect: because citizens' struggle for redress often has involved violence and intense sacrifice on the part of participants, many have been left scarred and embittered by their experiences – even when they have been successful in achieving their aims. In turn, this has heightened their skepticism about and decreased their support for China's political system as a whole. In this sense, protest has become a dangerous game for regime leaders. Moreover, as time has passed, and Chinese citizens have had more experiences with protest, they increasingly have moved away from localized, material demands that involve only a particular community to more expansive, ideal-driven demands that cut across many socioeconomic groups. And this particularly has been the case with younger Chinese (most notably among private-sector workers, environmental activists, urban homeowners, and Hong Kong residents) – with whom political leaders will need to reckon for some time to come.

CONCLUSION

Although outsiders might think that Chinese citizens live in constant fear of political repression and have no legal way to convey their collective complaints, in reality China's political system has allowed the public to collectively and publicly seek redress for their grievances, including not only through legal, institutionalized channels such as the "letters and visits" system and the courts, but also extra-legal methods such as marches and occupations. Far from being quiescent, China's citizens regularly have engaged in these activities when they have felt that they have been wronged. Over time, they have become increasingly edgy and empowered. Because institutionalized channels generally have failed to address citizen grievances, extra-institutional actions have become regular. However, these kinds of actions are not easy to control or predict. Thus, even though thus far China's top leaders have been able to successfully "ride the tiger" of popular protest, doing so has brought instability and uncertainty to the relationship between citizens and political authorities.[1]

In this already precarious situation, actions undertaken since 2012 by Xi Jinping have threatened to move state–society relations in a more volatile direction. Perhaps most notably, the Xi administration's methodical and violent suppression of human rights lawyers has removed a key institutional mechanism that has been used by aggrieved citizens to seek redress, and that has enabled the regime to adjust policies that are failing the populace and causing discontent. Simultaneously, this repression is strangling and scaring off from the legal profession many of China's most talented public service-oriented lawyers. Similarly, heightened oppression of Uighur and Tibetan minorities has pushed them in a more radical direction, leading to more violent and vehemently separatist actions. Though far less aggressive, official moves to constrict freedom of assembly and expression in Hong Kong also have elicited more oppositional views among residents there. Further, although wealthy mainland Han homeowners seem to have been able to continue to achieve some successes through activism under the Xi administration, the regime's attempts to stifle freedom of speech and inquiry via the Internet, ICTs, and mass media outlets – and within academia – are likely to stymie even well-off citizens' ability to achieve gains in a relatively non-confrontational fashion.

If people in China become unable to express their concerns through either institutionalized means or non-institutionalized protests, then their dissatisfaction will have no outlet or remedy within China's present political system, and they may come to see the need for systemic political change. And because they are now well-practiced at engaging in mass collective contention, they may be more likely to act on that perceived need. Meanwhile, protests on the part of Hong Kong residents and Tibetan and Uighur ethnic minorities will threaten the stability of CCP rule in the Autonomous Regions in which they reside. China's CCP-dominated political system may have been able to contain and benefit from popular contention from 1990 through the present, but in doing so it may have sown the seeds of greater regime-threatening unrest. In this context, if Xi Jinping's moves scare citizens into keeping their grievances to themselves, Xi is more likely to water those seeds than to crush them.

Notes

Introduction

1 See David Meyer, "Protest and Political Opportunities," *Annual Review of Sociology* 30 (2004): 125–45.

2 See Teresa Wright, *Party and State in Post-Mao China* (Cambridge: Polity Press, 2015).

3 http://english.cpc.people.com.cn/206972/206981/8188087.html [accessed April 8, 2015].

4 Constitution of Communist Party of China (adopted on Nov. 14, 2012). http://www.china.org.cn/china/18th_cpc_congress/2012-11/16/content_27138030.htm [accessed March 13, 2015].

5 http://en.people.cn/constitution/constitution.html [accessed March 10, 2015].

6 Yongshun Cai, "Local Governments and the Suppression of Popular Resistance in China," *China Quarterly* 193 (March 2008): 27, 30, 36.

7 Ibid., 28; Verna Yu, "Tales of Torture," *South China Morning Post*, June 27, 2015.

8 See Carl F. Minzner, "Riots and Cover-ups: Counterproductive Control of Local Agents in China," *Journal of International Law* 31:1 (2009): 53–123; and Christopher Heurlin, *Responsive Authoritarianism: Protest and Policy Change in Rural and Urban China* (Cambridge: Cambridge University Press, 2015).

9 See Murray Scot Tanner, "China Rethinks Unrest," *Washington Quarterly* 27(3) (Summer 2004): 137–56; and Jeremy Goldkorn, "Legal Daily Report on Mass Incidents in China in 2012," http://zzwave.com/plaboard/archive/3917864.shtml [accessed January 5, 2018].

10 Sun Liping, "China's Challenge: Social Disorder," *Economic Observer* 508 (Feb. 28, 2011): 10–11. http://www.eeo.com.cn/ens/feature/2011/05/09/200868.shtml [accessed June 16, 2015].

11 Kevin O'Brien, "Neither Transgressive nor Contained: Boundary-Spanning Contention in China," *Mobilization* 8:1 (February 2003): 51–64. Reprinted in Peter H. Gries and Stanley Rosen (eds.), *State and Society in 21st Century China* (London: Routledge, 2004), pp. 105–22.

12 Kevin O'Brien and Lianjiang Li, *Rightful Resistance in Rural China* (New York: Cambridge University Press, 2006).

13 See Huerlin, *Responsive Authoritarianism*.

14 Lianjiang Li, Mingxing Liu, and Kevin O'Brien, "Petitioning Beijing: The High Tide of 2003–2006," *China Quarterly* 210 (June 2012): 313–34.

15 Freedom House, "The Politburo's Predicament: Confronting the Limitations of CCP Repression," Jan. 2015: 17. https://freedomhouse.org/china-2015-politiburo-predicament#.VYCmdUb0ekk [accessed June 16, 2015].

16 Christian Göbel and Lynette Ong, "Social Unrest in China," Europe China Research and Advice Network, 2012. http://www.chathamhouse.org/sites/files/chathamhouse/public/Research/Asia/1012ecran_gobelong.pdf [accessed June 22, 2015].

17 Sarah Cook, "The Long Shadow of Chinese Censorship: How Chinese Media Restrictions Affect News Outlets around the World," Freedom House, Oct. 22, 2013. http://www.cima.ned.org/wp-content/uploads/2015/02/CIMA-China_Sarah%20Cook.pdf [accessed April 28, 2015]; Freedom House, "The Politburo's Predicament."

18 Steven Millward, "China now has 731 million internet users, 95% access from their phones," *Tech in Asia*, Jan. 22, 2017. https://www.techinasia.com/china-731-million-internet-users-end-2016 [accessed August 11, 2017].

19 http://www.statista.com/statistics/272385/age-distribution-of-internet-users-in-china/ [accessed April 12, 2015].

20 China Internet Network Information Center, "Statistical Report on Internet Development in China," July 2014. https://cnnic.com.cn/IDR/ReportDownloads/201411/P020141102574314897888.pdf [accessed June 22, 2015].

21 As of July 2017, blocked sites included Facebook, YouTube, Twitter, Google, and *The New York Times*.

22 Gary King, Jennifer Pan, and Margaret Roberts, "How Censorship in China Allows Government Criticism but Silences Collective Expression," *American Political Science Review* 107(2) (May 2013): 326–43.

23 These individuals are colloquially (and derogatorily) referred to as "fifty cent" party members due to the allegation that they are paid to make such posts. See Gary King, Jennifer Pan, and Margaret Roberts, "How the Chinese Government Fabricates Social Media Posts for Strategic Distraction, not Engaged Argument," *American Political Science Review* 111:3 (August 2017): 484–501.

24 Freedom House, "China 2014." https://freedomhouse.org/report/freedom-net/2014/china [accessed August 11, 2017].

25 Human Rights Watch, "China: Country Summary," January 2015. https://www.hrw.org/world-report/2015/country-chapters/china-and-tibet [accessed August 11, 2017].
26 Freedom House, "China 2014;" Freedom House, "The Politburo's Predicament."
27 Kevin O'Brien, "Rightful Resistance Revisited," *Journal of Peasant Studies* 40:6 (2013): 1051–62, at 1053.

Chapter 1. Popular Protest in the Post-Mao Era

1 Xi Chen, *Social Protest and Contentious Authoritarianism in China* (New York: Cambridge University Press, 2011).
2 Lee Feigon, *China Rising: The Meaning of Tiananmen* (Chicago, IL: Ivan R. Dee, 1990): 46–72.
3 Richard Baum, *Burying Mao: Chinese Politics in the Age of Deng Xiaoping* (Princeton, NJ: Princeton University Press, 1994): 27–65.
4 Stig Thorgersen, "Through the Sheep's Intestines – Selection and Elitism in Chinese Schools," *Australian Journal of Chinese Affairs* 21 (Jan. 1989): 29–56, at 33.
5 Stanley Rosen, "Contemporary Chinese Youth and the State," *Journal of Asian Studies* 68:2 (May 2009): 359–69, at 361, referencing Shi Zhong, "Chinese Nationalism and the Future of China," translated in Stanley Rosen, ed., "Nationalism and Neoconservatism in China in the 1990s," *Chinese Law and Government* 30:6 (Nov.–Dec. 1997): 8–27.
6 Local People's Congresses are at the lower level of China's state structure. They are elected every two years by the general population at the township/county level. Although non-Party members were not legally prohibited from running for these positions, in practice they were prevented from doing so.
7 Stanley Rosen, "China in 1987: The Year of the Thirteenth Party Congress," *Asian Survey* 28:1 (Jan. 1988): 35–51; Julia Kwong, "The 1986 Student Demonstrations in China: A Democratic Movement?" *Asian Survey* 28:9 (Sept. 1988): 970–85.
8 Rosen, "China in 1987," 36.
9 Kwong, "The 1986 Student Demonstrations," 982.
10 "Resolutely Combat Bourgeois Liberalization," *People's Daily*, Jan. 6, 1987.
11 Rosen, "China in 1987," 37.
12 Kwong, "The 1986 Student Demonstrations;" Rosen, "China in 1987."
13 State Education Commission, *Jingxin dongpo de 56 tian* (The Soul-Stirring 56 Days) (Beijing: Dadi Chubanshe, 1989): 138; cited in Yongshun Cai, "Local

Governments and the Suppression of Popular Resistance in China," *China Quarterly* 193 (March 2008): 40 (note 78).

14 Teresa Wright, *The Perils of Protest: State Repression and Student Activism in China and Taiwan* (Honolulu, HI: University of Hawaii Press, 2001).

15 "Recognize the Essence of Turmoil and the Necessity of Martial Law," *People's Daily*, June 3, 1989; Yuan Mu (news conference), Beijing Television Service, June 6, 1989 (FBIS, June 7, 1989, 12); Chen Xitong, *Report on Checking the Turmoil and Quelling the Counter-Revolutionary Rebellion* (Beijing: New Star Publishers, 1989).

16 Han was released in 1991, near death from tuberculosis. At present, he runs a Hong Kong-based labor activist organization, China Labour Bulletin. Wang was released in 1993, only to be re-arrested in 1995 for his continued activism. In 1998, he accepted exile in the US, where he completed his PhD in History at Harvard University. He currently teaches History at Qinghua University in Taiwan, and is the chair of the non-profit Chinese Constitutional Reform Association.

17 David Shambaugh, *China's Communist Party: Atrophy and Adaptation* (Berkeley, CA: University of California Press, 2008): 4.

18 Suisheng Zhao, "A State-Led Nationalism: The Patriotic Education Campaign in Post-Tiananmen China," *Communist and Post-Communist Studies* 31:3 (1998): 287–302; Ann-Marie Brady, *China's Thought Management* (New York: Routledge, 2011).

19 Murray Scot Tanner, "Unrest in China and the Chinese State's Institutional Responses," Testimony before the US-China Economic and Security Review Commission, Feb. 25, 2011. https://www.uscc.gov/sites/default/files/2.25.11Tanner.pdf [accessed June 22, 2015]; Christian Göbel and Lynette Ong, "Social Unrest in China," Europe China Research and Advice Network, 2012. http://www.chathamhouse.org/sites/files/chathamhouse/public/Research/Asia/1012ecran_gobelong.pdf [accessed June 22, 2015].

Chapter 2. Rural Protest

1 World Bank data. http://data.worldbank.org/indicator/SP.RUR.TOTL.ZS [accessed July 27, 2017].

2 James Kung, "Equal Entitlement Versus Tenure Security under a Regime of Collective Property Rights: Peasants' Preference for Institutions in Post-reform Chinese Agriculture," *Journal of Comparative Economics* 21 (1995): 82–111; James Kung and Shouying Liu, "Farmers' Preferences Regarding Ownership and Land Tenure in Post-Mao China," *The China Journal* 38 (July 1997): 33–63.

3 Cheng Ming [Contention] (Hong Kong), cited in Thomas Bernstein, "Unrest in Rural China: A 2003 Assessment," *Center for the Study of Democracy Paper* 13 (2004): 3–4.

4 Anshun Zhu, "Ruci jian fang wei na ban?" [Why did they build new houses?] in Shukai Zhao, ed., *Noncun, nongmin [The Countryside and the Peasantry]*, Qinghua University, 1999 (unpublished paper), 384. Cited in Kevin O'Brien and Lianjiang Li, *Rightful Resistance in Rural China* (Cambridge: Cambridge University Press, 2006): 43.

5 O'Brien and Li, *Rightful Resistance*, 45.

6 Thomas Bernstein and Xiaobo Lu, "Taxation without Representation: Peasants, the Central and Local States in Reform China," *China Quarterly* 163 (Sept. 2000): 742–63, at 746.

7 Zhang Wu, "Protest Leadership and Repertoire: A Comparative Analysis of Peasant Protest in Hunan in the 1990s," *Journal of Current Chinese Affairs* 42:2 (2013): 167–94; O'Brien and Li, *Rightful Resistance*; Thomas Bernstein and Xiaobo Lu, *Taxation Without Representation in Contemporary Rural China* (Cambridge: Cambridge University Press, 2003).

8 Ibid.

9 Isabelle Thireau, "From Equality to Equity," *China Information* 5:4 (1991): 42–57, at 56; Bernstein and Lu, "Taxation without Representation," 757; Kevin O'Brien, "Implementing Political Reform in China's Villages," *Australian Journal of Chinese Affairs* 32 (1994): 33–59, at 53.

10 Zhang Wu, "Protest Leadership and Repertoire."

11 Hiroki Takeuchi, *Tax Reform in Rural China: Revenue, Resistance, and Authoritarian Rule* (Cambridge: Cambridge University Press, 2014); and Christopher Heurlin, *Responsive Authoritarianism in China: Land, Protests, and Policy Making* (Cambridge: Cambridge University Press, 2016).

12 Bernstein and Lu, "Taxation without Representation," 753.

13 O'Brien, "Implementing Political Reform," 39.

14 Bernstein and Lu, "Taxation without Representation," 755.

15 Josephine Ma, "Create a Uniform System for Village Polls, Says Jimmy Carter," *South China Morning Post*, Sept. 9, 2003, 5; Jie Chen, "Sociopolitical Attitudes of the Masses and Leaders in the Chinese Village," *Journal of Contemporary China* 14:44 (Aug. 2005): 445–64, at 453; John James Kennedy, "The Implementation of Village Elections and Tax-for-Fee Reform in Rural Northwest China," in Elizabeth Perry and Merle Goldman, eds., *Grassroots Political Reform in Contemporary China* (Cambridge, MA: Harvard University Press, 2007).

16 Takeuchi, *Tax Reform in Rural China*.

17 Huerlin, *Responsive Authoritarianism*, 51.

18 Yingfang Chen, *Land Takings and the Urbanization of the Periurban Country-side – Investigation of Shanghai* (征地与郊区农村的城市化 – 上海市的调查) (Beijing: Wenjiang Press, 2003); and Xinming Yan, *Research on Employment and Social Security Among Landless Farmers* (失地农民的就业和社会保障研究) (Beijing: China Labor and Social Security Press, 2008), cited in Huerlin, *Responsive Authoritarianism*, 52.

19 Huerlin, *Responsive Authoritarianism*, 53.

20 China Land Resources Yearbook, various years, cited in Christopher Heurlin, *Responsive Authoritarianism*, 58.

21 Ethan Michelson, "Justice from Above or Below? Popular Strategies for Resolving Grievances in Rural China," *China Quarterly* 193 (2008): 43–64.

22 Christian Göbel and Lynette Ong, "Social Unrest in China," Europe China Research and Advice Network, 2012. http://www.chathamhouse.org/sites/files/chathamhouse/public/Research/Asia/1012ecran_gobelong.pdf, 11 and 37 [accessed June 17, 2015].

23 Huerlin, *Responsive Authoritarianism*, 56–7.

24 Ibid.

25 William Hurst, Mingxing Liu, Yongdong Liu, and Ran Tao, "Reassessing Collective Petitioning in Rural China," *Comparative Politics* 46:4 (July 2014): 459–78.

26 Rong Wang, "Engaging Government for Environmental Collective Action: Political Implications of ICTs in Rural China," in Wenhong Chen and Stephen Reese, eds., *Networked China: Global Dynamics of Digital Media and Civic Engagement* (New York: Routledge, 2015): 76–96.

27 Christopher Heurlin and Susan Whiting, "Villagers Against the State: The Politics of Land Disputes," paper presented at the annual meeting of the American Political Science Association, Chicago, August 30, 2007, p. 20.

28 Lianjiang Li, "Political Trust and Petitioning in the Chinese Countryside," *Comparative Politics* 40:2 (Jan. 2008): 209–26.

29 Hurst et al., "Reassessing Collective Petitioning," 471.

30 Zeng Zhimin, "Wukan: The Whole Story," *The China Nonprofit Review* 5 (2013): 17–101, at 30 and Zhao Yang (赵扬), "Moving towards cooperative governance – Where is Wukan headed? (走向合作治理 – 乌坎往何处去 Zouxiang hexuo zhili wang hechu qu)," *Building Society* (社会建设 Shehui jianshe) (5) (2013): 53, cited in Anne Christine Lie, "Rural Protests and New Dimensions of Political Space in China: Perceptions of the News Media and Social Media in Wukan Village," paper presented at the conference on Political Participation in Asia: Defining and Deploying Political Space, Stockholm University, Nov. 22–24, 2015, 2.

31 Lie, "Rural Protests," 3.

32 Personal communication with Anne Christine Lie, Feb. 17, 2016, drawing on Zeng Zhimin, "Wukan: The Whole Story."

33 Lie, "Rural Protests," 3–4.

34 Zeng Zhimin "Wukan: The Whole Story," 49; personal communication with Anne Christine Lie, Feb. 17, 2016.

35 Lie, "Rural Protests," 4–5, 9.

36 Ibid., 5; Shannon Tiezzi, "Democracy with Chinese Characteristics: The Case of Wukan," *The Diplomat*, April 3, 2014. http://thediplomat.com/2014/04/democracy-with-chinese-characteristics-the-case-of-wukan/ [accessed February 10, 2016].

37 Echo Hui, "Wukan Village's Future under Threat as Ex-cadres Retake Party Reins," *South China Morning Post*, March 4, 2014.

38 Lianjiang Li, "Political Trust in Rural China," *Modern China* 30:2 (April 2004), 228–258, at 247.

39 Ibid.; Jianrong Yu, "Conflict in the Countryside: The Emerging Political Awareness of the Peasants," *Social Research* 73:1 (Spring 2006), 141–58, at 149.

Chapter 3. Labor Protest

1 China Labour Bulletin, cited in Javier Hernandez, "Labor Protests Multiply in China as Economy Slows, Worrying Leaders," *New York Times*, March 14, 2016. http://www.nytimes.com/2016/03/15/world/asia/china-labor-strike-protest.html?smprod=nytcore-ipad&smid=nytcore-ipad-share [accessed March 15, 2016]; China Labour Bulletin, referenced in James Griffiths, "'We The Workers': On the Front Lines of China's Record-Level Labor Unrest," CNN, Feb. 22, 2017. http://www.cnn.com/2017/02/22/asia/china-labor-unrest-we-the-workers/index.html [accessed July 28, 2017].

2 "Tiananmen – Ten Years On," *China Labour Bulletin* 48 (May–June 1999), 3.

3 Beijing Workers Autonomous Federation Preparatory Committee, "Provisional Memorandum," May 28, 1989.

4 Andrew Walder and Xiaoxia Gong, "Workers in the Tiananmen Protests: The Politics of the Beijing Workers' Autonomous Federation," *The Australian Journal of Chinese Affairs* 29 (Jan. 1993): 1–29, at 12.

5 Dorothy Solinger, *Contesting Citizenship in Urban China: Peasant Migrants, the State, and the Logic of the Market* (Berkeley, CA: University of California Press, 1999), 44–9.

6 Ibid., 50, 65, 87, 135–6.

7 Feng Wang, "Boundaries of Inequality: Perceptions of Distributive Justice among Urbanites, Migrants, and Peasants," University of California, Irvine Center for the Study of Democracy Paper 07-09 (2007), 3; Kam Wing Chan, "Recent Migration in China: Patterns, Trends and Policies," *Asian Perspective* 24:4 (2001), 127–55, at 131; Solinger, *Contesting Citizenship*, 47 and 243–4.

8 Linda Wong, "Chinese Migrant Workers: Rights Attainment Deficits, Rights Consciousness and Personal Strategies," *China Quarterly* 208 (Dec. 2011): 870–92.

9 Dorothy Solinger, "Labour Market Reform and the Plight of the Laid-off Proletariat," *China Quarterly* 170 (June 2002): 304–26.

10 Ross Garnaut, Ligang Song and Yang Yao, "The Impact and Significance of State-owned Enterprise Restructuring in China," *The China Journal* 55 (Jan. 2006), 35–63, at 53.

11 Mark Frazier, "China's Pension Reform and Its Discontents," *The China Journal* 51 (Jan. 2004), 97–114, at 101 (fn. 11); William Hurst and Kevin O'Brien, "China's Contentious Pensioners," *China Quarterly* (2002), 345–60 at 349 (fn. 22). The legal retirement age was 55 for women and 60 for men.

12 Qiao Jian, "2003 nian: Xin yilun jiegou tiaozheng xia de laodong guanxi" (Labor relations in 2003, under a new round of structural adjustment), in *2004 nian: Zhongguo shehui xingshi fenxi yu yuce*, ed., Ru Xin, Lu Xueyi, and Li Peilin (Beijing: Shehui kexue chubanshe, 2004), 285; Timothy Weston, "The Iron Man Weeps: Joblessness and Political Legitimacy in the Chinese Rust Belt," in Peter Gries and Stanley Rosen, eds., *State and Society in 21st Century China* (New York: Routledge, 2004), 73.

13 Ching Kwan Lee, *Against the Law: Labor Protests in China's Rustbelt and Sunbelt* (Berkeley, CA: University of California Press, 2007), 26.

14 Ibid., p. 48.

15 Feng Chen, "Industrial Restructuring and Workers' Resistance in China," *Modern China* 29:2 (April 2003): 237–62, at 247.

16 Lee, *Against the Law*, 99.

17 Ibid., 70; Weston, "The Iron Man Weeps," 70; Cai, *State and Laid-off Workers*, 32.

18 Dorothy Solinger, "Clashes between Reform and Opening: Labor Market Formation in Three Cities," in Bruce Dickson and Chao Chien-min eds., *Remaking the Chinese State: Strategies, Society, and Security* (London: Routledge, 2001): 103–31; William Hurst, *The Chinese Worker after Socialism* (Cambridge: Cambridge University Press, 2012); Frazier, "China's Pension Reform."

19 Human Rights Watch, "Paying the Price: Worker Unrest in Northeast China," 14:6 (July 2002) https://www.hrw.org/reports/2002/chinalbr02/chinalbr0802-03.htm

20 Human Rights Watch, "Paying the Price;" Weston, "The Iron Man Weeps."
21 Solinger, "Labour Market Reform."
22 China Labour Bulletin Strike Map. http://maps.clb.org.hk/strikes/en# [accessed June 20, 2016].
23 Simon Denyer, "As China Slashes Coal Jobs, Miners Protest in Party's Revolutionary Base," *Washington Post*, March 1, 2016. https://www.washingtonpost.com/world/as-china-slashes-coal-jobs-miners-protest-in-partys-revolutionary-base/2016/03/01/e59535e1-8f7c-46ca-9d85-602eccc42fb7_story.html?hl=1&noRedirect=1 [accessed June 20 2016].
24 China Labour Bulletin, "Mass Protests by China's Coal, Iron and Steel Workers on the Decline," Aug. 8, 2016. http://www.clb.org.hk/content/mass-protests-china%E2%80%99s-coal-iron-and-steel-workers-decline [accessed October 17, 2017].
25 *State Administration for Industry and Commerce Statistical Collection* (2003) and *National Bureau of Statistics of China* (2006).
26 Chloe Froissart, "Escaping the Party's Thumb: A Few Examples of Migrant Workers' Striving for Autonomy," *Social Research* 73:1 (Spring 2006): 197–218, at 213, fn. 1.
27 Lee, *Against the Law*, 39.
28 Solinger, *Contesting Citizenship*, 79 and 129.
29 Anita Chan, "Recent Trends in Chinese Labour Issues: Signs of Change," *China Perspectives* 57 (Jan.–Feb. 2005): 1–35, at 27.
30 Chua Chin Hon, "Beijing Signs Pact to Protect Migrant Workers," *The Straits Times*, October 16, 2004. It should be noted that these reforms were very slow in coming. (I am grateful to Dorothy Solinger for this point.)
31 China Labour Bulletin, "Speaking Out: The Workers' Movement in China, 2005–2006," China Labour Bulletin Research Reports 5 (Dec. 2007), 32.
32 Josephine Ma, "'Make Sure Migrant Workers Get Paid,'" *South China Morning Post*, January 8, 2005, p. 6.
33 China Labour Bulletin, "Speaking Out," 7.
34 Mary E. Gallagher, "China's Workers Movement and the End of the Rapid-Growth Era," *Daedalus* 143:2 (Spring 2014): 81–95, at 86.
35 Ibid., 85.
36 "Woguo nongmin gong de shengcun xianzhuan" (How migrant workers in our nation subsist), *Banyue tan* (China Comment), reported in *Xinhua*, May 18, 2006; Social Trends Analysis and Forecasting Topic Group, Chinese Academy of Social Sciences, "Zhongguo jinru quanmian jianshe hexie shehui xin jieduan" (China enters a new stage in building a harmonious society), in Tuo Xin, Lu Xieui, and Lin Peilin, eds., *2007 nian: Zhongguo shehui xingshi fenxi yu yuce*

(2007: An analysis and forecast of trends in Chinese Society) (Beijing: Shehui Kexue Wenxian Chubanshe, 2006); Lee, *Against the Law*, 164–5.

37 Lee, *Against the Law*, 161 and 163.

38 China Labour Bulletin, "Speaking Out," 3.

39 Biqiang Wang, "Building a Fence: Labor Subcontracting," *Caijing*, May 21, 2012, cited in Gallagher, "China's Worker's Movement," 86; Freedom House, "Freedom in the World 2014: China" https://freedomhouse.org/report/freedom-world/2014/china#.VTqfeZP0ekk [accessed March 18, 2016].

40 China Labour Bulletin, "Speaking Out," 26.

41 Lee, *Against the Law*, 57.

42 China Labour Bulletin #11 (Feb. 1995), 9 and 11.

43 Pun Ngai, "Becoming Dagongmei (Working Girls): The Politics of Identity and Difference in Reform China," *The China Journal* 42 (July 1999): 1–18, at 6; Anita Chan, *China's Workers under Assault: The Exploitation of Labor in a Globalizing Economy* (Armonk, NY: M.E. Sharpe, 2001).

44 "Laboring over Workers' Rights," *Bejing Review* 46:52 (Dec. 25, 2003).

45 Social Trends Analysis and Forecasting Topic Group, Chinese Academy of Social Sciences, "Zhongguo jinru quanmian jianshe hexie shehui xin jieduan."

46 China Labour Bulletin, "Searching for the Union: The Workers' Movement in China 2011–13," 1–49, at 18. http://www.clb.org.hk/sites/default/files/archive/en/File/research_reports/searching%20for%20the%20union%201.pdf [accessed January 6, 2018].

47 Social Trends Analysis and Forecasting Topic Group, Chinese Academy of Social Sciences, "Zhongguo jinru quanmian jianshe hexie shehui xin jieduan." See also China Labour Bulletin, "Searching for the Union."

48 See Parry P. Leung, *Labor Activists and the New Working Class in China: Strike Leaders' Struggles* (New York: Palgrave, 2015).

49 Chris King-Chi Chan, "Community-based Organizations for Migrant Workers' Rights: The Emergence of Labour NGOs in China," *Community Development Journal* 48:1 (Jan. 2013): 6–2, at 10, citing Alex Jingwei He and Genghua Huang, "NGOs Defending Migrant Labour Rights in the Pearl River Delta Region: A Descriptive Analysis," *Hong Kong Journal of Social Sciences* 35 (2008), 41–71 [in Chinese].

50 Alex Jingwei He and Genghua Huang, "Fighting for Migrant Labor Rights in the World's Factory: Legitimacy, Resource Constraints and Strategies of Grassroots Migrant Labor NGOs in South China," Journal of Contemporary China 24: 93 (2015): 474–85, at 482. For similar NGO leader sentiments, see also 484–485.

51 Ibid.

52 James Griffiths, "China on Strike," CNN, March 29, 2016. http://www.cnn.com/2016/03/28/asia/china-strike-worker-protest-trade-union/index.html [accessed January 6, 2018].

53 Solinger, *Contesting Citizenship*, 34.

54 Ching Kwan Lee, "State and Social Protest," *Daedalus* 143:2 (Spring 2014): 124–34, at 130.

55 Quoted in Denise Tsang, "Hong Kong Factories Swept up in Wave of Pay Rises," *South China Morning Post*, June 16, 2010, cited in Florian Butollo and Tobias ten Brink, "Challenging the Atomization of Discontent: Patterns of Migrant-Worker Protest in China during the Series of Strikes in 2010," *Critical Asian Studies* 44:3 (2012): 419–40, at 425.

56 China Labour Bulletin, "Searching for the Union;" Hernandez, "Labor Protests Multiply."

57 China Labor Watch, "Thousands of Foxconn Workers Strike Again in Chongqing for Better Wages, Benefits," Oct. 8, 2014. http://www.chinalaborwatch.org/newscast/395 [accessed March 18, 2016].

58 Freedom House, "The Politburo's Predicament: Confronting the Limitations of CCP Repression," January 2015, 27. https://www.freedomhouse.org/sites/default/files/12222014_FH_ChinaReport2014_FINAL.pdf [accessed March 18, 2016].

59 Griffiths, "China on Strike."

60 Hernandez, "Labor Protests Multiply."

61 Gallagher, "China's Workers Movement," 83.

62 Lee, "State and Social Protest," 132.

Chapter 4. Homeowner Protest

1 Zhengxu Wang, Long Sun, Liuqing Xu, and Dragan Pavlićević, "Leadership in China's Urban Middle Class Protest: The Movement to Protect Homeowners' Rights in Beijing," *China Quarterly* 214 (June 2013): 411–31, at 412.

2 Yongshun Cai, "Civil Resistance and Rule of Law in China: The Defense of Homeowners' Rights," in Elizabeth Perry and Merle Goldman, eds., *Grassroots Political Reform* (Cambridge, MA: Harvard University Press, 2009), 176–7.

3 Benjamin Read, "Inadvertent Political Reform via Private Associations: Assessing Homeowners' Groups in New Neighborhoods," in Perry and Goldman, eds., *Grassroots Political Reform*, 155; Cai, "Civil Resistance," 176–7.

4 Cai, "Civil Resistance," 177–8.

5 Ibid., 179–80.

6 Luigi Tomba, "Residential Space and Collective Interest Formation in Beijing's Housing Disputes," *China Quarterly* 184 (Dec. 2005): 934–51, at 935.

7 Matthew S. Erie, "Property Rights, Legal Consciousness and the New Media in China: The Hard Case of the 'Toughest Nail-house in History,'" *China Information* 26:1 (2012): 35–59, at 37.

8 Cai, "Civil Resistance," 183–94, 191.

9 Ibid., 181–3.

10 Cai, "Civil Resistance;" Erie, "Property Rights."

11 Erie, "Property Rights," 41–2.

12 Cai, "Civil Resistance," 186–90; Erie, "Property Rights," 50–1.

13 Cai, "Civil Resistance," 188–9 and 192–3; Erie, "Property Rights," 41.

14 Cai, "Civil Resistance," 190–1; Erie, "Property Rights," 41.

15 Erie, "Property Rights," 35–6.

16 Personal communication with Benjamin Read, August 22, 2016.

17 Read, "Inadvertent Political Reform," 157; Read, "Assessing Variation in Civil Society Organizations: China's Homeowner Associations in Comparative Perspective," *Comparative Political Studies* 41:9 (Sept. 2008): 1240–65, at 1247; Kevin Lo, "Approaching Neighborhood Democracy from a Longitudinal Perspective: An Eighteen-Year Case Study of a Homeowner Association in Beijing," *Urban Studies Research* (2013), Article ID 639312.

18 Lo, "Approaching Neighborhood Democracy," 2.

19 Read, "Assessing Variation," 1249–50.

20 Ibid., 1248.

21 Lo, "Approaching Neighborhood Democracy," 3; Feng Wang, Haitao Yin, and Zhiren Zhou, "The Adoption of Bottom-up Governance in China's Homeowner Associations," *Management and Organization Review* 8:3 (November 2012), 559–83, at 562.

22 Ngai-Ming Yip and Yihong Jiang, "Homeowners United: The Attempt to Create Lateral Networks of Homeowners' Associations in Urban China," *Journal of Contemporary China* 20:72 (November 2011), 735–50, at 739.

23 Ying Wu and Junhua Chen, "The Constructive Significance of Homeowners' Rightful Protest in China," in Ngai-Ming Yip, ed., *Neighbourhood Governance in Urban China* (Cheltenham: Elgar, 2014), 169.

24 Benjamin Read, "Assessing Variation," 1255–7; Tomba, "Residential Space," 944; Luigi Tomba, "Gating Urban Spaces in China: Inclusion, Exclusion and Government," in Samer Bagaeen and Ola Uduku, eds., *Gated Communities: Social Sustainability in Contemporary and Historical Gated Developments* (London: Earthscan, 2010), 30.

25 Zhengxu Wang et al., "Leadership," 415–20; Yongshun Cai and Zhiming Sheng, "Homeowners' Activism in Beijing: Leaders with Mixed Motivations," *China Quarterly* 215 (Sept. 2013), 513–32, at 518; Benjamin Read, "Democratizing the Neighbourhood? New Private Housing and Home-Owner Self-Organization in Urban China," *The China Journal* 49 (Jan. 2003), 31–59, at 50.

26 Cai and Sheng, "Homeowners' Activism," 519–20.

27 Ibid., 519.

28 Ibid., 522–8.

29 Zhengxu Wang et al., "Leadership," 13; Ronggui Huang, "Are Residents' Committees able to Contain Homeowner Resistance?" in Ngai-Ming Yip, ed., *Neighbourhood Governance*, 73; Read, "Democratizing the Neighbourhood?" 45–6.

30 Tomba, "Gating Urban Spaces," 33.

31 Cai and Sheng, "Homeowners' Activism," 516.

32 Feng Wang et al., "The Adoption of Bottom-up Governance," 561.

33 Tomba, "Gating Urban Spaces," 33.

34 Zhengxu Wang et al., "Leadership," 414.

35 Yip and Jiang, "Homeowners United," 736–9. See also Read, "Democratizing the Neighbourhood?" 51.

36 Personal communication with Dragan Pavlicevic and Zhengxu Wang, July 19, 2016; Yip and Jiang, "Homeowners United," 739–47; personal communication with Ngai-Ming Yip, July 14, 2016.

37 Huang, "Are Residents' Committees," 80; Read, "Democratizing the Neighbourhood?" 47–8.

38 Lo, "Approaching Neighborhood Democracy," 6.

39 Personal communication with Benjamin Read, August 22, 2016.

Chapter 5. Environmental Protest

1 World Bank, "China Overview." http://www.worldbank.org/en/country/china/overview [accessed October 28, 2016].

2 Ran Ran, "Perverse Incentive Structure and Policy Implementation Gap in China's Local Environ Politics," *Journal of Environmental Policy & Planning* 15:1 (2013): 17–39, at 17.

3 Edward Wong, "On Scale of 0 to 500, Beijing's Air Quality Tops 'Crazy Bad' at 755," *New York Times*, Jan. 12, 2013; Elizabeth Economy, *The River Runs Black: The Environmental Challenge to China's Future* (Ithaca, NY: Cornell University Press, 2010).

4 Eleanor Albert and Beina Xu, "China's Environmental Crisis," Council on Foreign Relations, Jan. 18, 2016. http://www.cfr.org/china/chinas-environmental-crisis/p12608 [accessed October 28, 2016]. See also Elizabeth Economy, "Environmental Governance in China: State Control to Crisis Management," *Daedalus* 143:2 (Spring 2014): 184–97.

5 Bryan Tilt, "Industrial Pollution and Environmental Health in Rural China: Risk, Uncertainty and Individualization," *China Quarterly* 214 (June 2013): 283–301, at 296.

6 Jonathan Kaiman, "Inside China's 'Cancer Villages,'" *The Guardian*, June 4, 2013. https://www.theguardian.com/world/2013/jun/04/china-villages-cancer-deaths [accessed January 17, 2017].

7 Andrew Mertha, *China's Water Warriors: Citizen Action and Policy Change* (Ithaca, NY: Cornell University Press, 2010): 24, 47.

8 Thomas Johnson, "The Politics of Waste Incineration in Beijing: The Limits of a Top-Down Approach?" *Journal of Environmental Policy and Planning* 15:1 (2013): 109–28, at 110; "Keep the Fires Burning: Waste Incinerators Rile the Public, But Are Much Better Than Landfill," *The Economist*, April 25, 2015. http://www.economist.com/news/china/21649540-waste-incinerators-rile-public-are-much-better-landfill-keep-fires-burning [accessed October 28, 2016].

9 H. Christoph Steinhardt and Fengshi Wu, "In the Name of the Public: Environmental Protest and the Changing Landscape of Popular Contention in China," *The China Journal* 75 (2016): 61–82, at 62.

10 Ru Xin, Lu Xueyi, and Li Peilin, eds., *2010 nian: Zhongguo shehui xingshi fenxi yu yuce* (An Analysis and Forecast on China's Social Development (2010)) (Beijing: Shehui kexue wenxuan chubanshe, 2010): 8, cited in Lu Jian and Chris King-Chi Chan, "Collective Identity, Framing and Mobilisation of Environmental Protests in Urban China: A Case Study of Qidong's Protest" *China: An International Journal* 14:2 (May 2016): 102–22, at 102.

11 Johnson, "The Politics of Waste Incineration," 110, citing *The Beijing News*, "Zhongguo duo chengshi laji weicheng, guanli quexian zhi luan paifang" (Multiple Chinese cities are surrounded by waste, management inadequacy results in dumping), Nov. 1, 2010.

12 Mertha, *China's Water Warriors*, 65.

13 "Environmental Impact Assessment," Government White Paper, China. http://www.china.org.cn/english/MATERIAL/170391.htm [accessed November 1, 2016].

14 Yanhua Deng and Guobin Yang, "Pollution and Protest in China: Environmental Mobilization in Context," *China Quarterly* 214 (June 2013): 321–36, at 328.

15 Hung Chin-fu, "Citizen Journalism and Cyberactivism in China's Anti-PX Plant in Xiamen, 2007–2009," *China: An International Journal* 11:1 (April 2013): 40–54, at 49.

16 Wanxin Li, Jieyan Liu, and Duoduo Li, "Getting their Voices Heard: Three Cases of Public Participation in Environmental Protection in China," *Journal of Environmental Management* 98 (2012): 65–72, at 66.

17 Rachel E. Stern, "The Political Logic of China's New Environmental Courts," *The China Journal* 72 (2014): 53–74, at 56; Jennifer Holdaway, "Environment and Health Research in China: The State of the Field," *China Quarterly* 214 (June 2013): 255–82, at 263.

18 Mertha, *China's Water Warriors*, chapters 1–2.

19 Stern, "The Political Logic," 53–7.

20 Ibid., 57.

21 Yu-wai Li, Bo Miao, and Graeme Lang, "The Local Environmental State in China: a Study of County-Level Cities in Suzhou," *China Quarterly* 205 (March 2011): 115–32, at 124–6.

22 Stern, "The Political Logic," 60.

23 Holdaway, "Environment and Health Research," 259–60; Guobin Yang, "Contrasting Food Safety in the Chinese Media: Between Hegemony and Counter-hegemony," *China Quarterly* 214 (June 2013): 337–55, at 339.

24 Tilt, "Industrial Pollution and Environmental Health," 294–6.

25 Mertha, *China's Water Warriors*, 57, referencing Jennifer L. Turner, "Clearing the Air: Human Rights and the Legal Dimension of China's Environmental Dilemma," statement to the Congressional/Executive Commission on China Issues Roundtable: "The Growing Role of Chinese Green NGOs and Environmental Journalists in China," January 27, 2003.

26 Ronggui Huang and Ngai-ming Yip, "Internet and Activism in Urban China: A Case Study of Protests in Xiamen and Panyu," *Journal of Comparative Asian Development* 11:2 (2012): 201–23, at 212–16.

27 Rong Wang, "Engaging the Government for Environmental Collective Action: The Political Implications of ICTs in Rural China," in Wenhong Chen and Stephen Reese, eds., *Networked China: Global Dynamics of Digital Media and Civic Engagement* (New York: Routledge, 2015), 76–96.

28 "China's Internet users total 710 mln," *Xinhua*, August 3, 2016. http://en.people.cn/n3/2016/0803/c90000-9094951.html [accessed January 17, 2017].

29 Wang, "Engaging the Government," 76–96. See also Huang and Yip, "Internet and Activism in Urban China," 218.

30 Mertha, *China's Water Warriors*, 11–12.

31 Holdaway, "Environment and Health Research in China," 271.

32 Anna Lora-Wainwright, "The Inadequate Life: Rural Industrial Pollution and Lay Epidemiology in China," *China Quarterly* 214 (June 2013): 302–20, at 313–15; Tilt, "Industrial Pollution and Environmental Health," 291–8; Deng and Yang, "Pollution and Protest in China;" Benjamin Van Rooij, "The People vs. Pollution: Understanding Citizen Action against Pollution in China," *Journal of Contemporary China* 19:63 (Jan. 2010): 55–77; Ran Ran, "Perverse Incentive Structure," 25–30.

33 Thomas Johnson, "The Health Factor in Anti-Waste Incinerator Campaigns in Beijing and Guangzhou," *China Quarterly* 214 (June 2013): 356–75, at 359.

34 Ibid., 371–2; Huang and Nip, "Internet and Activism in Urban China," 208–14.

35 Deng and Yang, "Pollution and Protest in China," 323.

36 Shai Oster and Mei Feng, "In Booming China, A Doctor Battles a Polluting Factory," *Wall Street Journal*, July 19, 2006. http://www.wsj.com/articles/SB115325157476810126 [accessed January 20, 2017].

37 Huang and Nip, "Internet and Activism in Urban China," 208.

38 Yu Xiaogang, quoted in Lydia McMullen-Laird, "Yu Xiaogang wins prize for community conservation," *China Dialogue*, March 30, 2016. https://www.chinadialogue.net/culture/8785-Yu-Xiaogang-wins-prize-for-community-conservation/en [accessed January 20, 2017].

39 Graeme Lang and Ying Xu, "Anti-Incinerator Campaigns and the Evolution of Protest Politics in China," *Environmental Politics* 22:5 (2013): 832–48, at 839, citing Wang Q., Li, J., and Qiu, Q., "Fired Up About Trash Crisis," *China Daily – Hong Kong Edition*, Nov. 27, 2009, 7.

40 Deng and Yang, "Pollution and Protest in China," 327.

41 Jian Lu and Chris King-Chi Chan, "Collective Identity," 120.

42 Johnson, "The Health Factor," 369–70; Johnson, "The Politics of Waste Incineration," 121–4.

43 Huang and Yang, "Internet and Activism in Urban China," 211; Li et al., "Getting their Voices Heard," 70.

44 Steinhardt and Wu, "In the Name of the Public," 77.

45 Fung Yat-yiu, "Dalian Tries PX Activists," Radio Free Asia, Jan. 22, 2013. http://www.rfa.org/english/news/china/trial-01222013170318.html [accessed January 23, 2017].

46 Mertha, *China's Water Warriors*, 65–93.

47 Ibid., 94–109.

48 Deng and Yang, "Pollution and Protest," 323–6.

49 Yanhua Deng and Kevin J. O'Brien, "Societies of Senior Citizens and Popular Protest in Rural Zhejiang," *The China Journal* 71 (Jan. 2014): 172–88, at 176–7.

50 Deng and Yang, "Pollution and Protest;" Deng and O'Brien, "Societies of Senior Citizens."

51 Holdaway, "Environment and Health Research in China," 263.

52 Stern, "The Political Logic," 60–7; Steinhardt and Wu, "In the Name of the Public."

53 Bo Zhang, Cong Cao, Junzhan Gu, and Ting Liu, "A New Environmental Protection Law, Many Old Problems? Challenges to Environmental Governance in China," *Journal of Environmental Law* 28 (2016): 325–35, at 325–31.

54 Stern, "The Political Logic;" 60–7; Steinhardt and Wu, "In the Name of the Public;" Zhang et al., "A New Environmental Protection Law," 329.

55 Zhang et al., "A New Environmental Protection Law," 331–4.

56 Johnson, "The Politics of Waste Incineration," 123.

57 Steinhardt and Wu, "In the Name of the Public," 64–6, 82.

Chapter 6. Nationalist Protest

1 Yinan He, "History, Chinese Nationalism and the Emerging Sino-Japanese Conflict," *Journal of Contemporary China* 16:50 (2007): 1–24, at 4–8.

2 Suisheng Zhao, "A State-Led Nationalism: The Patriotic Education Campaign in Post-Tiananmen China," *Communist and Post-Communist Studies* 31:3 (1998): 287–302, at 295.

3 Licheng Qian, Bin Xu, and Dingding Chen, "Does History Education Promote Nationalism in China? A 'Limited Effect' Explanation," *Journal of Contemporary China* 26(104) (March 2017): 199–212; and Jackson S. Woods and Bruce J. Dickson, "Victims and Patriots: Disaggregating Nationalism in Urban China," *Journal of Contemporary China* 26(104) (March 2017): 167–82.

4 He, "History," 18.

5 Peter Hayes Gries, *China's New Nationalism: Pride, Politics, and Diplomacy* (Berkeley, CA: University of California Press, 2004): 125–7; Shannon Tiezzi, "The 'China Can Say No' Effect," *The Diplomat*, Aug. 7, 2014. http://thediplomat.com/2014/08/the-china-can-say-no-effect/ [accessed February 27, 2017].

6 Evan Osnos, "Angry Youth: The New Generation's Neocon Nationalists," *The New Yorker*, July 28, 2008, cited in Teresa Wright, "China's Rising Generation: College-Educated Youth in the Reform Era," in Zhiqun Zhu, ed., *New Dynamics in East Asian Politics* (New York: Continuum International, 2012): 245.

7 Wright, "China's Rising Generation," 245–6.

8 Charles Hutzler, "Yuppies in China Protest Via the Web – And Get Away With It: Nationalistic Dissidents Press For Hard-Hitting Policies on Japan, Taiwan, U.S." *Wall Street Journal*, March 19, 2004, https://www.wsj.com/articles/SB107965358779459770 [accessed March 6, 2017].

9 Shih-Diing Liu, "China's Poplar Nationalism on the Internet. Report on the 2005 Anti-Japan Network Struggles," *Inter-Asia Cultural Studies* 7:1 (2006): 144–55, at 145–6.

10 Jeremy L. Wallace and Jessica Chen Weiss, "The Political Geography of Nationalist Protest in China: Cities and the 2012 Anti-Japanese Protests," *China Quarterly* 222 (June 2015): 403–29.

11 Ibid., 408.

12 Ibid., 410.

13 Gries, *China's New Nationalism*, 129.

14 Hutzler, "Yuppies in China."

15 Wallace and Weiss, "The Political Geography," 407, referencing Jessica Chen Weiss, *Powerful Patriots: Nationalist Protest in China's Foreign Relations* (New York: Oxford University Press, 2014).

16 Weiss, *Powerful Patriots*.

17 Ibid., 46–66, and Dingxin Zhao, "Nationalism and Authoritarianism: Student-Government Conflicts during the 1999 Beijing Student Protests," *Asian Perspective* 27:1 (2003): 5–34.

18 Ibid.

19 Ibid.

20 Weiss, *Powerful Patriots*, 127–50; Jim Yardley, "China Bans Anti-Japan Protest," *New York Times*, April 23, 2005, 1; Xu Wu, *Chinese Cyber-Nationalism: Evolution, Characteristics, and Implications* (Lanham, MD: Rowman and Littlefield, 2007).

21 Weiss, *Powerful Patriots*, 189–218; Wallace and Weiss, "The Political Geography."

22 Weiss, *Powerful Patriots*, 201–8.

23 Ibid., 209.

Chapter 7. Political Protest

1 Teng Biao, "Rights Defence (*weiquan*), Microblogs (*weibo*), and the Surrounding Gaze (*weiguan*): The Rights Defence Movement Online and Offline," *China Perspectives* 3 (2012): 29–39, at 30; Ethan Michelson, "Lawyers, Political Embeddedness, and Institutional Continuity in China's Transition from Socialism," *American Journal of Sociology* 113:2 (Sept. 2007): 352–414, at 362, 365–8, 370–3; and Yuwen Li, "Lawyers in China: A 'Flourishing' Profession in a Rapidly Changing Society?" *China Perspectives* 27 (Jan.–Feb. 2000): 20–34, at 21, 23.

2 Fu Hualing and Richard Cullen, "Climbing the Weiquan Ladder: A Radical-izing Process for Rights-Protection Lawyers," *China Quarterly* 205 (March 2011): 40–59, at 43.
3 Ibid., 44; Teng, "Rights Defence," 33; Eva Pils, *China's Human Rights Lawyers: Advocacy and Resistance* (New York: Routledge, 2014).
4 Pitman B. Potter, "4 June and Charter 08: Approaches to Remonstrance," *China Information* 25:2 (2011): 121–38, at 122.
5 Liu Xiaobo, "The Internet and I" (*wo yu hulianwang*), retrieved from http://www.epochtimes.com/gb/6/2/20/n1230054.htm; cited in Yuntao Zhang and John Tomlinson, "Three Constituencies of Online Dissent in China," *Chinese Journal of Communication* 5:1 (March 2012): 55–60, at 57.
6 Teng, "Rights Defence," 30–1.
7 Ibid., 32.
8 David Barboza, "Chinese Man Who Bragged of Privilege Gets Six Years," *New York Times*, January 30, 2011; "My Dad is Li Gang," Know Your Meme website: http://knowyourmeme.com/memes/events/my-dad-is-li-gang-%E6%88%91%E7%88%B8%E6%98%AF%E6%9D%8E%E5%88%9A [accessed December 19, 2017].
9 Maria Bondes and Gunter Schucher, "Derailed Emotions: The Transformation of Claims and Targets during the Wenzhou Online Incident," *Information, Communication, and Society* 17:1 (2014): 45–65.
10 "Grass-mud Horse," China Digital Times. http://chinadigitaltimes.net/space/Grass-mud_horse [accessed December 19, 2017].
11 See Teresa Wright, "The China Democracy Party and the Politics of Protest in the 1980's–1990's," *China Quarterly* 172 (December 2002): 906–26.
12 Fu and Cullen, "Climbing the Weiquan Ladder," 50; Teng, "Rights Defence," 35.
13 Fu and Cullen, "Climbing the Weiquan Ladder."
14 Zhang and Tomlinson, "Three Constituencies," 59.
15 Teng, "Rights Defence," 32–3, 39.
16 Ibid., 32, 36.
17 Potter, "4 June," 130.
18 Fu and Cullen, "Climbing the Weiquan Ladder;" Zhang and Tomlinson, "Three Constituencies."
19 Potter, "4 June;" Maura Elizabeth Cunningham and Jeffrey Wasserstrom, "Interpreting Protest in Modern China," *Dissent* (Winter 2011): 13–18; Wright, "The China Democracy Party."
20 Teng, "Rights Defence;" Fu and Cullen, "Climbing the Weiquan Ladder;" Chin-fu Hung, "The Politics of China's Wei-Quan Movement in the Internet Age," *International Journal of China Studies* 1:2 (Oct. 2010): 331–49.

21 "'Walking on Thin Ice:' Control, Intimidation and Harassment of Lawyers in China," Human Rights Watch, April 2008 https://www.hrw.org/reports/2008/china0408/china0408web.pdf [accessed March 27, 2017]; Eva Pils, "'If Anything Happens…' Meeting the Now-Detained Human Rights Lawyers," China Change, January 10, 2016. https://chinachange.org/2016/01/10/if-anything-happens-meeting-the-now-detained-human-rights-lawyers/ [accessed March 27, 2017]; Teng, "Rights Defence;" Fu and Cullen, "Climbing the Weiquan Ladder."

Chapter 8. Ethnic Minority Protest

1 "China's Population Mix," http://www.china.org.cn/e-groups/shaoshu/mix.htm [accessed May 11, 2017].
2 Yufan Hao and Weihua Liu, "Xinjiang: Increasing Pain in the Heart of China's Borderland," *Journal of Contemporary China* 21:74 (March 2012): 205–25, at 209–13.
3 Michael Dillon, *China: A Modern History* (New York: I.B. Tauris, 2012): 378–9; Hao and Liu, "Xinjiang," 207–13.
4 BBC News, "Tibet Profile – Overview," Nov. 13, 2014. http://www.bbc.com/news/world-asia-pacific-16689779 [accessed May 11, 2017]; Enze Han and Christopher Paik, "Dynamics of Political Resistance in Tibet: Religious Repression and Controversies of Demographic Change," *The China Quarterly* 217 (March 2014): 69–98, at 73–5.
5 Enze Han, "The Dog That Hasn't Barked: Assimilation and Resistance in Inner Mongolia, China," *Asian Ethnicity* 12:1 (Feb 2011): 55–75; David Sneath, *Changing Inner Mongolia* (Oxford: Oxford University Press, 2000): 114–15; William R. Jankowiak, "The Last Hurrah? Political Protest in Inner Mongolia," *Australian Journal of Chinese Affairs* 19/20 (Jan–Jul 1988): 269–88, at 276.
6 Jankowiak, "The Last Hurrah?"
7 Edward Gargan, "Tibetan Protest for Independence Becomes Violent," *The New York Times*, Oct. 3, 1987. http://www.nytimes.com/1987/10/03/world/tibetan-protest-for-independence-becomes-violent.html [accessed May 12, 2017]; Alice Yaoyao Dang, "Protests in Lhasa 1987–1989," *Contemporary Tibet* (Spring 2014). http://www.academia.edu/9725645/Protests_in_Lhasa_1987-1989 [accessed May 12, 2017].
8 Hao and Liu, "Xinjiang," 207.
9 Justin Hastings, "Charting the Course of Uyghur Unrest," *The China Quarterly* 208 (December 2011): 893–912, at 903.

10 Ibid., 900.
11 Justin Hastings, "Perceiving a Single Chinese State: Escalation and Violence in Uighur Protests," *Problems of Post-Communism* 52:1 (Jan.–Feb. 2005): 28–38, at 32.
12 Hastings, "Charting the Course;" Hao and Liu, "Xinjiang."
13 Hastings, "Charting the Course," 893.
14 Ibid., 911.
15 Ibid., 894–912; Hao and Liu, "Xinjiang," 205.
16 Maura Elizabeth Cunningham and Jeffrey Wasserstrom, "Interpreting Protest in Modern China," *Dissent* (Winter 2011): 13–18, at 17.
17 Shohret Hoshur, translated by Mamatjan Juma and written in English by Roseanne Gerin, "Killings in Xinjiang's Guma Sparked by Anger at Prayer Restrictions," Radio Free Asia, Feb. 23, 2017; Uyghur Human Rights Project, "Briefing: Ban on 'Islamic' Names an Absurd Intrusion into Uyghurs' Private Lives." http://uhrp.org/uaa-and-uhrp-reports-and-briefings-press-releases/briefing-ban-%E2%80%9Cislamic%E2%80%9D-names-absurd-intrusion [accessed May 4, 2017].
18 Maya Wang, "Chinese Netizens Attack Minority Uyghur Muslims: How China's Censorship Undermines its Own Goal," Human Rights Watch, Feb. 26, 2017. https://www.hrw.org/news/2017/02/26/chinese-netizens-attack-minority-uyghur-muslims [accessed May 13, 2017].
19 Han and Paik, "Dynamics of Political Resistance," 76–7.
20 Han and Paik, "Dynamics of Political Resistance," 73–4; Cunningham and Wasserstrom, "Interpreting Protest in Modern China," 16–17; Shan Wei, "Explaining Ethnic Protests and Ethnic Policy Changes in China," *International Journal of China Studies* 1:2 (Oct. 2010): 509–29, at 509.
21 Lobsang Choephel, Sangyal Dorjee, Dawa Dolma and Pema Ngodup, translated by Dorjee Damdul and written in English by Paul Eckert Young, "Farmer Stages First Tibetan Self-Immolation of 2017," Radio Free Asia News, March 19, 2017; "Security Crackdown Follows First Tibetan Self-Immolation in 2017," International Campaign for Tibet Report, March 28, 2017; "China: Major Tibetan Buddhist Institution Faces Further Demolitions," Human Rights Watch, March 29, 2017. https://www.hrw.org/news/2017/03/29/china-major-tibetan-buddhist-institution-faces-further-demolitions [accessed May 13, 2017].
22 Nimrod Baranovitch, "The 2011 Protests in Inner Mongolia: An Ethno-environmental Perspective," *China Quarterly* 225 (March 2016): 214–33, at 217.
23 Ibid.; Jonathan Watts, "Herder's Death Deepens Tensions in Inner Mongolia," *The Guardian*, May 27, 2011, https://www.theguardian.com/world/2011/

may/27/tensions-herders-miners-inner-mongolia [accessed December 21, 2017] and "China Executes Man for Running over Mongol Herder," *Yahoo News*, August 24, 2011.
24 "Chinese Mongolians Protest Again, Herders Beaten: Rights Group," *Reuters*, June 30, 2011.

Chapter 9. Protest in Hong Kong

1 Michael Davis, "Beijing's Broken Promises," *Journal of Democracy* 26:2 (April 2015): 101–10, at 102–3.
2 Edmund W. Cheng, "Street Politics in a Hybrid Regime: The Diffusion of Political Activism in Post-colonial Hong Kong," *China Quarterly* 226 (June 2016): 383–406, at 387; Sebastian Veg, "Legalistic and Utopian: Hong Kong's Umbrella Movement," *New Left Review* 92 (March/April 2015): 55–73, at 57.
3 Ngok Ma, "Civil Society in Self-Defense: The Struggle against National Security Legislation in Hong Kong," *Journal of Contemporary China* 14:44 (2005): 465–82, at 466.
4 Cheng, "Street Politics," 385; Alvin So, "The Transformation of Social Movements in Hong Kong after 1997," in J. Broadbent and V. Brockman, eds., *East Asian Social Movements: Power, Protest, and Change* (New York: Springer, 2011): 365; Sebastian Veg, "The Rise of 'Localism' and Civil Identity in Post-Handover Hong Kong: Questioning the Chinese Nation-State," *China Quarterly* 230 (June 2017): 323–47, at 324.
5 Cheng, "Street Politics," 384–7; Zheng Yongnian and Tok Sow Keat, "Beijing Responds to Hong Kong's Democratization Movement: From Bureaucratic Control to Political Leadership," *Asian Affairs* 33:4 (Winter 2007): 235–55, at 238.
6 So, "The Transformation," 365–9; Cheng, "Street Politics," 388–9.
7 Ma, "Civil Society," 466–7.
8 So, "The Transformation," 371–2; Ma, "Civil Society," 475–6.
9 Ma, "Civil Society," 465–77.
10 Ibid., 480; So, "The Transformation," 372–3.
11 Ma, "Civil Society," 465–74, 477–9.
12 Ibid., 478–80.
13 Ibid., 480–1.
14 Zheng and Tok, "Beijing Responds," 244.
15 Ibid., 247–8; Veg, "Legalistic and Utopian," 57.
16 Cheng, "Street Politics," 389.

17 Veg, "Legalistic and Utopian," 57; Davis, "Beijing's Broken Promises," 105; Cheng, "Street Politics," 397.

18 Veg, "Legalistic and Utopian," 68.

19 Veg, "The Rise of 'Localism,'" 328.

20 So, "The Transformation," 375–6.

21 Ibid., 376.

22 Joshua Wong, "Scholarism on the March," *New Left Review* 92 (March–April 2015): 43–52, at 44.

23 Ibid., 44.

24 Keith Bradsher and Kevin Drew, "Protesters March as New Hong Kong Leader Is Sworn In," *New York Times*, July 1, 2012.

25 Veg, "Legalistic and Utopian," 57.

26 Davis, "Beijing's Broken Promises," 106–8.

27 Veg, "Legalistic and Utopian," 57–9.

28 Ibid., 60–1.

29 Ibid., 60.

30 Victoria Tin-bor Hui, "The Protests and Beyond," *Journal of Democracy* 26:2 (April 2015): 111–21, at 112.

31 Hui, "The Protests," 112.

32 Wong, "Scholarism on the March," 46.

33 Cheng, "Street Politics," 393.

34 Shannon Tiezzi, "How a Hong Kong Newspaper Became an Occupy Movement Flashpoint," *The Diplomat*, October 17, 2014. http://thediplomat.com/2014/10/how-a-hong-kong-newspaper-became-an-occupy-movement-flashpoint/ [accessed July 27, 2017].

35 Cheng, "Street Politics," 393 and 397.

36 Hui, "The Protests," 114–15; Veg, "Legalistic and Utopian," 61.

37 Hui, "The Protests," 111.

38 Veg, "Legalistic and Utopian," 62–3.

39 Cheng, "Street Politics," 402.

40 Chris Lau, "Joshua Wong and other Occupy Leaders Allowed to Appeal against Jail Terms," *South China Morning Post*, Nov. 7, 2017; Natasha Khan, "Hong Kong Protest Leader Joshua Wong Freed on Bail," *Wall Street Journal*, Oct. 24, 2017.

41 Hui, "The Protests," 118.

Conclusion

1 I am grateful to an anonymous reviewer for this metaphor.

Index